Recruitment to legislative office is one of the core functions of political systems, yet we know little about how the process varies from one country to another. *Passages to Power* provides a comparative account of legislative recruitment which applies a common analytical framework and new survey data to nineteen advanced democracies. Legislative recruitment refers to the critical step as people move from lower levels of politics into parliamentary careers. Who succeeds in becoming a politician? Who fails? And why? Based on original research which adopts a 'new institutionalist' perspective, this book compares these issues in a wide range of countries. This important new study brings together an outstanding group of international scholars to look at recruitment around the world. The countries examined in depth include Australia, Canada, Finland, Germany, Japan, The Netherlands, New Zealand, the United Kingdom and the United States, along with a comparison of all member states in the European Union.

Passages to power

Passages to power

Legislative recruitment in advanced democracies

edited by

Pippa Norris

Kennedy School of Government, Harvard University

CAMBRIDGE
UNIVERSITY PRESS

PUBLISHED BY THE PRESS SYNDICATE OF THE UNIVERSITY OF CAMBRIDGE
The Pitt Building, Trumpington Street, Cambridge CB2 1RP, United Kingdom

CAMBRIDGE UNIVERSITY PRESS
The Edinburgh Building, Cambridge CB2 2RU, United Kingdom
40 West 20th Street, New York, NY 10011-4211, USA
10 Stamford Road, Oakleigh, Melbourne 3166, Australia

First published 1997

Printed in the United Kingdom at the University Press, Cambridge

Typeset in 10/12 Monotype Plantin   [SE]

A catalogue record for this book is available from the British Library

Library of Congress Cataloguing in Publication data

Passages to power: legislative recruitment in advanced democracies /
    edited by Pippa Norris.
       p.   cm.
    Includes bibliographical references and index.
    ISBN 0 521 59099 X. – ISBN 0 521 59908 3 (pbk.)
    1. Nominations for office.   2. Political parties.   3. Legislators–
    Recruiting.   4. Legislators.   5. Comparative government.
    6. Democracy.   7. Representative government and representation.
    I. Norris, Pippa.
    JF2085.P37   1997
    324.5–dc21   96-40357   CIP

ISBN 0 521 59099 X hardback
ISBN 0 521 59908 3 paperback

Contents

Figures

Tables

Notes about the contributors

HELENA CATT is a Lecturer in Political Studies at the University of Auckland, New Zealand. Her books include *Towards Consensus?* (1993), *Season of Discontent: By-elections and the Bolger Government* and *Voter's Choice: Electoral Change in New Zealand?*. She writes and teaches on comparative politics, New Zealand politics, democracy and electoral systems.

LYNDA ERICKSON is Associate Professor in the Department of Political Science at Simon Fraser University in Burnaby, British Columbia, Canada. Her areas of specialisation are Canadian parties and women in politics in Canada. She has co-authored *Grassroots Politicians: Party Activists in British Columbia* (1991), and has written on the nomination and selection of party leaders and parliamentary candidates in Canada.

HARUHIRO FUKUI, formerly a Professor of Political Science at the University of California, Santa Barbara, now teaches at the University of Tsukuba, Japan. He specialises in Japanese politics and foreign policy, and is the author of *Party in Power: The Japanese Liberal-Democrats and Policy-Making* (1970), co-author of *The Textile Wrangle: Conflict in Japanese–American Relations, 1969-71* (1979), and editor of *Political Parties of Asia and the Pacific* (1985), as well as several other books and journal articles and chapters in edited volumes.

VOITTO HELANDER is Associate Professor of Political Science at the University of Turku. He has written several books and articles on interest organisations and corporatism, professions, local politics, public administration and parliamentary activities. These include *Consultation and Political Culture* (with Dag Anckar, 1983).

PAUL S. HERRNSON is Professor of Government and Politics at the University of Maryland. He is the author of *Party Campaigning in the 1980s* (1988), and *Congressional Elections: Campaigning at Home and in Washington* (1995), and co-editor of *Risky Business? PAC Decisionmaking in Congressional Elections* (1994), *The Interest Group Connection* (1997) and *Multiparty Politics in America* (1997).

MONIQUE LEIJENAAR is Associate Professor of Political Science at the University of Nijmegen, The Netherlands. She has published several books and articles on local politics, election studies, and women and politics. She is co-editor of *Gender and Power* (1991), and co-author of *Equality in Participation and Decision-Making* (1991).

JONI LOVENDUSKI is Professor of Politics at the University of Southampton. Her main books include *Contemporary Feminist Politics* (1993), *Women and European Politics* (1986), and *Political Recruitment: Gender, Race and Class in the British Parliament* (1995). She has co-edited *The Politics of the Second Electorate* (1981), *The New Politics of Abortion* (1986), *Gender and Party Politics* (1993), *Different Roles, Different Voices* (1994) and *Women in Politics* (1966).

IAN MCALLISTER is Director of the Research School of Social Sciences at the Australian National University and was previously Professor of Government at Manchester University. His publications include, among other books, *The Loyalties of Voters: A Lifetime Learning Model* (1990); *Political Behaviour: Citizens, Parties and Elites in Australia* (1992) and *Russia Votes* (1996). He has previously taught at the University of New South Wales, Australia and held research positions at the University of Strathclyde and Queen's University, Belfast.

KEES NIEMÖLLER is Professor and Head of the Department of Methodology at the University of Amsterdam, and also Director of the Dutch National Election Studies. His main interests focus on electoral research, marketing and the use of databases in the social sciences. Recent publications include *The Dutch Voter* (1994).

PIPPA NORRIS is Associate Director of the Joan Shorenstein Center on the Press, Politics and Public Policy and Lecturer at the Kennedy School of Government, Harvard University. She works on comparative politics. Her main books include *Electoral Change Since 1945* (1996), *Political Recruitment: Gender, Race and Class in the British Parliament* (1995), *British Byelections* (1990), and *Politics and Sexual Equality* (1986). She has also edited or co-edited *The News Media and its Influences* (1997), *Women, Media and Politics* (1996), *Comparing Democracies: Voting and Elections in Global Perspective* (1996), *Women in Politics* (1996), *Different Roles, Different Voices* (1994), *Gender and Party Politics*, (1993), and the *British Elections and Parties Yearbook* (1991-3). She also co-edits the *Harvard International Journal of Press/Politics*. She has previously taught at

Edinburgh University and held visiting posts at the University of East Anglia and the University of California, Berkeley.

BERNHARD WESSELS is Senior Fellow at the Wissenschaftszentrum Berlin für Sozialforschung. He has been the Principal Investigator of studies of German Bundestag members and candidates since 1988 and is currently working on a major cross-national survey of members of the European Parliament. He has published widely on German political elites, political representation and political sociology, including *Konfliktpotentiale und Konsensstrategien* (1989), *Abgeordnete und Bürger* (1990), *Erosion des Wachstumsparadigmas: Neue Konfliktstrukturen im politischen System der Bundesrepublik?* (1991), *Politische Klasse und politische Institutionen* (1991), and *Parlament und Gesellschaft* (1993).

Preface

In common with many international projects involving a team of collaborators from different continents, this book has evolved over many years. The structure and framework developed from an early research agenda (Norris, Carty, Erickson, Lovenduski and Simms 1990). The contributors met to present their work at a series of meetings: the American Political Science Association in Washington, DC in 1993; the Workshop on the Future of the Australian Party System organised by Marion Simms in Canberra in 1994; the Conference on Party Politics in the Year 2000 organised by David Farrell and Ian Holliday in Manchester in 1995; the International Political Science Association World Congress in Berlin in 1995; and the European Consortium of Political Research Joint Workshops meeting in Bordeaux in 1995. We would like to thank all these organisations for providing opportunities for us to develop our collaboration.

In addition we appreciate the advice and suggestions about the project provided by all our colleagues in different meetings, including Karen Beckwith, Susan Carroll, Ken Carty, Robert Darcy, Lynda Fowler, Mark Franklin, Marianne Githens, Jim Lamare, Joni Lovenduski, Richard Matland, Susan Scarrow, Marian Simms, Donley Studlar, and Jack Vowles, among others. We are most grateful for data from the European Representation Study directed in conjunction with Jacques Thomassen, Bernhard Wessels and Richard Katz. Colleagues at the Shorenstein Center on the Press, Politics and Public Policy at the Kennedy School of Government, Harvard University, provided a stimulating environment to complete the project and Brett Hansard helped assemble the final manuscript. At Cambridge University Press, John Haslam has provided continuous encouragement and editorial support.

The surveys which form the heart of this project have been supported by a range of national research councils. The *1993 Australian Election Study* was funded by the Australian Research Council and conducted by Ian McAllister, David Gow, Roger Jones and David Denemark. The *British Candidate Study 1993* was funded by the Economic and Social

Research Council of the UK (Research Grant 0000-23-1991) and conducted by Pippa Norris and Joni Lovenduski. The *Canadian Candidate Project 1993* study was funded by the Social Sciences and Humanities Research Council of Canada. Lynda Erickson would also like to thank Jane Dyson, Gonzalo Carasco, Susan Fonseca, Christopher Kam, Jean-François Labell, Judy Morrison, Ken Stewart and Jeffrey Yip for their assistance with the project, Ken Carty for advice, Elizabeth Arnold, Cynthia Cusinatto, Rosemary Dolman, Sheila Gervais, Tom Flanagan and the national offices of the Canadian political parties for their participation in the project. The *New Zealand Study* was funded by the Foundation for New Zealand Research Science and Technology and conducted by Peter Aimer, Helena Catt, Raymond Miller, Jack Vowles and Jim Lamare.

Lastly this book would not have been possible without the cooperation of all the parliamentary candidates who generously set aside time in a busy schedule to participate in the surveys, and all the party officials who provided assistance, information and advice. We thank you all for your help.

PIPPA NORRIS
Harvard University

1   Introduction: theories of recruitment

Pippa Norris

Competitive democratic elections offer citizens a choice of alternative parties, governments and policies. But, equally important, campaigns provide voters with a choice of candidates for office. The nature of the ballot may vary: Dutch voters are offered a long list of names under a common party banner; Canadians face the choice of one candidate per party in their riding; in American primary elections citizens can pick from rival nominees within a party. But in all cases voters are selecting political leaders who may determine the future of their country. Which candidates get on the ballot, and therefore who enters legislative office, depends on the prior recruitment process.

The concept of *legislative recruitment* refers to the critical step as individuals move from lower levels into parliamentary careers. The chapters in this book work within a common conceptual framework which assumes that all such recruitment involves four levels of analysis (see Figure 1.1):

- the *political system*, notably the legal regulations, party system and electoral system, which structure candidate opportunities in the political market-place;
- the *recruitment process*, particularly the degree of internal democracy within party organisations and the rules governing candidate selection;
- the *supply* of candidates willing to pursue elected office, due to their motivation and political capital; and lastly,
- the *demands* of gatekeepers (whether voters, party members, financial supporters or political leaders) who select some from the pool of aspirants.

These levels can be understood as nested, in a 'funnel of causality', so that supply and demand works within party recruitment processes, which in turn are shaped by the broader political system. The core question pursued in subsequent chapters concerns how individual actors interact within different institutional contexts. By comparing how the recruitment

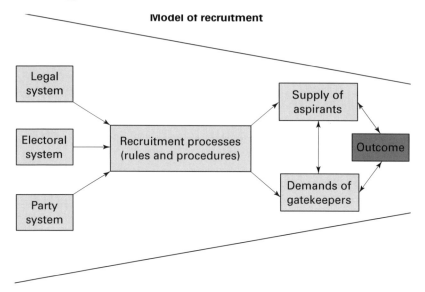

Figure 1.1 Model of recruitment.

process works in a range of advanced industrialised democracies we can explore how far variations in the institutional setting have a major impact upon the outcome.

The book compares established democracies including nineteen advanced industrialised societies in North America, Western Europe, Scandinavia and the Pacific. The research design is based upon a contextual analysis of the recruitment process within the major parties in each country combined with elite-level surveys of individual parliamentary candidates in elections held during the early 1990s. Most chapters deal with the recruitment process in general elections while the conclusion covers candidates running for election to the European Parliament. Similar, or functionally equivalent, questions were asked in each survey, allowing comparison of factors such as the social background and political experience of candidates. This approach provides significant cross-national variations in the institutional context, while allowing a richer and denser understanding of the specific process of recruitment within parties in each country. The conclusion seeks to test theories of recruitment in a systematic manner across member states of the European Union. The aim of this introduction is to suggest why political recruitment matters, to map out common perspectives in the literature and to outline the approach adopted by this book, and to identify the core features of the recruitment process which will be covered by subsequent chapters.

Normative concerns about political recruitment

The recruitment process represents one of the basic functions of every political system which has long raised normative concerns about the consequences of the recruitment process for political careers, the social diversity of legislative elites, and the democratic distribution of power within parties.

What is the impact of recruitment on political careers?

Many previous studies have analysed political careers, where recruitment represents the first step in a lifetime's parliamentary service (Mezey 1979; Jewell 1985; Buck 1963; Blondel 1973; King 1981; Riddell 1993; Schlesinger 1966, 1991). Through recruitment people are choosing their leaders. In the long run *who* gets into the legislature, perhaps rising during a twenty- or thirty-year career into the highest offices of state, may have more important repercussions for the future of the country than other electoral choice. In many countries recruitment into parliament is a filtering mechanism which determines who is eligible for government office. Some who pursue legislative careers will ultimately rise to become Cabinet Ministers, party leaders and heads of state. There are alternative pathways into political elites, including the military, media or bureaucracy, but experience of elected office remains the most common route in most democracies (Blondel 1987, 1995). As Kazee (1994, 165) argues, the effectiveness of government in any society depends in large part upon the quality of the leaders who seek office. The personal experiences, political attitudes and abilities which politicians bring to public life can vary substantially across different political systems, depending upon the qualifications which are regarded as relevant for elected office. Unlike those who become physicians or civil engineers, there are no standardised and internationally recognised qualifications to be a politician. Unlike vacancies in executive management, there are no specified and well-defined job descriptions. Politicians can adopt multiple legislative roles (see Searing 1994). Whether the recruitment process favours those who can raise independent financial resources, those who have worked their way up the party ladder, or those with considerable experience in local government, may produce very different types of legislators. In turn, this may influence effective governance.

As ideal types, routes into political careers can be classified as relatively hierarchical or lateral. Many established parliamentary systems, particularly in unitary states, are characterised by a clearly demarcated and well-trodden ladder into the higher echelons of power. In Britain, for example, the steps are well defined. Labour and Conservative politicians commonly rise from constituency party office and local government service to become a parliamentary candidate, then, if elected, a back-bench MP, perhaps a junior minister, and ultimately, the pinnacle of power, a cabinet minister or Secretary of State (see chapter 9). British politicians can rarely miss or by-pass a step in the established hierarchy. Westminster provides stable and institutionalised political careers. This process reinforces common experiences as politicians are socialised into the familiar routines of the corridors of power. With relatively moderate levels of incumbency turnover, any outsiders at Westminster are soon absorbed into 'the best club in London' (for detailed accounts see Riddell 1993; Norris and Lovenduski 1995). Vertical segmentation and differentiation reinforce minimum transfers between political elites, for example few higher civil servants ever enter parliament. Similar patterns are evident in Germany (see Wessels chapter 5), the Netherlands (Leijenaar and Niemöller chapter 7) and Australia (see McAllister chapter 2). In Japan the pathway to power is even more closed, since many new members of the Diet 'inherit' their seat through long-standing family connections and well-established koenkai machines. About a quarter of Diet members enter as 'hereditary' or 'nisei' (second generation) candidates (see Fukui chapter 6).

In contrast in federalist systems with a division of powers, like the United States, there are complex and diverse (although not random) routes into legislative office, with horizontal or lateral career moves, and a more permeable elite. Hence aspirants may move from the US House into the Senate, from Gubernatorial office into the Presidency, or from a Cabinet post into the judiciary (see Ehrenhalt 1992; Fowler and McClure 1989; Kazee 1994). The 'revolving door' in American politics also facilitates rotation between the private and public sectors, for example from the news media into the White House executive, or from Congress into a lobbying firm. Canadian politics is also characterised by a relatively open system, with a high level of incumbency turnover, where progress in political careers does not require many years of party or local government service (see Erickson chapter 3), while Finland also shares many of these characteristics (see Helander chapter 4).

The differences between these career paths to Westminster, the Diet and Capital Hill may have a significant impact, not only on the type of politician who succeeds in these systems, and the qualifications and experience of people who embark upon political careers, but also upon the cohesiveness and permeability of the legislatures. Most importantly, many established democracies have experienced an increased *professionalisation* of legislative careers (Buck 1963; King 1981). To use the Weberian distinction, in many countries amateurs who live *for* politics have been increasingly replaced by professionals who live *from* politics (Weber 1958). This shift signifies a move from amateurs who may enter public service as a temporary step, perhaps at the end of a long and distinguished life in business, the law or journalism, towards a full-time life-long career with its own training, qualifications and rewards. This trend means that more and more representatives tend to be experienced politicians, adept campaigners and skilled legislators, with many years of public service.

This pattern has caused concern about whether greater professionalisation weakens the linkages between citizens and their representatives, and whether the power of incumbents allows them to restrict opportunities for new challengers to enter parliament, as discussed in subsequent chapters on Australia (McAllister chapter 2), The Netherlands, (Leijenaar and Niemöller chapter 7), Japan (Fukui chapter 6) and Germany (Wessels chapter 5). Yet at the same time in other countries there are concerns that too many amateurs may be entering parliament without the necessary prior political experience or legislative skills, a pattern noted in Canada (Erickson chapter 3) and in Finland (Helander chapter 4). Clearly there is a fine balance between the necessary experience required for effective governance and the circulation of political elites which allows new blood to enter parliaments. In many countries there is concern that the recruitment process has shifted out of kilter on one side or other of this delicate equilibrium.

Does recruitment produce diverse leaders?

The recruitment process also determines the composition of parliaments, who gets into power, and therefore whether legislatures reflect society at large. This process has long raised concerns about the legitimacy of representative bodies. In comparing the social composition of parliaments we can draw a distinction between the larger pool of *aspirants* who are interested in pursuing elected office, the smaller group of *candidates* who are nominated to stand, and the smallest group of *legislators* who are elected into parliaments. Like a game of musical chairs, some fall by the wayside at every stage of the process. If the recruitment process involves a totally neutral competition for office, then parliaments will perfectly mirror the supply of aspirants who come forward. But unless MPs are picked purely at random, the recruitment process filters some over others, on a systematic basis. Some candidates fail while others succeed, depending upon factors such as their party service, formal qualifications, legislative experience, speaking abilities, financial resources, political connections, name-recognition, group networks, organisational skills, ambition for office or incumbency status. The criteria which are relevant for success can vary from one country to another.

The central concern here is that as a result of this filtering process legislators are often atypical of the electorate. One long tradition in the literature has traditionally focussed on political elites, notably the socio-economic background of leaders in government, the civil service, business and industry, and the military (Thomas 1939; Ross 1955; Aaronovitch 1961; Bottomore 1964; Parry 1969; Scott 1991; Mellors 1978; Putnam 1976; Loewenberg and Patterson 1979; Aberbach, Putnam and Rockman 1981). These studies established that legislatures worldwide include more of the affluent than the less well-off, more men than women, more middle-aged than young, and more white-collar professionals than blue-collar workers. Moreover, over time the paucity of working-class MPs has been exacerbated, with the growth of representatives from a professional background like lawyers, businessmen and journalists (Norris 1996a). In recent decades traditional issues about social class have received less attention than concern about the persistent under-representation of women and ethnic minorities (Lovenduski and Norris 1993; Randall 1987). Worldwide women are 9 per cent of parliamentarians, and 5.6 per cent of cabinet ministers (United Nations 1995). The proportion of women MPs has declined in recent years, following the abandonment of quotas in Central and Eastern Europe. Identifying the differences and similarities in the pathways to power which cause this pattern, and analysing their consequences, is one of the primary aims of this book.

One major stream of literature has been concerned to understand the consequences of the composition of elites for political representation (Birch 1964, 1971, 1993; Pitkin 1967; Penock and Chapman 1968; Eulau and Wahlke 1978; Converse and Pierce 1986; Esaiasson and Holmberg 1996). In the older literature, based on the responsible party model of representative democracy, it was commonly assumed that *what* members stood for, particularly their party affiliation, was more important than *where* they came from (Edinger and Searing 1967; Schleth 1971; Matthews 1985:45). Yet a growing body of work has demonstrated that the social background of legislators may matter not just for the symbolic legitimacy of elected bodies, but also for the attitudes and behaviour of representatives. Studies have found that the class, generation, gender and education of elected members produces attitudinal differences within parties in Germany (Wessels 1985: 50–72) and

Sweden (Esaiasson and Holmberg 1996: 31–48). Gender differences among legislators have been found to be significant predictors of their attitudes in Britain (Norris and Lovenduski 1995), Scandinavia (Karvonen and Per Selle 1995) and the United States (Thomas 1994). This suggests that the development of a more diverse legislature may influence not just its legitimacy but also its dominant policy agenda, and perhaps its style of politics.

Is the recruitment process democratic, open and fair?

The last controversy in the literature revolves around how far the process of recruitment is internally democratic within parties, which concerns the appropriate division of power between party leaders and grassroots members. At the turn of the century Ostrogorski (1902) established a long tradition which suggests that *who* selects candidates, whether party leaders, members or grassroots voters, may have important consequences for the distribution of power within parties, and perhaps for party discipline in parliament. Institutionalists have studied recruitment to understand the distribution of power within party organisations, who has the power to select, and the formal rules governing the process (McKenzie 1955; Eldersveld 1964; Epstein 1970; Painebanco 1988; Ranney 1965; Rush 1969; Ware 1996; Katz and Mair 1994, 1992).

Parties can be classified according to the degree of centralisation of the selection process, on a continuum ranging from the most open systems determined mainly by voters (such as the Canadian Conservatives or the US Democrats), to the most closed systems determined mainly by party leaders (such as the Mexican PRI or Forza Italia). Between these poles, a range of actors may play a role: voters, party members, local delegates, factions, affiliated groups, regional officers and national party leaders (see Ware 1995; Gallagher and Marsh 1988; Lovenduski and Norris 1993).

Normative theories concerning the importance of internal party democracy, and its consequences, continue to be strongly debated. Proponents of responsible party government argue that democracy works most effectively where parties provide an alternative set of programmes on the major issues facing the country, voters choose parties based on their policies and performance, and free and fair elections are held at regular intervals to allow alternation of the parties in power. As such democracy provides all citizens with an opportunity to hold parties collectively responsible for their actions. In contrast advocates of 'strong' or 'participatory' democracy argue that the choice of parties in elections once every four or five years provides only limited opportunities for citizen control over their leaders. To supplement this system, it is suggested, core party activists in local areas or all grassroots party members need to be able to exercise influence over their leaders through internal party mechanisms, including determining the selection of party candidates, leaders and policy platforms. This debate poses unresolved issues about whether representatives should be accountable to the whole electorate, to grassroots party members, to a smaller group of party activists, or to the party leadership.

The new institutionalism research design

The process of recruitment therefore raises significant normative concerns about how the process should operate according to rival conceptions of democracy, and empirical issues about how the process does operate in practice. While the importance of recruitment is widely acknowledged, there have been few systematic studies into the shadowy pathways to power prior to election in most countries. Comparative studies comparing the process in different countries, using a common theoretical framework, remain even scarcer (for detailed reviews of the literature see Matthews 1985; Czudnowski 1975; and comparative studies by Loewenberg and Patterson 1979; Mezey 1979; Norris 1996a; and Gallagher and Marsh 1988). This means that although we have well-developed theories of voting behaviour and elections, which have been examined and replicated in many different national contexts, as a result of this neglect it sometimes appears as if candidates are born by miraculous conception, politically fully clothed, the day the campaign is announced. We lack powerful and well-tested theories which could unify comparative research on candidacies. Building on the literature which is available, this book seeks to develop our theoretical and empirical knowledge by exploring routes to power in a wide range of parties in advanced industrialised democracies. The core questions explored by subsequent chapters concern *who* becomes a candidate, *how*, and *why* this happens.

A thorough review of the literature (Fowler 1993) highlights the variety of theoretical and methodological approaches to understanding legislative recruitment, and the fragmentation of the field. We have already discussed some of the predominant perspectives which have focussed on the insights recruitment provides into political careers, issues of social representation, and the process of party politics. Each approach has provided important clues to understand part of the puzzle of legislative recruitment. While establishing a rich foundation on which to build, these approaches need to be melded into a more integrated and comprehensive theoretical framework. The book works within a *new institutionalism* perspective, an increasingly popular approach which suggests that the attitudes and behaviour of individual actors need to be understood within their broader institutional context (March and Olsen 1989; Powell and Dimaggio 1991). Many studies have focussed on the formal recruitment process as set out in legal regulations, constitutional conventions and official party rules (see, for example, Rush 1969; Ranney 1965). These studies often assume that the formal processes determine the outcome. The obvious weakness of this approach is that formal rules may have little bearing on informal practices. Constitutions may exercise *de jure*, not *de facto*, authority. The focus on party structures neglects the attitudes, priorities and concerns of *selectors*, whether party leaders, members, voters or non-party financial supporters, or interest groups. Moreover institutional approaches have also paid little attention to the motivation and experience of candidates. In contrast behavioural approaches have used surveys of elites to understand the attitudes of party selectors or candidates (see, for example, Gallagher and Marsh 1988; Bochel and Denver 1983). Yet the micro-behavioural perspective assumes that these attitudes are static, and generalisable irrespective of the broader context. For example, it assumes that selectors are looking for the same qualifications in candidates irrespective of the type of seat, type of party, or type of rules governing the process. Yet a change in the procedures, for example a party's adoption of affirmative action quotas to boost women's representation, may encourage more women to aspire for office, and may alter the attitudes of selectors towards female nominees.

We can start to rectify this gap by combining the analysis of the macro-level institutional structure of recruitment – the political systems and recruitment processes within parties – with the micro-level analysis of the attitudes of the candidates and selectors using individual-level survey data. This assumes a multi-method approach, ideally combining qualitative sources (depth interviews with core actors, participant observation of selection procedures, and organisational analysis of party structures) and quantitative sources (surveys of candidates, aspirants and party selectors). The *new institutionalism* approach used in this book assumes that the politics of recruitment is not simply reducible to either the attitudes, preferences and concerns of individual actors, or the legal and constitutional structures within which they work. Instead there is a process of interaction: the rules and procedures of political systems structure behaviour, attitudes and opinions in predictable and orderly ways.

The analytical framework of legislative recruitment

The chapters which follow work within a broadly common framework, although the stress on different components varies, as befits each particu-

Table 1.1. *The context of the electoral and party systems*

	Australia	Canada	Finland	Germany	Japan	Netherlands	New Zealand	UK	USA
Electoral system lower house	AV	FPTP	Open regional party list	FPTP+ closed regional party list	SNTV (to 1993) then mixed	Open national party list	FPTP (to 1993) then mixed	FPTP	FPTP
No of seats	148	295	200	656	500	150	120	650	435
No of constituencies	148	295	15	329	–	1	120	650	435
Legislative turnover per election	80	60.8	65.3	79.4	72.7	71.1	71.9	–	–
Legislative turnover per annum	7.5	13.1	8.7	5.76	8.19	10.9	9.4	–	–
Party system	Two-and-a-half	Moderate multiparty	Fragmented multiparty	Moderate multiparty	Predominant one-party	Fragmented multiparty	Two party (until 1993)	Two party	Two party
Effective number of parties in lower house	2.42	2.35	4.88	2.78	3.95	5.38	2.16	2.26	2.00
Total number of parties in lower house	4	6	10	6	10	10	4	9	2

Notes: The figures are calculated for the most recent general election (mid-1990s) to the lower house. Incumbency turnover is calculated as net change from one general election to the next from 1980–93. The effective number of parliamentary parties (ENPP) is based on the formula of Rein Taagepera and Matthew Shugert, *Seats and Votes* 1989. New Haven: Yale University Press. FPTP=First past the post or single member plurality elections. AV=Alternative vote. SNTV=Single non-transferable vote. Legislative turnover is the proportion of members replaced per election or per annum.

Sources: Lawrence LeDuc, Richard Niemi and Pippa Norris (eds.). 1996. *Comparing Democracies.* Newbury Park, Ca: Sage for all data except that on incumbency, which is from Richard Matland and Donley Studlar 'Turnover Patterns and Explanations of Variations in Turnover in Parliamentary Democracies', Paper presented at the European Consortium of Political Research, Bordeaux 1995.

lar political system. In this approach recruitment processes are under-stood as a structured market-place. We distinguish between components of recruitment: the *structure of opportunities* set by the political system, the *rule-governed process* of recruitment within parties, the *demands* of each party, and the *supply* of candidates.

The structure of opportunities

The political system within each country sets the structure of opportuni-ties for political careers. In particular the legal regulations, electoral rules and system of party competition determine the broad pool of eligibles. A cross-national comparison highlights systemic factors which are often taken for granted by participants. The elected offices available within the political system vary according to whether there is a bicameral or uni-cameral parliament; how many seats there are in each chamber; whether there is a federal or unitary system; how frequently elections are held; and the rate of incumbency turnover. The status, power and rewards of leg-islative office vary according to the career structure in government; the function and powers of the parliament; the full- or part-time demands of the legislature; and the material rewards of office. The 'costs' of standing for election vary according to campaign spending regulations and public funding; the share of the costs borne by candidates; and the loss of alter-native career rewards. The party and electoral systems vary according to the number and type of parties contesting elections; the type of electoral system used for different offices. These factors influence the costs and benefits of becoming a candidate in different countries.

To explore these issues the book compares recruitment to the lower house of legislatures in a range of parties in advanced industrialised democracies. The significant contrasts between these political systems help to highlight the similarities and differences in recruitment under different conditions (see Table 1.1). The book includes major world powers like Japan and Germany, as well as smaller polities like Finland, The Netherlands and New Zealand. Some systems are federalist, where national parliaments share power with regional or state-level legislatures (Australia, Canada, United States, Germany), while others were highly centralised (Britain, New Zealand). Using Sartori's classification (1976), the comparison includes classic exemplars of predominant party systems (Japan prior to 1993), two-party systems (New Zealand prior to 1993, Britain, the United States, Australia), moderate pluralism (Germany, Canada, Finland), and polarised pluralism (The Netherlands). Some of the political systems have proved remarkably resilient to changes in the major parties in power (Britain, Australia) while others have experienced substantial party fragmentation in recent years (New Zealand, Canada, Japan). Some use majoritarian electoral systems (Canada, Australia) while others are highly proportional (The Netherlands, Germany). Legislative turnover is highest in Canada and Finland, and lowest in Australia and Germany. The conclusion compares candidates from twelve member states running in a single election to the European Parliament. In short, the countries included in this book allow the similarities and contrasts in patterns of recruitment to be understood in many different contexts.

Recruitment processes

In most countries recruitment usually occurs within political parties, influenced by party organisations, rules and cultures. Yet recruitment allows multiple routes. Where parties have weak mass-branch organisations – such as in the United States or Russia – politicians hungry for power can turn to interest groups, the media or financial donors to provide the essential springboard to power. Hence in the United States we have the development of the 'political entrepreneur' who brings their own skills, organisation and resources to the primary campaign (Ehrenhalt 1992). The process of selection in Canada and Finland also seems highly permeable by outsiders. Nevertheless in all democracies except for the United States, which uses primaries by voters, one of the core functions of parties is to determine who can be nominated under their party label from among the pool of eligibles. The party rules and procedures determine the process which all aspirants have to go through to become official nominees.

Selector demand

Within this context the attitudes of selectors control the *demand* for candidates and determine the criteria which are seen as appropriate to select political leaders. As subsequent chapters demonstrate, the particular qualifications which determine who rises into legislative office vary in different parties. The role of *party service* varies widely. For example, this is regarded as an essential qualification in Australia (see McAllister chapter 2) and in Germany where aspirants need to work hard for the party over many years (Ochsentour) before being rewarded with a candidacy (Wessels chapter 5). In Japan candidates need to inherit a line or *keiretsu* with local officials and politicians, and a *koenkai* electoral machine to mobilise support (see Fukui chapter 6). In Britain parliamentary candidates have usually previously held office in local government (Norris and Lovenduski 1995). In The Netherlands party service was seen as essential in the past, but the criteria have widened in recent years (see Leijenaar and Niemöller chapter 7). Yet in Canada and Finland political experience and party credentials are not regarded as critical resources for becoming a candidate (see Erickson chapter 3 and Helander chapter 4), while in America these qualities can even be regarded as a liability for political entrepreneurs in many states (see Herrnson chapter 10).

The role of *financial resources* also varies substantially. Money is indispensable for election to the Japanese Diet, where it costs candidates at least Y200 million ($200,000) to run an effective campaign, sixty times as much as in Britain or The Netherlands (see Fukui chapter 6). New regulations have tightened how the money can be raised and spent, but have not reduced its importance. Liberal Democrat Party candidates in Japan have to raise the bulk of this money themselves. In the United States candidates operate like political entrepreneurs, spending much of their time raising campaign dollars, since the average House incumbent spent $511,000 in 1993–4 (see Herrnson chapter 10; Stanley and Niemi 1995; Ehrenhalt 1992). Yet there are few electoral costs for candidates who run in New Zealand (see Catt chapter 8), or in Britain (see chapter 9). In Germany generous public subsidies of party election campaigns means that individual candidates for the Bundestag are not selected on the basis of their fund-raising abilities (see Wessels chapter 5). Therefore the demands facing aspirants and candidates for office vary substantially between political systems.

Candidate supply

Lastly supply factors include the political capital and motivation of candidates. *Political capital* can be understood to include the resources aspirants bring to the process. This may include not just financial assets but also such things as political connections, party experience, career flexibility, educational qualifications and legislative skills. Motivation refers to the drive which makes aspirants want to stand. Motivations differ: some may aspire to office because of family traditions, political ambitions, a willingness to be a party standard-bearer, or encouragement from community supporters. Motivation is often understood in terms of individual psychological drives but the literature stresses that candidate motivation is shaped, ordered and structured by its institutional context (Fowler 1993). Some may run in one context but not another. We therefore need to analyse individual motivation, and perceptions of the rules of the game, to see how these influence strategic behaviour in the pursuit of political careers.

The components within this framework can be seen as analytically distinct yet, just as supply and demand interact in the economic marketplace, so these factors interact in the recruitment process. The political system sets the general context, the recruitment process sets the steps from aspiration to nomination, while selector demand and candidate supply determine the outcome. Changes in the rules governing the electoral system, for example the switch from first-past-the-post to a mixed member system in New Zealand, can have a major impact on the selection process within party organisations. And, in turn, changes in party processes, such as affirmative action programmes, can have a significant influence on who runs for office, and the criteria gatekeepers use to judge applicants.

The challenge in comparative politics is to sharpen our theoretical framework, to develop new insights about political careers, and to understand individual attitudes and behaviour within its institutional context. While few doubt the importance of political ambition, there are serious difficulties in determining (rather than simply assuming) the underlying motivation of politicians (Williams and Lascher 1993). The barriers and opportunities faced by those running for office remain a continuing puzzle. The following chapters therefore seek to throw new light on legislative recruitment by exploring how far the outcome is affected by the structure of opportunities in the political system, the processes of recruitment within parties, the demands of gatekeepers and the supply of candidates.

2   Australia

Ian McAllister

If studies of legislative recruitment have demonstrated anything over the past three decades, it is that the process of candidate selection is multi-causal (Putnam 1976; Fowler and McClure 1989; Matthews 1985). One factor common to national elections in almost all liberal democracies is membership of, and sponsorship by, a political party. Once the legal eligibility criteria have been met, a minimal requirement for legislative recruitment is usually party membership. But once this precondition has been met, it is also evident that party service can be a significant factor. Parties often reward their loyalists, particularly in political systems which have substantial numbers of safe seats or where there are opportunities for co-option or for indirect election. Moreover, with the increasing pro-fessionalisation of politics, there exists a growing pool of party profession-als who seek (and sometime expect) such electoral rewards (see Wessels chapter 5). Indeed, without such incentives, it might be difficult for parties to meet the required level of recruitment to sustain their full-time, professional staff.

Party service, like certain types of occupation, may be regarded as a supply-side resource, providing aspirants with political experience, confidence and knowledge which makes them more willing to pursue a political career. But service may also be a demand factor. Party selec-torates have a role in choosing candidates who possess particular social or other characteristics. Selectors may value party service, or they may con-sider such experience to be attractive to the wider electorate (Bochel and Denver 1983; Gallagher and Marsh 1988). The impact of party service on recruitment is likely to be strongest within party systems characterised by strong, mass-branch political organisations, such as Australia, Britain or Germany. Party systems which are characterised by weaker mass-branch organisations, most notably Canada and the United States, are likely to provide fewer opportunities for party service to be used as a path to legislative recruitment (see Erickson in chapter 3).

This chapter focusses upon the role of party service in legislative recruitment in Australia. Three questions are addressed: (1) how important is party service as a springboard to elected office in Australia, compared to other career paths; (2) are those candidates who use party service as a path distinct from other candidates; and (3) does party service improve the vote that a candidate receives, and if so, why?

Australia is a particularly appropriate case study for an analysis of party service. In principle, it follows the model of responsible party government, whereby the parties determine recruitment to the legislature and it is the majority party, not the individual legislator, which controls legislative decision-making (Harmel and Janda 1992; Katz 1987; Rose 1974). This, coupled with the strong discipline that the parties can impose within parliament, means that in Australia 'the over-riding theme seems to be government of the people, by the party, for the party' (Jaensch 1983, 53; Rydon 1986). To test the impact of party service, data are analysed from the *Australian Election Study* candidate sample, which interviewed all major candidates standing in the March 1993 federal election.

The centrality of Australian parties

Political parties have been central to the operation of the Australian political system throughout the twentieth century. This has remained true in the past two decades, in contrast to many other countries where the mass media, the failure of parties to deal with economic problems, and the rise of interest groups have all combined to undermine the traditional party roles (Dalton 1988: 191). The continuing importance of Australian parties has its roots in the political culture, which has combined Benthamite utilitarianism with a strong theme of egalitarianism, nurtured in the early years of white settlement (Collins 1985; Bean 1993). The net effect has been to enhance the role of parties as vehicles for organising the political system, even before the establishment of the federal system in 1901 (Loveday et al. 1977). Their influence is seen throughout the political system, particularly in the high levels of party discipline enforced among MPs and in strong party identification among voters.

The parties operate rigid discipline within parliament to the extent that dissent from the party line is virtually unheard of, and the real decisions concerning legislation are arrived at within the party room. Labor was the first to achieve effective discipline at both the electoral and parliamentary levels, but the Liberals, of necessity, soon followed (Rydon 1986: 188). As Jaensch (1994: 239) puts it, 'legislative voting is redundant, except on the rare "conscience votes" or the even rarer case when a member of the Liberal or National parties has come under pressure from constituents or the local or state party base'. The upper house, the Senate, was designed to protect the interests of the states against domination by both political parties and the federal government, but since the Second World War it, too, has fallen under the influence of party. In order to gain election to the Senate, a candidate requires a place near the top of the party ballot. As a result, the Senate has became 'a happy hunting ground for the party faithful' (Emy 1974: 294).

Parties also occupy a central role among voters. Party identification in Australia has been relatively stable since 1967, when the first data were collected, and it closely follows the vote. In 1993, only 12 per cent of survey respondents failed to volunteer a party identification when asked to do so, only 4 percentage points more than the proportion of non-partisans in 1967, a quarter of a century before (Figure 2.1). The only significant change in patterns of partisanship has been in its strength. Between 1979 and 1993 the proportion of 'very strong' partisans almost halved while the proportion of weakest partisans increased from 19 to 32 per cent. Nevertheless, viewed comparatively, the levels of partisanship in Australia are exceptional, and set it apart from many other advanced industrial democracy. At least part of the explanation rests with the system of compulsory voting, which ensures that even the most apathetic citizens must vote and must have some familiarity with parties, coupled with the frequency of state and federal elections.

Once having established their indispensability to the Australian political system, the major political parties have molded political institutions and behaviour to ensure that they remain there. In common with other advanced industrial democracies with strong party systems, legislative recruitment depends on a party label; without it, election to the federal parliament is all but impossible. Since 1949 only three independents have ever sat in the federal parliament. One of these, Sam Benson, had previously been first elected as a Labor member and subsequently expelled from the party. Only two of these 1,948 contests, then, involved an independent who was first elected under that label. New political parties have been equally unsuccessful electorally. Since federation in 1901, only once has a minor political party won more than 10 per cent of the vote; that occurred in 1990 when the Australian Democrats won 11.3 per cent of the first preference vote.

Analyzing party service

The impact of party service is analysed with data derived from the candidate component of the 1993 *Australian Election Study* survey, conducted among all major party candidates (Labor, Liberal, National and Democrat) at the 1993 federal election, as well as identifiable green and

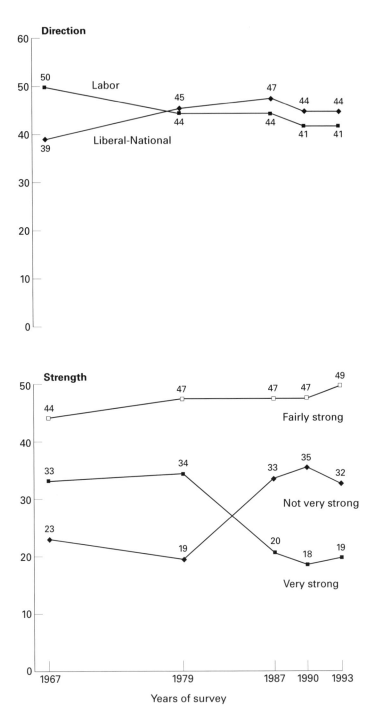

Figure 2.1 The direction and strength of party identification in Australia, 1967–93.
Sources: 1967 and 1979 *Australian National Political Attitudes Surveys*:
1987, 1990 and 1993 *Australian Election Study* surveys.

other environmental candidates. Of the 613 candidates who were in one of these categories in the election, 415 (or 67.7 per cent) responded to the survey. Although the Liberal and National (formerly Country) parties are separate, independent parties, they have been in permanent coalition since the early 1920s, except for 1932–4, 1939–40, 1973–4 and a short period in 1987. In practice, they are also ideologically very close (see McAllister 1992) and are treated as a single entity in the analyses presented here.

Party service involves a variety of activities. Parties present a range of opportunities for participation among their members. Indeed, one of the reasons for the introduction of the mass-based political party at the turn of the century was to provide a mechanism for inducting large numbers of people into the party, who would then be available for mobilisation and propagandisation within the electorate. Participation in the party organisation is determined mainly by the type of organisation in question (Painebanco 1988). Parties with strong mass-branch relations provide multiple opportunities since there is considerable interchange between the branch and the centre; potential political careerists can seek to make a political impact in one or other of these domains, secure in the knowledge that both are important power centres. By contrast, strongly centralised parties ensure that participation in centrally organised party activities will bring greater rewards while, conversely, caucus or cadre parties predominantly emphasise local participation (Katz and Mair 1994). In line with the increasing demands placed on party organisations to contest elections, formulate policies and regulate a host of other activities, most parties have placed increasing reliance on participation by their members. Surveys indicate that candidates and campaign activists have a high and increasing level of party involvement. Miller and Jennings (1986: 77) show that about seven out of ten campaign activists in the US were party officeholders during the 1980s. In Australia, Joan Rydon (1986: 115) suggests a similar level of party involvement among Australian federal MPs. Norris and Lovenduski (1995: 89) report much higher levels of party office-holding among British major party candidates in the 1992 general election: no less than 95 per cent of Labour candidates and 90 per cent of Conservative candidates had held local party office.

Party service may be defined in many ways, and the emphasis placed on each will be determined by the type of party in question, the political system within which it operates, and other factors such as the degree of recent electoral success that it has enjoyed. There is a basic distinction, however, between party service which is of a voluntary and unpaid nature, and party service which involves holding a regular, paid job. While voluntary work implies loyalty, it also suggests a degree of amateurism; if individuals are recruited into politics through this path, it may involve a conditional commitment, since most will have had a regular job which could be taken up again if their political careers proved to be unsuccessful. In contrast, holding a paid job implies professionalism and a high level of commitment to making politics the individual's chosen career. If the political career fails, there may be no other skill to which the party professional may turn.

Voluntary party service is defined here in terms of strictly party-related activities, such as holding local or branch office, and by an extended period of party membership. All of these branch-centred activities demonstrate a level of party commitment, particularly at the local level. *Professional* party service is concerned with employment by the party, either directly in a national headquarters or in a regional office, or in a minister's or elected representative's office. In systems that have strong, centralised parties, large party bureaucracies are a functional necessity, for without them the party's ability to formulate policy and maintain regular day-to-day activities would be difficult to sustain. Both types of party service are, of course, not mutually exclusive and may overlap in significant ways; voluntary party service can (and often does) provide a path to professional service, and vice versa. But in general, voluntary and professional party service attract different types of individuals and, as this chapter will demonstrate, have different consequences.

The candidate component of the *Australian Election Study* asked respondents a range of questions about their level of party political involvement at different stages during their lives; the figures reported in this paper are based on the 388 candidates who stood for one of the major parties, Labor, Liberal, National or Australian Democrat. Table 2.1 shows that most of the candidates had held office at some levels of the party and in respect of several different tasks. The most common type of party office-holding was being elected as a local branch official, which was mentioned by 66 per cent of the candidates, followed by representing the branch at an annual conference, which just over half of the candidates mentioned. Being elected to a state or federal party position was comparatively rare, numbering just 31 and 13 per cent of the respondents, respectively. In general, the differences between all candidates and their counterparts who were elected, are comparatively small.

Candidates were asked how long they had been a party member, with the average period of time being 12.3 years, reflecting a fairly significant commitment prior to their selection. The comparable figure for MPs was just over twenty-two years. In contrast to voluntary party service, professional party service was much rarer among the candidates; just over one in ten said that they had been employed in an MP's or minister's office,

Table 2.1. *Party service among Australian candidates and MPs*

	All candidates	MPs only
Voluntary party service		
Elected positions (per cent)		
Conference delegate	55	72
Local branch	66	80
State position	31	31
Federal position	13	14
(At least one of these)	(75)	(86)
Professional party services (per cent)		
Employed by MP, minister	11	8
Employed by party	5	12
(At least one of these)	(15)	(18)
Length of party membership (years)	12.3	22.4
(N)	(388)	(85)

Source: 1993 AES, candidate sample.

while just under half that said that they had been employed by their political party. Once again, the levels of professional party service were not significantly greater among MPs – 18 per cent compared to 15 per cent among the candidate sample as a whole.

Given the major differences in the method of election, party control and organisation of the lower and upper houses in Australia, and the organisational and ideological differences between the major political parties, we would expect significant house and party variations in these aspects of party service. These expectations are confirmed by the results in Table 2.2. Senate candidates are nearly three times more likely to have been employed by the party and more likely to have held an elected party office, compared to their lower house counterparts. Party employment and party office-holding at the branch level would appear to be an important prerequisite for legislative recruitment to the upper house. However, Senate candidates tend to have been party members for a shorter period: just under twelve years compared to over fifteen years for House of Representatives candidates.

There are also consistent differences in party affiliation, though they are most marked between the Australian Democrats and the two major parties, the Labor and Liberal-National parties. Democrats are significantly less likely to have held any of the four party positions. In general, such office-holding is more significant among Labor candidates

Table 2.2. *Party service and its characteristics*[a]

	Party employment (per cent)	Elected party position (mean)	Length of party membership (years)	(N)
House				
Representatives	12	1.5	15.5	(325)
Senate	21	2.2	11.6	(63)
(p)	(0.00)	(0.00)	(0.01)	
Party				
Labor	22	2.0	17.1	(119)
Liberal-National	11	1.7	13.6	(148)
Democrat	14	1.2	5.8	(121)
(p)	(0.04)	(0.00)	(0.00)	
Gender				
Male	14	1.7	12.9	(307)
Female	19	1.6	9.7	(81)
(p)	(0.38)	(0.48)	(0.00)	
Marginality				
Very safe	6	1.4	12.5	(98)
Safe	16	1.5	11.5	(132)
Marginal	13	1.4	10.9	(95)
(p)	(0.06)	(0.44)	(0.56)	
Localism[b]				
Lives in constituency	12	1.5	12.2	(252)
Lives outside constituency	13	1.3	9.5	(63)
(p)	(0.87)	(0.06)	(0.03)	

Notes:
[a] Party employment is per cent employed by an MP, minister or by the party. Elected party positions are the number of positions defined in Table 2.1. Significance levels are based on t-values for dichotomous variables, chi-squares for other variables. Marginality is defined as follows: very safe, ≥60 per cent of two party preferred vote; safe, 53–59 per cent; marginal <53 per cent.
[b] Estimated only for House of Representatives candidates.
Source: 1993 AES, candidates sample.

than among the Liberal-Nationals, though the differences are not large. Labor candidates are more likely to have held a paid party position (22 per cent) compared to either the Liberal-Nationals (11 per cent) or the Democrats (14 per cent). Finally, Labor candidates have generally served the party for a longer period of time (just over seventeen years) than their Liberal-National competitors (just under fourteen years); Democrat candidates have the shortest period of membership, just under six years, on average.

The remaining factors examined in Table 2.2 – gender, marginality of the constituency, and localism – exhibit few party differences. However, it is notable that women candidates have significantly shorter periods of party membership, a reflection of the requirement among all of the parties, but particularly within Labor, to recruit women to stand for elected office (Studlar and McAllister 1991).

There are no significant differences in the marginality of the House of Representatives seats that candidates are recruited for, at least based on their levels of party service, which suggests that selectors do not discriminate on that criterion. However, candidates who are local are more likely to have held more party positions, and to be more long-standing party members. There are, then, important dimensions to party service, encompassing whether the nature of the work was voluntary and unpaid, or professional and paid. Although Table 2.1 demonstrated that there were differences between major party candidates on some of these dimensions, most notably in the house that candidates stood for, and in their party affiliation, it is perhaps surprising that the differences were not larger. This finding tends to confirm Miller and Jennings' (1986: 77–8) observation about the similar levels of office-holding among Democrat and Republican activists. It also suggests that party organisations may well place similar imperatives on their members and that similar career structures exist within each party. The next section examines how these two aspects of party service relate to reasons for standing in the first federal election.

The motivational bases of party service

Ever since party members became the subject of analysis in the 1950s, scholars have attempted to identify the motivational bases for political involvement. The earliest studies suggested that, contrary to expectation, the major incentives to party involvement lay in social solidarity and career goals, rather than in policy orientation or in partisan commitments (Clarke and Wilson 1961; Eldersveld 1964). More recent research has suggested that policy and partisan explanations for involvement may have been underestimated, at least at the level of party activists, who form the organisational core of almost all political parties (Miller and Jennings 1986). Much of the difficulty in identifying motivations exists because different organisational levels within the party will produce different motivations; the motivations of inactive, mass members will, for example, differ from those of highly active election candidates.

Table 2.3. *Reasons for contesting first federal election*[a]

	Per cent say 'very important'	Factor loadings (decimals omitted)		
		1	2	3
Pragmatist				
Political situation in the electorate was good	19	*78*	−15	06
Personal and work situations in my life were right	41	*70*	32	03
I thought I could win	23	*67*	−33	−11
Defeatist				
I thought it would be good experience	30	01	*77*	06
I did not want the incumbent to run unopposed	23	−12	*72*	02
Partisan				
I was encouraged by supporters	45	16	−06	*84*
I was asked to run by the local party	48	17	17	*80*
Eigenvalues		1.8	1.4	1.1
Per cent variance explained		25	21	16

Notes:
[a] Varimax rotated factor loadings from a principal components factor analysis with utilities in the main diagonal. Scale reliabilities for the first three factors (Cronbach's alpha) are .55, .39 and .53.
Source: 1993 AES, candidate sample.

But it might also be expected that different types of party service would lead to different motivations for political involvement, with high levels of party commitment leading to partisan motivations. Equally, however, it is possible that motivations provide the basis for choosing different types of party service. For example, partisan motivations may engender a strong party commitment. Since the data used here are cross-sectional, it is impossible to address the question of causality. Moreover, since the motivations relate primarily to the first federal election campaign that the candidates contested (which may or may not be the one analysed here), and we include incumbents as well as challengers within the sample, we are introducing some imprecision into the estimates. The first stage in the analysis is to identify the factors that motivate party involvement. Since the target group in this case is those who have already been selected as candidates by their respective parties, the survey asked the respondents what motivations they had for standing in their first federal election.

The explanations fall into three broad categories, shown by the pattern of factor loadings in Table 2.3. The first explanation is mainly *pragmatic* and is concerned with the likelihood of winning the seat, as well as with the candidate's own personal circumstances. The political explanations attract about one in five respondents who said that it was 'very important' to them, while the personal explanation gains more substantial support, 41 per cent. The second explanation is labelled as *defeatist*, and respondents see the important reasons for contesting the election as experience, and the desire not to see the incumbent run unopposed; in other words, these are largely negative reasons for standing in the election. The third explanation is *partisan* and involves being asked by the party to run and being encouraged by supporters; both attract the support of nearly half of the candidates.

The major reasons for first running for office are, then, mainly partisan; indeed, if the respondents are classified according to which of the three factors they score highest on, 58 per cent emerge as partisans. However, it is notable that the partisan reasons that are given for standing in the first election relate to exogenous factors – encouragement by supporters and being asked to run by the local party – rather than by any sense of serving the party through establishing a political career, or for ideological reasons. Candidates who considered themselves to be pragmatists in their first electoral contest make up 24 per cent of the sample, followed by defeatists, who make up the remaining 18 per cent. The motivations for seeking elective office – at least in the first contest – are primarily partisan and altruistic, rather than personal and careerist.

The extent to which these motivations are related to professional and voluntary party service is shown in Table 2.4. In this analysis (and in the subsequent regression models presented in Figure 2.2), the estimates control for gender, cabinet membership, incumbency and party. An additional control in Table 2.4 is whether or not the candidate was standing for the Senate. In Figures 2.2 and 2.3 the number of cases is much reduced by calculating the estimates for House of Representatives candidates only, and separately for each of the three major parties. Party service is defined by two variables: professional service and voluntary service. Professional service is a composite of having been employed in some capacity by the party, as defined in Table 2.1; voluntary service combines the number of elected party positions each candidate reported, and length of party membership.

Party service is a significant influence on two of the three motivations for the first federal contest. In the case of pragmatism, increased voluntary service is more likely to lead to a stronger endorsement of this as a motivation, net of other things, while voluntary service significantly

Table 2.4. *Party service and reason for first federal candidature*[a]

| | (Standardised coefficients) | | |
	Pragmatist	Partisan	Defeatist
Party service			
Professional	0.00	−0.03	−0.04
Voluntary	0.09*	−0.05	−0.22*
Controls			
Gender	0.03	−0.03*	−0.10*
Senate candidate	−0.11*	0.02	0.00
Cabinet member	−0.05	−0.02	0.00
Incumbent	0.12*	0.06	−0.20*
Party (Liberal-National)			
Labor	−0.20*	0.12*	0.20*
Democrat	−0.31*	0.13*	0.12*
Constant	4.9	6.7	5.2
Adj. R-squared	0.12	0.02	0.15

Notes:
* p.05, two-tailed.
[a] Standardised coefficients from OLS regression equations predicting reasons for first federal candidature, as defined in Table 2.2. Party service combines party employment, elected party positions and length of party membership.
Source: 1993 AES, candidate sample.

reduces defeatism. In none of the three equations is professional party service a significant influence on the motivations given for standing in the first election. To that extent at least, it is voluntary party participation, rather than the more career-oriented professional form of participation, which influences the first contest. This is perhaps all the more surprising, since we might have expected someone with professional aspirations to view their first contest within a strongly partisan context.

The results are also notable for the importance of some of the control variables. Women are less likely to stand in their first election for partisan or defeatist motivations, but pragmatic considerations do count, though not significantly so. Senate candidates were less likely to stand for pragmatic reasons, reflecting the nature of Senate election where most senators are elected for a six-year term and casual vacancies are filled by co-option; in that context, standing for the Senate, or permitting one's name to be discussed within the party, reflects a pragmatic opportunity. In general, candidates knew what did *not* motivate them, rather than what did, the main exception being MPs who display a degree of pragmatism, as compared to challengers, as well as a rejection of defeatist motivations – not surprisingly. This is, of course, as likely to be a post hoc rationalisation on their part as an accurate reflection of their motivations at the time. There are also major party variations in these patterns. Labor and Democrat candidates are motivated more by personal and partisan motivations than their Liberal-National counterparts, with the latter being motivated more by pragmatism than anything else.

The impact of party service on the vote

Party service could influence the vote that candidates receive in a number of ways. The most straightforward way is where the influence of party service is direct, so that a candidate with more service would secure a larger vote than another candidate, similar in all other respects, who lacked the same level of party service. This could come about because the first candidate possessed better campaigning skills by virtue of their party experience, or because the candidate could count upon more resources, via the efforts of party colleagues. This *campaign hypothesis* is most likely to operate in mass-branch parties, such as the major Australian and British parties, where responsibility for managing the local election campaign falls upon the local party branch, rather than on the central organisation. Moreover, there is a wide range of literature which demonstrates that campaigning efforts and skills can often influence the vote, particularly in marginal constituencies (see, for example, Whiteley and Seyd 1994).

An alternative means by which party service could influence the vote is indirect, via the party gatekeepers – the selectorate. Where candidate selection is primarily a local responsibility, the most widely valued characteristics 'are aspirants' track records in the party organisation and in the constituency' (Gallagher 1988: 248). Successful candidates are usually those who have spent time in the constituency, been actively involved in organisation activities, and gained a public profile through broader community activities, such as through business, sporting or other non-political associations. Although some parties actively seek non-members – or at the very least, less active members – this applies only to a handful of parties. In addition, the campaigning skills and experience of potential candidates are an attribute that selectors are always acutely interested in, particularly where the electoral system is based on single member constituencies. Thus the *selection hypothesis* predicts that party service will influence the vote indirectly, via the attributes that selectors, rather than voters, emphasise.

Testing the campaign and selection hypotheses in the context of available survey data is beyond the scope of this study. A definitive test of the campaign hypothesis would require detailed information about campaign activities, while testing the selection hypothesis would require information about the selection process and the other candidates. Moreover, two further complications to testing them in the Australian context are the system of compulsory voting and the sophisticated level of party factionalism that exists within both parties, but particularly within the Labor Party. Compulsory voting means that candidates have little incentive to conduct intensive local campaigns, since 95 per cent of the voters will turn out to cast a ballot. Similarly, the local Labor Party selection process is complicated by the need to balance factional representation among candidates, a trend that also exists, albeit in a much less organised way, in the Liberal Party (McAllister 1991).

Nevertheless, we can make some attempt to test the two hypotheses. If the *campaign hypothesis* were to hold, then we would expect that voluntary party service would have a direct effect on the vote, estimated across the parties as a whole. In other words, the campaigning skills and resources of the candidates, measured by their voluntary party service, should influence the vote that they receive, net of party and other effects. In the case of the *selection hypothesis*, the assumption is that party service will exercise its greatest impact within the party organisation, through the nomination process. A party loyalist will therefore have a better chance of securing a winnable seat, since he or she will have credentials that the party considers worth rewarding; these may be either voluntary or professional service. The selection hypothesis therefore implies that party service influences the vote indirectly, within the party.

To test these hypotheses, the analysis must be restricted to examining candidates who stood for the House of Representatives, since Senate candidates are elected under a different electoral system. Since the campaign hypothesis predicts that party service will influence the vote in the context of inter-party competition, the estimates are made for all major party candidates. Since the selection hypothesis suggests that party service predicts the vote through intra-party competition, this must be tested separately for each of the three major parties. These estimates are shown in Figures 2.2 and 2.3 in the form of path models. The models show the effects of party service and motivations for contesting the first election on the vote, but they also control for gender, incumbency, cabinet status and (in Figure 2.2 only) party. In Figure 2.3, the Democrat model controls only for gender since the Democrats have no MPs and, obviously, no cabinet or shadow cabinet members.

The results show little support for the campaign hypothesis in Figure 2.2. There is no statistically significant path between voluntary party

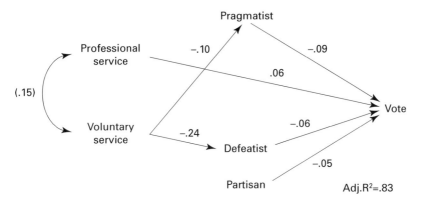

Figure 2.2 Testing the campaign hypothesis. Path model showing standardised regression coefficients. The estimates control for (but do not show) gender, incumbency, cabinet or shadow cabinet status and party. Only paths significant at p<.05 are shown.
N=325 major party House of Representatives candidates.
Source: 1993 *AES*, candidate sample.

service and the vote. Indeed, the only link between party service and the vote involves professional party activity, and then the path is a modest, albeit significant, one. Among the motivations, all three have an impact on the vote: as we would expect, pragmatism increases the vote, while defeatism reduces it, net of other things. Partisan motivations, which may reflect co-option to stand for an unwinnable seat as well as strong partisanship, also reduce the vote that a candidate receives. The lack of support for the campaign hypothesis is explained not only by compulsory voting, which renders local party activity largely redundant, but the importance of professional party service reflects the public profile that many party professionals establish within federal politics. The Labor Party national secretary and the Liberal Party director, as well as other officials, gain considerable media exposure as spokespersons for their respective parties. In several cases they have entered federal politics; it is not surprising, then, since federal election campaigns are largely conducted through the mass media, that they gain more attention and, consequently, more votes than their competitors.

In contrast, there is more support for the selection hypothesis in Figure 2.3. In each of the models, one or other aspect of party service is a significant positive predictor of the vote that a candidate receives, relative to other candidates within his or her own party. The only caveat to this pattern occurs among Democrat candidates where professional service is

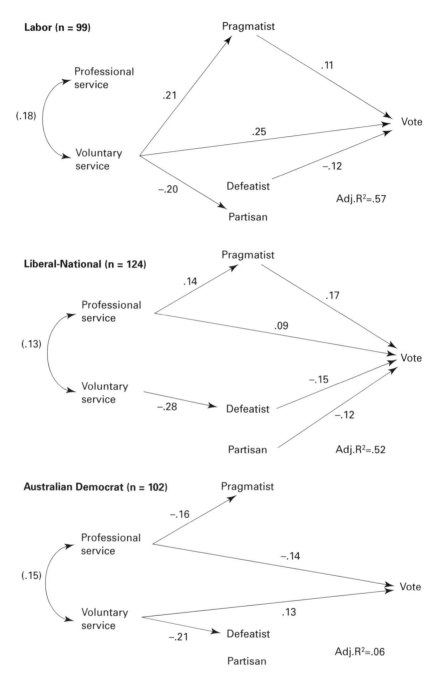

Figure 2.3 Testing the selection hypothesis. Path models showing standardised regression coefficients. The estimates control for (but do not show) gender, incumbency, and cabinet or shadow cabinet status in the Labor and Liberal–National models and gender only in the Australian Democrat model. Only paths significant at p<.10 are shown. Source: 1993 *AES*, candidate sample.

a negative predictor of the vote, while voluntary service acts to increase it. However, given the lack of overall explanatory power for the Democratic model – the total variance explained is 6 per cent, compared to 57 per cent for Labor candidates and 52 per cent for the Liberal-Nationals – together with their minority status, this should not cause us to reject the hypothesis. Indeed, the impact of voluntary service in the Labor model is considerable; the standardised coefficient of .25 suggests that it is about as important in predicting the vote as all three motivations for contesting the first election combined.

The fact that professional and voluntary party service work in different ways in the two main parties also tells us something about how the selectorates within each of the parties value party service. The Labor Party, with its strong and highly democratic branch structure and trade union traditions, values voluntary party service and local party loyalty. Moreover, while professional party activity is an important path for legislative recruitment, it is more likely to occur through election to the Senate, where simply being allocated a favourable position on the party ballot secures election. For example, while 17 per cent of Labor candidates to the House of Representatives had been full-time party employees, the figure for Labor Senate candidates was 45 per cent. In contrast, the Liberal-Nationals, though also parties with strong local roots, also combine elements of cadre organisation, with local notables exercising considerable influence. In this context, it is not surprising that voluntary party service has no influence on the vote, while professional service does have a significant influence.

Conclusions

Party service does, then, significantly improve the vote, but it exercises its influence via the nomination process, rather than via the conduct of the election campaigns. It also operates in different ways for different parties. Among Labor candidates, voluntary service increases the vote, reflecting their particular organisational structure and party culture; among Liberal-National candidates, it is professional service that counts for more, reflecting a looser local branch structure, often dominated by several prominent personalities. Democrat candidates show a different pattern altogether: while voluntary service increases the vote, professional service reduces it, in almost equal proportions.

Comparative studies of legislative recruitment have emphasised the wide range of factors which influence the decision surrounding who stands for elective office and, among those who form the potential pool of candidates, who is selected by the party (Putnam 1976; Gallagher and

Marsh 1988; Lovenduski and Norris 1993). Within this latter stage of the recruitment process, many preconditions have been identified. This chapter has focussed on one of these preconditions: the role of party service. In countries that have strong, disciplined party systems, like Australia, the political parties place an additional hurdle for potential candidates: the requirement that they have served the party effectively. Since voters rarely discriminate between candidates based on their personal or political characteristics, the parties possess great power to nominate those of their members they favour.

Party service is an important path for legislative recruitment in Australia. Election candidates display high levels of voluntary party service, and significant numbers have been employed by the party in some professional capacity, particularly in the Labor Party. Although partisan motivations for standing for election are the most important considerations for candidates, these are only weakly related to party service and have comparatively little influence on the vote that candidates attract. Both voluntary and professional party service increase the likelihood of election, but they operate in different ways within the parties. Within the Labor Party, voluntary party service increases the likelihood of gaining a winnable House of Representatives seat, while professional party service increases the likelihood of gaining a favourable position on the party's Senate list. Within the Liberal-National parties, voluntary services counts for little, and it is professional party service that is more likely to reap electoral rewards.

This is clear evidence of the extent to which party service, through knowledge and familiarity with the party organisation, both local and central, enhances a candidate's election prospects. Service to the local party will bring the aspiring candidate into contact with the local power-brokers and party officials; provide an entree to the formal committees and informal groups that take important local decisions; and provide essential political intelligence about the constituency as a whole. Service in a professional capacity will also provide knowledge about formal party decision-making, but it will also provide access to a range of informal networks and contacts, which can be invaluable when seeking a nomination. Moreover, the Australian political system, with state and federal levels of government, upper and lower houses in each and multiplicity of electoral systems, provides a structure of political opportunities, particularly for party professionals, which is perhaps greater than is found in any other advanced democracy.

3 Canada

Lynda Erickson

Selection of party candidates for the Canadian House of Commons is a comparatively open process, largely controlled locally by the members of party constituency associations. Few formal requirements are demanded of those who stand for selection, and the resources required for winning a candidacy are modest. Moreover, with a high turnover rate among Members of Parliament, many non-incumbents are well placed competitively. While these features may lead us to expect healthy candidate competition for seats, such rivalry is meagre, even among the most established and successful parties. Indeed, following the 1993 general election, when almost 70 per cent of the newly elected House had not sat in the previous parliament, virtually a fifth of these new members took their seats without having faced any competition to become their party's candidate.

This chapter will explore these features of candidate selection among the parties in Canada, focussing on the experience of the 1993 election. The first section outlines the traditions and historical evolution of party selection practices, and the procedures used by each of the parties in selecting their candidates. The next section discusses local control of selections, the degree of competition for candidacies and the issue of democracy within parties. The chapter concludes by examining the characteristics of those who succeed in becoming candidates and legislators in this system.

The chapter draws on data from the *Canadian Candidate Study* conducted by the author in the 1993 General Election. The study examined party selection and party candidates among five national parties: the Progressive Conservative, Liberal, New Democratic, Reform and Bloc Québécois. It incorporates a variety of data, including the *Candidate Survey* (N=629), the *Constituency Association Survey* (N=471), aggregate data on election results and constituency characteristics, detailed telephone interviews with a random sample of fifty candidates, and interviews with party officials (Erickson 1995b).

The opportunity structure

The electoral system and the legal context

Canada uses a single member plurality system to elect all of the members of its lower house, like Britain and the United States.[1] The logic of such a system is nominally candidate oriented and locally focussed. Yet, as in Britain and the USA, parties monopolise national elections, and independents are rarely elected. Moreover, Canadian parties determine who will run under their label, unlike American parties which have lost control over the selection of their candidates. Also, local candidates rarely determine the outcome in Canadian elections (Ferejohn and Gaines 1991). Therefore, while nominally candidate-focussed, the electoral system has not produced a system of independent candidates.

Extensive rules surround much election activity, but direct legal regulation of party selection has been minimal. Candidates must meet legal requirements concerning nomination deposits, deadlines for filing, and the number of electors who must sign nomination papers. The only law directly addressing the selection process, introduced in 1970, requires national party leaders to certify each of their party candidates. This gives leaders a veto over who may run under their party label. Although seldom used directly by party leaders (Carty and Erickson 1991) this provides a mechanism for central control.

Legal regulation of election financing also has implications for aspiring candidates, in particular local spending and reimbursement regulations. In Canadian elections, spending limits are imposed on candidates' campaigns, and candidates are eligible for reimbursement of half their expenditures if they receive at least 15 per cent of the vote in their constituency. These regulations reduce the importance of personal wealth or financial backing for candidates.

Legislative turnover rates

The opportunity structure is also set by turnover rates which affect the prospects of success for new candidates. In some countries low turnover may discourage the overall level of competition for candidacies. In Canada, the relatively high turnover rate for the House of Commons provides many opportunities for aspiring politicians.

Change in the membership in the House has three components: retirement, electoral defeat, and the addition of new seats. *Retirement* usually occurs when a member decides not to run for re-election. Members may

[1] Canada's upper house of parliament, the Senate, is an appointed body.

also stand down because they have not been reselected as their party's candidate, but this is unusual as party norms typically protect MPs from such internal party challenges. *Electoral defeat*, in which MPs lose their seats to another party, is the most significant component in Canadian turnover. As Atkinson and Docherty note, 'most MPs who leave the job do so involuntarily' (1992:305). But turnover also has implications for the retirement rate. When MPs anticipate electoral defeat, many may decide to retire voluntarily. The third component of change, the addition of new seats to the legislature, has occurred with constituency boundary redistributions required by population change. Between 1968 and 1993, thirty-one new seats were added to the House: eighteen in 1979 and thirteen in 1988.

Electoral volatility in Canada is comparatively high (Blake 1991) producing considerable legislative turnover compared to other developed democracies. Matland and Studlar (1995) compared elections from 1980 to 1993 in twenty-five developed countries. Their study found most parliaments experienced turnover of about a third (31 per cent) of their members every election. In contrast, in Canada the average parliamentary turnover was over half of all MPs per election (53 per cent), the highest of any democracy under comparison. Measured on a yearly basis, the average turnover for all democracies was 9.47 per cent per annum, but 13.4 per cent in Canada.

The party system

Canada's national party system has recently seen dramatic fragmentation (Erickson 1995a). In 1993 Canada changed from a two-and-a-half party to a moderate multi-party system based on deep regional divisions. From 1935 until 1984, the centrist Liberal Party dominated government, holding office for all but seven of those years. During this era the major opposition party, the Progressive Conservatives, placed itself close to the Liberals on the ideological spectrum, but was so rarely successful in winning government that internal conflicts developed in response to its semi-permanent opposition status in the House of Commons (Perlin 1980). However, in 1984 the Conservatives successfully dislodged the Liberals from office, winning a landslide majority in the House, and they won a second majority government.

From 1935 to 1988, smaller parties presented candidates for election to the House, but only the Cooperative Commonwealth Federation (CCF) and its organisational reincarnation, the New Democratic Party (NDP), consistently won at least some ridings (that is, constituencies or seats). A social democratic party, the NDP had never held more than 15 per cent of House seats, but it was an important player in national politics because of its potential to take seats from the major parties.

Table 3.1. *Canadian election results, 1988–93*

Party	Candidates 1988 (No.)	1993 (No.)	Votes 1988 %	1993 %	Seats 1988 (No.)	1993 (No.)	Seats 1988 %	1993 %
Liberal	294	295	32	41	83	177	28	60
Progressive Conservative	295	295	43	16	169	2	51	0.7
NDP	295	294	20	7	43	9	15	3
Reform	72	207	2	19	0	52	0	18
Bloc Québécois	0	75	0	14	0	54	0	18
Other parties 1988–8 1993–9	536	913	5	3	0	0	0	0
Independents	54	51	.17	.6	0	1	0	0.3
No party*	100	100	.2	.4	0	0	0	0

Note:
* Includes candidates whose party has failed to meet the requirements of a registered political party and those who made a written request that 'no affiliation' be their designation on the ballot.
Source: Elections Canada (1993).

The 1993 election shattered this two-and-a-half-party system (see Table 3.1). Regional pressures had begun to undermine support for the governing Conservative party in the early 1990s. The challenge came from the separatist party, the Bloc Québécois (BQ), in Quebec, and the Reform Party, a neo-conservative populist party based in western Canada. By 1993, the Conservative government had become so unpopular that the leader, Brian Mulroney, resigned. But even a newly selected leader, Kim Campbell, could not draw enough support to keep the party alive electorally. Although initially the new leader did boost Conservative support, by the final days of the campaign the party's popularity had slumped again. In the 1993 election the Conservatives experienced an unprecedented collapse, winning only 16 per cent of the popular vote. Reduced from 160 to only 2 seats, the Conservatives lost their status as an official party in the House of Commons.[2]

The *New Democratic Party* also faced an electoral crisis in 1993. Although it experienced a surge in popularity in the early 1990s, by election time the national party had to work to protect even its safest seats.

[2] According to the rules of the House, a party must have twelve sitting members in order to be granted status as an official party in the Commons.

Winning just 7 per cent of the popular vote, the party's representation in the House dropped to nine seats and, like the Conservatives, the NDP lost its official party status in the House.

The *Bloc Québécois* (BQ) was created in 1990 as a Parliamentary group committed to sovereignty for Quebec. In 1993 it contested seats only in Quebec, but it won 49 per cent of the popular vote there and fifty-four of the province's seventy-five seats. Despite its recent creation, as the second largest party in the Commons it became the official opposition.

The *Reform Party*, also a newcomer to Canadian politics, contested its first election in 1988 when it ran seventy-two candidates in Western Canada. The party won just 2 per cent of the national vote and no seats in the election, although it gained an MP in a by-election held shortly afterward. In the 1993 election, the party expanded its reach regionally and ran candidates (207) in all provinces except Quebec. With 19 per cent of the national vote, the party won fifty-two seats, all but one in western Canada.

Only the *Liberal Party* represented continuity in the party system. It resumed its former place as the dominant organisation in the national party system, winning 177 seats or 60 per cent of the House membership. The Liberals formed a majority government, under the leadership of Jean Chrétien, albeit having attracted only 41 per cent of the national vote.

Throughout the 1980s, the electoral lists were dominated by the three traditional parties. The Conservatives, Liberals and NDP ran candidates in virtually every constituency and, between them, they nominated 59 per cent of all those who ran in the 1980, 1984 and 1988 elections. Of the other parties contesting those elections, only a couple ran in more than half of the country's constituencies in any one election. During the 1980s about eleven parties contested each election. About 1,509 candidates fought each contest, including about 116 with no official party affiliation, and only one unaffiliated candidate was elected throughout this decade.

In the 1993 election, the splintering of the traditional party system was reflected at the candidate level as well as in the voting results. A record 2,155 candidates and 14 parties fought the election.[3] The three traditional parties nominated among them only 41 per cent of contestants, although they were the only parties running in virtually all ridings. Two minor parties nominated candidates for more than half the ridings across the country, and the National Party had the potential to be a 'spoiler' in few constituencies.[4] Just over 150 candidates ran as independents or with no affiliation, and one succeeded, a former Conservative MP who

[3] In order to gain the status of an official party for the purposes of the election and thereby have its name on the ballot in those ridings in which it nominates candidates, a party must have fielded at least fifty official candidates.
[4] The National Party won 1.4 per cent of the national vote.

decided to run as an independent after his nomination had been vetoed by his party leader. In Canada, as in Australia or Britain, without a party label independents stood little chance of ever entering parliament.

The recruitment process within Canadian parties

The most striking and perhaps puzzling features of selection practices within Canadian parties, compared with elsewhere, is that they have traditionally had a strongly local cast in terms of who decides, they remain fairly permeable and open, yet at the same time there is so little competition for candidacies. Explaining this pattern is the task of this chapter.

Local control

Initially rooted in the cadre-like character of the early parties in the system, the pattern of decentralised control was subsequently reinforced by norms of local democracy and grassroots participation. Yet, while history and the weight of democratic norms protected local autonomy, other factors, working in a contrary direction, recently led to some involvement of national party organisations.

Party candidates have typically been chosen by local party associations meeting in public assemblies to select their constituency standard-bearers (Carty and Erickson 1991). Any number of individuals could be nominated, and the local members who attended the assemblies decided among the nominees. If more than two people were nominated, a majority vote was required and a series of ballots was held, usually at the one meeting. The person who received the fewest votes dropped off with each ballot. In many cases, however, the meetings were a formality, either because the MP or another notable local figure was seeking the candidacy, or simply because only one person came forward for nomination.

In selecting their candidates, local party associations have usually opted for people who resided in or near the constituency's boundaries. Outsiders could not easily parachute in, particularly to ridings which the party had some chance of winning. Rules and practices surrounding candidate selections were also determined largely by the local parties. Little intervention or supervision from regional or national party levels was evident and, typically, there was limited outside assistance in recruiting prospective candidates.

The origins of this local control lie in the politics of nineteenth-century Canada when political parties were mainly cliques of notables supporting a leader, and parties outside of Parliament were loose networks of local supporters tied to the parties through leading figures in local communities. There were no national party organisations, and even the notion of formal party membership had no real meaning. The idea that local supporters should determine their candidate, and the rules by which these candidates were chosen, gained a strong hold in this context, retaining its legitimacy even after the parties developed national organisations, created national party constitutions, introduced formal memberships, and began to hold regular national conventions. Nor was the parochial focus of the process fundamentally challenged by the entrance of new, more mass-based parties, such as the CCF, into the system. Infused with notions of grassroots participation, such parties have reinforced norms of local independence in candidate selection.

National party involvement

Pressure grew for national party involvement in candidate selection with increasing party organisation, more election regulation, and the nationalisation of election campaigns. The introduction of broadcasting regulations that gave more air time to parties which nominated more candidates made it important to contest virtually all constituencies across the country. Accordingly, outside party officials began to intervene when, in hopeless ridings, no one came forward to run under their banner. Also, as parties became increasingly institutionalised, they began to standardise their procedures and structures. Some of the regulations introduced, such as rules on party membership, had implications for candidate selection. In addition, with the leader's veto, a means by which to impose national party preferences and a national party agenda with respect to candidates was realised in law, even if, in practice, the mechanism was rarely used.

Pressures for more national party involvement in selection intensified in the late 1980s. Partly this reflected a growing concern about group and issue mobilisation that threatened takeovers of local selection by outsiders whose allegiance to the parties was limited. Local selection rules were typically few, resulting in very limited requirements of those standing for the candidacy and of those voting at selection meetings. Since the number of even nominal members choosing the local candidate was usually small – an estimated 250 votes would have won half the contested party nominations for the 1988 election (Erickson and Carty 1991) – local selection was easily captured.

In some constituencies, 'single issue' groups such as anti-abortion organisations had mobilised their members to join a particular local party. Although such groups had limited success in capturing nominations, they raised concern about manipulation of the process. Other constituencies had been witness to fierce contests between aspiring candidates who had mobilised ethnic communities to join a local party and support them for the nomination. Sometimes these struggles continued after the selection meetings, involving appeals to regional party officials and complaints concerning the local rules and procedures – or lack thereof. There were few such situations but they attracted considerable media attention, and parties began to worry that the number of such instances would escalate and foster internal divisions. More pressure for greater national party involvement also came from those critical of the narrow range of Canadians represented on the benches in Parliament. In particular, women's groups demanded that national party organisations adopt procedures that would result in more female candidates in competitive ridings.

Finally, national parties were aware the candidate teams they were mounting faced increasing public scrutiny. The national media were commenting on who was running under the different party labels in terms of documenting the representation of women or other minorities, and examining the political or private personae of individual candidates. While the national parties were being held accountable for the composition of their candidates teams, their lack of influence left them vulnerable to the vagaries of the loosely structured, permeable selection process in which many candidates were effectively self-selecting. Consequently, national party organisations became even more interested in expanding their role in candidate selection. This inevitably produced some tension between local forces and national party objectives. The central–local tension focussed around different issues in different parties, and was not equally important for all parties, but it shaped some modifications in the recruitment process for the 1993 election.

Recruitment rules and practices were developed and altered in the late 1980s and early 1990s in the context of uncertainty for the parties. In a system in which the turnover of seats was already comparatively high, the instability of the party system could be seen as an added challenge or an opportunity. Few seats could be designated as safe for any party, a discouraging situation for potential recruits who were seeking candidacies that promised a long-term career. On the other hand, there would be more candidacies that were electorally competitive.

The Liberals and national involvement

Each party approached recruitment for the 1993 election with a different agenda. The Liberals, who had held the lead in the opinion polls for much of the time since the 1988 election, were concerned to have a team of candidates that would stand up to national scrutiny and would be attractive to the electorate, especially in the absence of a charismatic party leader. The new party leader, Jean Chrétien, had been chosen in 1990, and, although he had a long history in politics, prior to the election he had a lacklustre image among the electorate.

The Liberals' efforts to address concerns about candidate selection in their party were part of a larger process of party reorganisation begun after their second consecutive election loss in 1988. In response to concerns that the national party had so little influence in shaping their candidate team, the Reform Commission that examined the party's organisation recommended implementing a national framework of selection rules. Accordingly, the party added a clause to its national constitution which gave its National Campaign Committee power to establish rules of procedure for the selection of candidates.

The rules adopted for the 1993 election established a national framework for selection procedures with provision for regional variations. By these rules, prospective nominees for party candidacies had to be approved by provincial campaign chairpersons, who were themselves appointed by the national leader. These chairpersons were also given other powers they could use to influence the outcomes of selection, including deciding the schedule for filing nomination papers and for holding selection meetings. But the provision that drew the most attention allowed the party leader to by-pass a nomination meeting and appoint the local party candidate. Such appointments could be used for a number of purposes, including to avoid divisive local contests focussed around issues such as abortion, to increase the number of women candidates in competitive ridings, as well as to place 'star' candidates on the party's election team.

In keeping with its attempts to have some control over the process, the national party imposed a general freeze on the selection process until the regulations for each province were set in place. By the time most local associations had begun serious planning for their selection meetings the party's front-running position in the polls made Liberal candidacies very attractive in many constituencies.

The NDP and representative recruitment

The agenda driving change in the NDP was a desire to recruit more women and minority candidates. The goal was to nominate female candidates in half the constituencies in the country, and to have 15 per cent of its candidates from racial minorities, the disabled, or aboriginal groups. In the 1988 election, 28 per cent of the party's candidates, but only 12 per cent of its MPs, were women. In response to this situation, the women's organisation within the party had campaigned actively in support of a mandatory policy on gender equity in the selection process. At the party's 1991 national convention, these women succeeded in getting a resolution passed in support of mandatory guidelines, and a constitutional amendment adopted that gave the party's Federal Council the authority to intervene in the selection process in order to establish rules that would 'achieve affirmative action goals' (Edney 1991).

Notwithstanding these developments, it soon became apparent that strong norms in the party concerning local democracy would make the imposition of mandatory outcomes impossible. The provisions subsequently adopted by the NDP stipulated that local associations should follow procedures that would facilitate, but not require, the achievement of affirmative action goals (Erickson 1995b). Usually, those procedures were designed regionally by groups of representatives from local associations. The national party undertook to oversee the affirmative action plans in associations with MPs who were not seeking reselection.

In 1991 when the NDP began working on its policies on women and minority candidates, its popularity ratings were averaging 25 per cent in the opinion polls, suggesting it would do comparatively well in the next election. However, as election-time drew closer, the party's ratings dropped and what had looked like a party whose candidacies were promising began to seem like one in which even its safest ridings were at risk.

Conservative continuity

In contrast, the Conservatives were less concerned with revising their selection procedures or increasing the influence of the national party in the process. As the party with the most sitting members, it could expect many uncontested and generally unproblematic nominations as MPs signalled their desire to run again for the party. Overall, the party's selection process was relatively unstructured by national regulations, with only sketchy national guidelines laid out for the local parties. Since most of the associations that had open candidacies held their selection meetings after the new leader was chosen, but before the election campaign had progressed very far, a majority of new candidates was chosen at a time when the party was in a reasonably competitive position.

New party practices: reform and the BQ

The new parties followed traditional practices of local selection. But each had their own special policies for candidate selection. The Reform Party, in particular, devoted considerable attention to developing its procedures in this area, as reflected in its guidelines for local associations. As a party movement, Reform had attracted a number of enthusiastic recruits, many of whom were interested in standing. Since Reform's ideological position is staked to the right of the rest of the parties, some it attracted were extremists who could be embarrassing to the party in an election campaign. Because it had been particularly critical of the political class, the party was concerned that the candidates on its slate would stand up to popular scrutiny of their public personae and personal lives. Yet the national party organisation was limited in the control it could exert over the composition of its candidate team, because the party's ideological attraction for the public was also partly grounded in its reputation for grassroots' involvement and influence in party decisions. The national organisation could not be seen as imposing candidates or restricting the choices of local associations. Consequently, the national party produced an extensive set of *voluntary* guidelines for its local associations to use in their candidate search and selection procedures. In addition, a long questionnaire was distributed to local associations for prospective candidates to complete voluntarily.

In the Bloc Québécois, the party constitution says the local riding association members are to select candidates but provides for the supervision of local selection by the Quebec organisation. The rules and procedures for selection meetings are set by the central Electoral Committee, which grants permission for selection meetings to be held, and which can intervene in the nomination process in critical situations. According to the rules drawn up for the 1993 election, the Electoral Committee could oppose a prospective nominee for a candidacy prior to a selection meeting 'pour des raisons graves' (Bloc Québécois 1993: 1). Similarly, in exceptional circumstances, the party leader could appoint a local candidate.

One aspect of the Bloc's approach to local control that sets it apart from the other parties is the lack of residency rules for membership in local associations. The other four parties had at least some requirements in this regard. In the BQ, there were no such limits. Although this is somewhat contentious within the party, it is consistent with a notion of community that extends to the province as a whole and may derive some impetus from the party's overall focus on Quebec as a distinct community in Canada.

Localised selection, competition and party democracy

The local character of party selection continued to prevail as parties chose their candidates for the 1993 general election: most candidates were still chosen by local party associations at local selection meetings.

The Liberal leader used his power to appoint only fourteen candidates (5 per cent of those who ran under the party's label). For the NDP a number of candidates were appointed in ridings in which the party had effectively no local association, and, similarly, the BQ leadership appointed candidates in a small number of ridings where local party activity was minimal. But overall, according to the Candidates Survey, only 3 per cent of candidates were appointed by party officials from outside their local riding.

Yet while local selection was the norm, there were limits to local autonomy and choice. First, there was evidence from the Liberal Party, particularly in Ontario, that outside party officials did intervene in some instances when controversy threatened. For example, challenges to incumbent reselection were effectively eliminated and in some instances the party leadership denied controversial aspirants the right to run for a nomination (see, for example, Delacourt and McInnes 1993; Ward 1993).[5]

Even more serious for party democracy, in many local associations members had little, if any, choice. As noted earlier, norms in all the parties tend to protect incumbents from challenge. Thus, virtually all MPs who indicated their interest in running for re-election faced no official challenge to their reselection. But uncontested selection was not limited to MPs. Among non-incumbents, 42 per cent of candidates did not face any rivals. Moreover, in the contests that did occur, the pool of prospective candidates was very limited. Half of those candidates who faced competition faced only one opponent. Only a fifth of those who won in a competitive ballot faced more than two opponents at their selection meeting.

Although competition for new candidacies was related to the electoral prospects of a local party, restricted choice was not limited to associations with the poorest chances of winning. As Table 3.2 shows, among the new candidates who won their seats, 18 per cent had won their nominations by acclamation at a local selection meeting. A further third had faced only one other aspirant.

Other data in Table 3.2 confirm that the lack of competition within the

---

[5] Although some of the Liberals' attempts to manage nominations may have been designed to avoid controversy, in many instances it still erupted, especially with respect to the leader's appointments. Press coverage tended to focus on opposition to the appointments and editorials on the practice were disapproving. In the Constituency Survey, even some Liberal respondents wrote in negative comments about the practice of and provisions for leader appointments. However, not all Liberals' comments concerning leader appointments were negative, and when asked about the influence the national party leadership has over the selection of party candidates only 30 per cent of Liberals responding to the Constituency Survey said it was too great. Still, by comparison, only 12 per cent of respondents from the other parties said the influence of national party leadership was too great.

Table 3.2. *Competition for nomination*

Competitiveness of selection	Electoral success 1993		Electoral competitiveness*			
	Won %	Lost %	Safest[a] %	Marginal[b] %	Unlikely win[c] %	Hopeless[d] %
No competitors**	21	47	32	30	38	65
Two competitors	29	28	27	29	38	24
Three competitors	23	15	14	26	20	9
More than three competitors	28	9	27	14	5	2
N	97	412	37	76	56	186

Notes:
* These data do not include Reform or BQ candidates.
** Includes 3 per cent not selected at a meeting.
[a] Seat won by 10 per cent margin in 1988.
[b] Seat won by less than 10 per cent or lost seat by 10 per cent or less in 1988.
[c] Between 10 and 20 per cent fewer votes than the winner in 1988.
[d] More than 20 per cent behind the winner in 1988.
Source: Canadian Candidate Survey 1993 (non-incumbents only).

traditional parties[6] was not limited to uncompetitive constituency associations. Using a measure of local competitiveness devised from the results of the last election, a third of the non-incumbents who ran in their parties' most competitive seats said they won their candidacy by acclamation. A further third faced only one other competitor for their position.

The results also indicate that when a local party assessed its chances of victory most favourably, competition for its new candidacies was far from guaranteed. Where seats were judged to be 'safe' by the local association fewer than half had a competitive race for their nomination. For those whose chances were characterised as 'good' a quarter had no competition, and a further third had only two aspirants on their nomination ballots (see Table 3.3).

Competition for new candidacies was most frequent in the Reform party (see Table 3.4). Almost two-thirds of Reform candidates faced competition for their position, and more than half had at least two other competitors on their selection ballot. Among the other parties, non-incumbent candidates for the Conservative and BQ parties were most

---

[6] This indicator is only used for the traditional parties. In the 1988 election Reform was just months old thus using results from that election as an indicator of its local competitiveness in 1993 would be inappropriate. The BQ did not exist in 1988.

Table 3.3. *Competition for nomination by perceived election chances*

| Competitiveness of selection | Perceived electoral competitiveness* | | | |
	Safe %	Good chance %	Unlikely %	Hopeless %
No competition**	56	24	48	66
Two competitors	12	29	30	20
Three competitors	6	26	18	9
More than three competitors	25	22	4	6
N	16	235	95	35

Notes:
* Question: 'When your candidate was being nominated, how did your local association assess its chances of victory in your constituency? Was victory considered to be: safe; we had a good chance; unlikely; hopeless?
** Does not include the five local associations in which no selections were held.
Source: Constituency Survey 1993 (non-incumbent only).

likely to face competition, and among the Tories a third faced two or more other aspirants. Even though the Liberals' position in the polls was good throughout the time selections were taking place, only half their non-incumbent candidates won their nomination in a contest, and just a quarter had more than one other competitor on their selection ballot. Only the NDP, whose election prospects at the time of most nomination contests were seen by their local parties as most bleak, had less competition for their candidacies than did the Liberals.[7]

In many local parties, the lack of competition for new candidacies was considered a problem. In the *Constituency Survey*, a majority of members said either it was a chore to find a candidate for the election (21%), or there was not enough competition for their nomination (33%). On the other hand, when asked whether their local party had discouraged any prospective candidates from seeking the nomination, a few of the local association respondents (17%) did say they had. This was more likely to be reported by associations in which three or more people had run for their candidacy. Few associations with just one or two nominees on their candidacy ballot said they had discouraged anyone from running.

[7] In the Constituency Association Survey, 60 per cent of NDP associations indicated that their local association assessed its chance of a local victory unlikely or hopeless at the time when their local candidate was being chosen. By comparison 20 and 19 per cent of Conservative and Liberal associations, respectively, indicated their association considered the chances of local victory unlikely or hopeless.

Table 3.4. *Competition for candidacies by party*

Competitiveness of selection	PC %	Liberal %	NDP %	Reform %	BQ %
No competition*	39	49	61	20	36
Two competitors	26	26	30	28	36
Three competitors	21	17	7	24	18
More than three	14	8	2	28	9
Total	111	109	138	123	33

Note:
* Includes 4 per cent of candidates who were appointed by local or outside officials.
Source: Candidate Study 1993 (non-incumbent only).

Whether or not local party members had some choice as they set about nominating their candidates was not the only problem for party democracy. The question of membership recruitment was also an issue. In some associations, becoming a candidate was less about gaining the support of committed party locals than about selling enough new party memberships to personal supporters. According to the Constituency Survey, in most associations (84 per cent) where there were contests for the party nomination, the successful aspirant had recruited people to join the party and vote for him or her at the selection meeting. In a third of the contested selections, the proportion of new members signed up by the various contestants more than doubled the total membership of the local party (see Table 3.5). High levels of recruitment were most frequent in the Liberal, Conservative and BQ parties. In the Reform Party, where competition for candidacies was greatest, high membership recruitment was a rare occurrence. Membership recruitment is facilitated by the rules of many local parties. In a third of the associations in the *Constituency Survey*, people had to be members for only fifteen days or less in order to vote at a selection meeting.

The outcome of the process

The outcome of the process can be analysed in terms of the major factors which are usually considered in the composition of political elites, namely the gender, occupational class and local roots of legislators. Canada's record for electing women to the national legislature was, until the 1980s, a very poor one. In the 1984 election the proportion of women MPs virtually doubled, to 10 per cent, and there were indications that the parties had become aware of the electoral advantages in having more

Table 3.5. *Membership recruitment patterns*

Recruited members as proportion of local membership	All %	PC %	Liberals %	NDP %	Reform %	BQ %
10 per cent or less	33	4	5	73	48	18
11 to 30 per cent	19	17	5	24	26	0
31 to 50 per cent	14	19	12	3	17	9
Over 50 per cent	35	60	78	0	8	73
N	215	48	40	33	83	11

Source: Canadian Constituency Survey 1993.

women candidates (Erickson 1991). In the 1988 election, the percentage of women in the House increased again, to 13 per cent. With this election Canada placed about mid-point in the representation of women among established democracies (Brodie 1991; Norris and Lovenduski 1995).

For women's groups, the 1993 election was seen as another opportunity to improve the representation of women in the House of Commons. The Royal Commission on *Electoral Reform and Party Finances* (1991) had targeted the issue of women's presence in the House as a critical problem of equity and fairness. The traditional parties continued to be interested in increasing their number of women candidates. Moreover, as the election approached it became apparent that the NDP and Conservative parties would be headed by women. The NDP had chosen Audrey McLaughlin as leader in December 1989, thereby breaking the barrier to that job. When the Conservatives chose Kim Campbell as their leader in June of 1993, she became Canada's first woman prime minister.

Going into the election, the NDP with its process-oriented affirmative action policy had the most rigorous approach for nominating more women, and the most ambitious target (Erickson 1995b). The Liberals set a target that 25 per cent of its candidates would be women, and their Women's Commission provided workshops, resource materials and encouragement for women aspirants. The Conservatives did not set any targets for the nomination of women candidates, however Kim Campbell, the leader, had often voiced her support for increasing the number of women in politics and, with a woman leader, the party's image in terms of being receptive to women candidacies seemed altered. Moreover, Conservative women's groups mounted support for women candidacies, encouraging women to come forward at the local level.

Neither Reform or BQ had any particular policies with respect to women candidates. For many in the Reform party, the project of increasing women's representation was highly suspect, catering as it did to what many of its members saw as a 'special interest'. The extensive guidelines for candidate selection drawn up by the national office did not include special proposals or programmes to advance female candidacies, nor did the party have a separate women's organisation to seek out and promote women nominees. Similarly, for the BQ the question of women's representation was not on its agenda. The party's primary project is to take Quebec out of Canada and thus create conditions that would make the party itself, and hence subsequent candidacies, redundant. The party had no special proposals or programmes to promote women candidacies, nor a women's organisation.

The focus on women in 1993 had some impact on the outcome. The percentage of women running for parties increased to one quarter of all candidates (see Table 3.6) although this varied considerably by party, and, as a result, the increase in terms of membership in the House was modest. In part due to an extraordinarily high turnover rate among MPs, a factor critical for increasing the number of women legislators (Darcy, Welch and Clark 1994; Young 1991), the percentage of women increased from 13 to 18 per cent of MPs. In comparative terms, Canada's rate of female MPs is above the levels in the United Kingdom (9 per cent) and the United States (11 per cent), and fairly comparable to many European countries, but it continues to be well below the rates of leading countries such as Sweden (40 per cent) and Norway (39 per cent).

Among the parties, those that were least successful electorally nominated the largest number of women. The NDP, which won only 9 seats, nominated 113 women. While the party's target of 50 per cent women candidates was not achieved, the substantial increase in its women candidates from 1998 (28 per cent to 39 per cent) suggests the mandated procedures did have some effect.

The Conservatives, who won just two seats, ran sixty-seven women, 23 per cent of their total candidates. This was thirty more than they ran in the previous election – an increase that occurred in spite of the fact that the party had had a high proportion of incumbents and only fourteen of them were women. It seems the symbolism of having a woman leader had an effect in attracting women to run for the party. Although the Liberals had publicly set a goal that a quarter of its candidates would be women, the nomination of women became a difficult issue. When by March 1993 the party appeared to be short of its target objective, the leader began to exercise his power to designate candidates and appointed a number of women. By election time he had appointed nine women (out of fourteen appointments), and the party still fell short of its goal. It ran sixty-four women, 22 per cent of its total candidates, up from 17 per cent in 1988.

Table 3.6. *The social background of candidates and legislators*

	Candidates	Legislators
Gender		
Women	24	18
Men	76	82
Education:		
High school or less	9	9
College or technical	9	9
Some university	19	14
University degree	30	31
Postgraduate degree	34	37
Employment status:		
In paid work	37	41
Self-emlployed	40	44
Fulltime education	5	5
Retired	5	5
Homemaker	2	0
Unemployed	7	0
Selected occupations:		
Senior management	8	10
Professionals	43	42
Middle management	11	9
Small business owners	8	8
Technical and paraprofessional	3	2
Sales and service	6	5
Administrative	4	6
Clerical	1	0
Skilled trades	3	3
Labouring occupations	1	0
Farmers	5	10
N	625	134

Source: Canadian Candidate Survey 1993.

The proportion of women on the electoral slates of the Reform and BQ parties was substantially lower than it was for the traditional parties. The BQ ran ten women (13 per cent of their total number of candidates), while Reform ran twenty-three women (11 per cent of their total).

What explains the paucity of women? While women remain under-represented in party candidacies, especially the most competitive ones, there is no evidence that this is a result of the prejudices of local party members who vote at selection meetings. When women put their names forward for selection, they were equally as successful as their male counterparts (Erickson 1995b). Still, party practices appear to affect the number of women who come forward. Aggressive policies such as the active recruitment of women by regional and national party officials, and the mandatory affirmative action procedures undertaken by the NDP, may affect the number of women who put their names forward.

Candidates characteristically shared a fairly common background. Given the local nature of the selection process, it should come as no surprise that most of the candidates resided in the ridings in which they competed. This was to be expected of MPs, two-thirds of whom lived in their constituencies, usually for many years. But even among new candidates, 78 per cent said they lived in the riding in which they sought a seat, and almost 60 per cent had lived there for more than ten years.

In terms of their class and educational characteristics, Canadian candidates and legislators reflect a pattern well known in other Western democracies: they are well educated and overwhelmingly middle-class (see Table 3.6). About two-thirds had a university degree, and over half had a postgraduate degree. Fewer than 10 per cent had only a high school diploma or less. Most were employed; the rest were typically in full-time education or were retired, and few were unemployed or homemakers. Reflecting the importance for politicians of flexible occupations, many were self-employed. Reflecting the common occupational bias, half the candidates who were employed were senior managers or professionals yet surprisingly, given the historical link in Canada between MPs and being a lawyer, only 10 per cent were lawyers. About a fifth were in middle management positions or owned their own small business. In common with other parliamentary elites, almost no Canadian candidates were drawn from working-class jobs: 3 per cent were in skilled trades and less than one per cent were in labouring occupations. The occupational pattern among legislators was very similar except that none was in a labouring or clerical occupation. Although working-class representation is limited across all established democracies, Canada has particularly weak recruitment channels for class representation.

Amateurs or professionals?

In many other countries party service and political experience characterise the recruitment pool from which candidates are drawn (see McAllister chapter 2). Yet strikingly in Canada, with caucus-cadre party organisations, political background and party credentials are not critical resources. Canadian candidates are, in many respects, political amateurs. Only a quarter (27 per cent), *including the incumbents* had ever run for election to the House before. Among non-incumbents, only 12 per cent had previously run for election to the House before and 6 per cent had

Table 3.7. *The political backgrounds of candidates*

	Incumbents* N=107	Non-incumbents N=359 N=158
Political experience		
Previous candidate for		
House of Commons		
Traditional parties	100	14
New parties	–	6
Ran for provincial legislature:		
Traditional parties	10	13
New parties	–	5
Elected to provincial legislature:		
Traditional parties	7	4
New parties	–	2
Candidate for local government:		
Traditional parties	41	29
New parties	–	24
Elected to local government:		
Traditional parties	36	25
New parties	–	17
Party experience		
Held local party office:		
Traditional parties	47	54
New parties	–	41
Held provincial party office:**		
Traditional parties	26	25
Held national party office:		
Traditional parties	26	15
New parties	–	12

Notes:
* The number of incumbents in the new parties was too small.
** Reform Party and the BQ have no equivalent of provincial wings of traditional parties.
Source: Canadian Candidate Survey 1993.

run for a provincial legislature. Fewer than 5 per cent had been elected to a provincial legislature. This lack of experience was apparent among candidates for both the new parties and the traditional ones. Even among the latter only 14 per cent of non-incumbents had previously run for the House of Commons and 13 per cent had run for provincial office (see Table 3.7).

Table 3.8. *Importance of candidate qualities for local members*

Qualities:	Mean score*	N
Personal energy and enthusiasm	3.6	461
Committed to constituency	3.6	461
Supports their political views	3.5	455
Likely to win votes	3.5	458
Good speaker	3.3	458
Local resident	3.2	459
Good personal appearance	3.0	460
Stable home life	2.9	451
Well educated	2.9	459
Experienced party worker	2.6	461
Political experience	2.5	454
Nationally well known	1.7	457

Note:
* Responses were scored: Very important=4; Quite important=3;
Not very important=2; Not at all important=1.
Source: Canadian Constituency Survey 1993.

Nor was local politics a common experience for most candidates. Only a third of candidates had ever run for local office. Among non-incumbents only a fifth had ever been elected to local government. Compared to the political experience of the British MPs and parliamentary candidates (Norris and Lovenduski 1995), or those in Australia, Germany or Finland discussed in this book, the Canadian candidates stand in stark contrast. Almost a third of the candidates in Britain had stood for Parliament before, about two-thirds had been candidates for local government, and from 44 to 66 per cent had been elected to local government.

This lack of political experience appears to reflect the Canadian party culture. In the Constituency Survey, respondents were asked to indicate how important it was to party members that candidates had certain qualities. Just 12 per cent believed political experience to be very important. In the list of thirteen qualities respondents were asked to assess, political experience was almost at the bottom of the list (see Table 3.8). This was true of both the traditional and newer parties. If, as Norris and Lovenduski suggest (1995), British candidates need only to demonstrate *some* political experience, in Canada it seems candidates do not even have to do that.

Nor is party involvement a critical factor when parties select their new candidates, contrary to Australia (see McAllister chapter 2). Among non-incumbent candidates, almost one-fifth were *not* active in their party before they sought nomination in 1993. Of those who were active, a third devoted little time (less than five hours per month) to party work.[8] A majority of candidates had held party office, but again many (42 per cent) had not. In contrast in Britain from 87 to 96 per cent of MPs and candidates had held local party office.

Again, as Table 3.8 demonstrates, the lack of party activity among candidates reflected opinion in local parties that a background in party affairs is not that important for candidates. Being an experienced party worker was scored comparatively low, like political experience in general. Only 14 per cent said their local party members thought being an experienced party worker was a very important quality for their local candidate. Political and party amateurism appear to be of little consequence for many aspiring politicians, and may even be an advantage.

Conclusions

Party selection in Canada and the candidates to which the process gives rise provide a useful comparison for other countries whose electoral systems are similarly centred on single-member constituencies or ridings. Locally focussed, but party-controlled, the candidate selection system is highly permeable. Even in 1993, an election year in which many competitive candidacies were up for grabs, the overall level of competition for party nominations was modest. Incumbency restricted competition in some local parties, but still new candidacies were routinely won with little or no competition. This was evident even when seats were electorally promising. In addition, in many battles nominees succeeded by signing up more new members than their competitors. With little choice available for many local party members, and recruitment practices that often swamp the established membership of local associations, the phenomenon of party primaries does not guarantee that local party democracy is well preserved.

The candidates that emerged from this process in 1993 were, in many respects, similar to those who run for national office in other advanced democracies. They were well educated, and a majority were professionals

---

[8] Reflecting the enthusiasm of those involved in new political movements, the candidates for the two new parties were most active in their parties: 63 per cent of Reform candidates and 75 per cent of BQ candidates said they devoted more than five hours a month to party activities. By comparison, 43 per cent of PC candidates and 54 per cent of Liberal ones said they spent that much time.

or senior managers. Working-class representation was particularly low, even in comparison to other countries. A quarter of the candidates were women, but among the parties the proportion of female candidates was highest in the least successful parties. Finally, in a reflection of the local character of the process, candidates were overwhelmingly locally based, with almost two-thirds having lived for more than ten years in the ridings for which they sought election.

In terms of the candidates' political experience, neither the party nor other political requirements of candidates were very demanding. Aspiring candidates did not need to demonstrate their experience in prior national, provincial or even local elections in order to win a party nomination. Perhaps more problematic for the parties is that the level of party activity required was also modest. Candidacies should be among the most prized positions the parties are able to bestow. That many who attain these positions are not very active partisans is testimony to the weakness of Canadian parties as participatory organisations.

4   Finland

Voitto Helander

This chapter focusses on the recruitment of candidates for parliamentary election in Finland. On the one hand pathways to the Parliament, the Eduskunta, have been paved by procedures which are relatively highly formalised and standardised. On the other hand it has been emphasised that the Finnish recruitment system is highly decentralised (Gallagher 1988: 245; Gallagher, Laver and Mair 1995: 129–35; Ranney 1981: 76–89). For this reason a description of the opportunity structure, including the electoral system and legal regulations governing the process, makes a natural starting point for the analysis. Subsequent sections outline the fragmented multi-party system in Finland, and consider how supply and demand affect the outcome. The main questions are: what kinds of person become candidates and get elected? And to what extent do elitist tendencies characterise the selection process?

At the empirical level both supply and demand factors (Norris and Lovenduski 1995) are taken into consideration. The *demand-side* analysis is focussed on the intra-party selection process. We analyse the strategies used by the district (constituency) party leadership to bring about as good an array of candidates as possible. For this reason we consider how far the national party leadership has flexibility in compiling the final list, how far the district party organisations have taken advantage of the opportunities which the Electoral Act provides, and to what extent the district party leadership has tried to manipulate the list in relation to the preferences expressed by the party members and the local party branches. The activities of the district party organisations were analysed in connection with the parliamentary election of March 1995.[1]

---

[1] A survey covering the salaried officials of the parties represented in the Eduskunta was completed in January–February 1995. As many as ninety-three or 88.6 per cent (n=105) of those surveyed responded to the questionnaire. On the basis of the data particularly the gatekeeper role of the district party leadership was under consideration with the aim of explaining similarities and differences between the parties. The questionnaire included questions on the activities of the local party branches as proposers of aspirants for the party primaries. The implementation of the party primaries was also under consideration with a special focus on the measures taken by the district party leadership for balancing the final list.

The other main questions concern the *supply side*. This focusses upon what kind of resources and motivation the candidates possess. The analysis considers three issues. First, in terms of social background and political experience: what differences are there between those who became a candidate and those who failed? Second, concerning the motives of the candidates, and what kind of conceptions do they have of the role of a deputy. Third, in terms of political careers: is the pathway to parliament covered by a red carpet, or does success require a long and thorny path through many unsuccessful efforts? To shed light on these issues a survey of candidates was completed in the Turku (southern) constituency in the 1995 general election.[2]

The structure of opportunities

The opportunities to become a legislator in Finland are strongly influenced by the electoral system and the legal regulations surrounding the recruitment process. The 200 members of the unicameral Finnish Parliament are elected for a four-year term on the basis of proportional representation. For electoral purposes the country is divided into fifteen constituencies. Fourteen multi-member constituencies vary in size from seven to thirty-one members, with the exception of the single-member self-governing province of Aland. This means that in practice an electoral threshold exists in the smallest constituencies, even though there are no formal national or constituency thresholds.

Until 1969 the parties established the rules for the selection of candidates and the running of campaigns. The principal criticism against the old system concerned its highly centralised character. Both the process of candidate-nomination and campaign work were in the hands of the national party leadership (Sundberg 1989: 55–7; Sundberg 1995: 46). As a consequence certain legislative measures were introduced in the late 1960s. These included the adoption of the Party Act, the Decree on Public Party Subsidies and the 1969 Electoral Act through which the dis-

---

The party rules (if there were any) and all information on the aspirants and the results of the party primaries were gathered with the party district survey. The party district data were completed by the official electoral statistics.

[2] The principal aim of the survey addressed to the candidates of the Turku constituency was to chart the supply-side factors included in the selection process. The questionnaire included items on the candidates' social and political background and associational affiliations. Their motives on representation were also under consideration. The survey comprised all those 176 candidates put up in the Turku constituency by political parties or non-party electoral alliances. One hundred and fourteen or 64.7 per cent of the candidates returned the questionnaire. There was not any systematic bias as far as the response rate of different educational, occupational, age, gender and party groups was concerned.

parity between the parties was radically reduced. All forms of undemocratic organisation as regards intra-party activities were outlawed. At first the parties were entitled to a monopoly in putting up candidates (Sundberg and Gylling 1992: 276–7), although this was repealed some years later, because it met with heavy criticism from the viewpoint of democracy (Pesonen 1995: 14.)

According to the new 1975 Electoral Act both political parties and individual eligible voters are entitled to put forward candidates. The procedure is different for each. A registered party is entitled to put up candidates equalling the number of seats in the multi-member constituency. The number of candidates, however, may total fourteen even in the smallest constituencies. Two or more parties are entitled to join together to form an electoral alliance (bloc), in which case the number of candidates may not exceed the seats assigned to the constituency.

For an association of individual eligible voters to put up an electoral list at least one hundred eligible persons must sign the list. These lists can join an electoral alliance with other lists but they are not allowed to establish such an alliance with political parties; hence, there cannot be any 'mixed' electoral coalitions between party lists and electoral lists.

Finland uses an *open* list system where voters prioritise among candidates. Every candidate in assigned a number. The voter casts his or her ballot for an individual candidate by writing down the number of the candidate on the ballot. The number of seats assigned to each party or electoral alliance is determined by the proportion of the total vote gained by its candidates. The distribution of seats to individual candidates is determined by their ranked order as expressed by the voters' individual preferences. The seats are allocated to the parties (electoral alliances) by the d'Hondt formula.

Each candidate of a party list or an electoral alliance is assigned a comparison number based on the following formula. The candidate who has received the most votes is assigned a comparison number equalling the total vote of the electoral alliance. The second in order is assigned one half of the total vote of the electoral alliance. The third in order receives a comparison number equal to one third of the vote and so on. All candidates in an electoral alliance are ranked according to these figures. When the comparison numbers have been counted for all candidates in the constituency the seats gained by each party list or electoral alliance are determined according to the order of the comparison numbers. The deputy delegates are determined by the ranked order in each party list or electoral alliance.

The order of the names on the party-list, or on the list of an electoral alliance, does not have any effect on the final result. By far the most usual way to build up a list is to put the names in alphabetical order. The other method in use has been to present the names of the candidates in the order resulting from the party primary. This kind of method is regularly applied by the Social Democrats. In an electoral alliance the candidates of different parties or lists are assigned successive electoral numbers.

The Electoral Act lays down certain general principles about the process of candidate selection. These include provisions on putting forward aspirants and managing candidate nomination. Every local party branch which is based on personal membership is entitled to nominate persons for the party primary. The Electoral Act further provides that a person supported by at least fifteen members of one party branch, or thirty members of separate party branches in the same constituency, must be taken onto the list for the party primary. The procedure also secures the right to participate for persons who have been disapproved of by the branch leadership. The nomination procedure presupposes that the person under consideration has given written approval for the candidacy. As far as the franchise in the party primary is concerned the Electoral Act provides that every party member of full legal age has the right to vote, using a secret ballot.

Legally all parties must hold a primary unless no more than the number of candidates assigned to the constituency have been nominated. If the party has no internal rules for candidate selection the Electoral Act provides the framework although the law does not regulate such practical issues as joining an electoral alliance, the timetable of a party primary, and the number of aspirants for which a party member may vote.

Most parties have drawn up model rules in line with the provisions of the Electoral Act for organising candidate selection at the constituency level. These include such matters as the way in which the party branches or individual party members can make proposals for the nomination process; whether a party member is entitled to vote for only a single or for several aspirants; and whether the voting may be completed by postal ballot or in some other way.

After the party primary has been completed a decision on the final list is taken by the district party organisation. According to the Electoral Act the district party organisation may depart from the order of the party primary on the approval of the party's central board. The right to change is limited to one quarter of the nominees who succeeded in the party primary. Moreover the district party organisation is not allowed to remove those aspirants who have received most votes.

The party system

During the last half century the party system in Finland may be characterised as a fragmented multi-party system. The most successful

Table 4.1. *Parliamentary elections in Finland, 1945–95: elected members (N)*

Year	FPDU/LWA	SDP	FRP	CP	LPP	CL	NCP	SP	OTHER	Number of parties in parliament
1945	49	50	–	49	9	–	28	14	1	7
1948	38	54	–	56	5	–	33	14	–	6
1951	43	53	–	51	10	–	28	15	–	6
1954	43	54	–	53	13	–	24	13	–	6
1958	50	48	–	48	8	–	29	14	3	7
1962	47	38	–	53	13	–	34	14	3	8
1966	41	55	1	49	9	–	26	12	7	8
1970	36	52	18	36	8	1	37	12	–	8
1972	37	55	18	35	7	4	34	10	–	8
1975	40	54	2	39	9	9	35	10	2	10
1979	35	52	7	36	4	9	47	10	–	8
1983	27	57	17	38	–	3	44	11	3	8
1987	20	56	9	40	–	5	53	13	4	8
1991	19	48	7	55	1	8	40	12	10	9
1995	22	63	1	44	–	7	39	11	12	10

Notes:

FPDU = Finnish People's Democratic Union 1944–90; (included the Finnish Communist Party). Since 1990 'Left Wing Alliance' (LWA).

SDP = Social Democratic Party of Finland 1899– .

FRP = Small Farmers' Party of Finland, 1962–66; since 1966 Finnish Rural Party.

CP = Agrarian Union 1906–1965, Center Party since 1965.

LPP = National Progressive Party 1918–51; Finnish People's Party 1951–65; since 1965 Liberal People's Party.

CL = Christian League of Finland 1958– .

NPC = National Coalition Party 1918– .

SPP = Swedish People's Party 1906– .

OTHER = Included in 'Other' are the Swedish Left (one member in 1945); the Liberal Union (one member in 1962, the Constitutional Party (one member in 1975 and 1983), the Unity Party (one member 1975); and the Green Party (two members in 1983, four in 1987 and ten in 1991).

party (the Social Democrats in 1995) has never won more than 28.3 per cent of the vote or more than 63 seats out of the 200 in parliament. The number of parties winning parliamentary mandates has varied from six to ten, with eight parties as the average in the post-war Eduskunta.

When assessing the party system one point worth noting is the ease with which a party may be established in Finland. The Party Act 1968 presupposes that to be registered as a party an association must gather at least 5,000 signatures from persons eligible for Parliament. The relative ease with which a party can be established caused a flood of parties in the early 1990s. If a party does not succeed in gaining any seats in the Eduskunta at two successive elections it is removed from the party reg- istry. The party field has not been so badly fragmented as the number of parties with parliamentary seats might suggest. Since 1945 the share of the parliamentary mandates gained by the four biggest parties has never fallen below 80 per cent. Seen from this viewpoint the Finnish party system may be regarded as a four-party system with some more or less stable smaller parties completing it.

The Finnish party system has deviated from its Scandinavian counter- parts in certain respects. One conspicuous feature has been the relatively strong position of the Communists (the Finnish People's Democratic Union). The stronghold taken by the Center Party (CP) has also been a deviating feature from the Scandinavian party-model. In a similar way the position of the Social Democratic Party (SDP) has not been comparable to other Scandinavian countries, where the social democrats are by far the biggest or even a hegemonic party.

Since the early 1970s several changes in the party system have taken place. The Communists were for a time split into two separate parties. After strong competition between the majority wing and the Stalinists a reunification took place in the late 1980s under the name of the Left Wing Alliance (LWA). The support of the party fell from one quarter of the vote in 1945 down to 10 per cent in the early 1990s. Instead of being a big party it had become a middle-sized one on the Finnish scale.

The Swedish People's Party (SPP), representing the interests of the language-minority, has retained its support but the Liberals have almost completely lost their parliamentary representation. At the end of 1994 a new party, the Young Finns' Party, was established. The party succeeded in gaining two seats at the 1995 parliamentary election. In the 1960s two other parties emerged onto the parliamentary scene. The Finnish Rural Party (FRP) has – like other populist parties – had its ups and downs during the past two decades. On the contrary, another newcomer, the Christian League of Finland (CL) has established its position as a small party with relatively stable support all over the country. Since the early

1980s the Green movement has perhaps more than any other new political group had an impact on the Finnish party system. The movement was transformed in the 1980s into two parties with the Green League (GL) having taken the parliamentary position as a middle-sized party.

One conspicuous feature of the Finnish parties has been the development toward catch all-type parties. This particularly concerns the Social Democrats and the Center Party. But the tendency also characterises the other large and middle-sized parties. These developments have an impact on the relationships between the parties. One consequence has been the disappearance or fading of the ideological borderlines between the parties which were characteristic of the immediate post-war years. All parties are now eligible as cabinet parties. Finnish cabinets have often crossed the borderline between the socialist and non-socialist parties. A recent change in the Constitution includes a clear shift toward majority parliamentarism. As a consequence the formation of cabinets has become easier, and opportunities to establish effective coalitions have greatly increased.

The supply of candidates

As other chapters have noted, we can make a distinction between *professional* career politicians who have devoted many years to working their way up the ladder of party and local government office, and political *amateurs* who enter without such a background. One critique often directed at the Finnish electoral system, with the high weight put on voters' personal preferences, has concerned the quality of the candidates, particularly their lack of political experience and knowledge of societal issues. To maximise support parties are apt to recruit national celebrities onto their lists. The recruitment of persons who have often appeared in public, such as sportsmen, beauty queens, actors and television stars, may, according to this critique, bring in many members of Parliament who are politically inexperienced. To eliminate these kinds of tendencies proposals have been made to change the electoral system toward the 'closed' (or long) lists used in other Scandinavian countries.

It is true that parties have to certain extent tried to draw onto their lists persons who are well known and attractive but politically completely inexperienced. Particularly the non-socialist parties have recruited onto their lists certain national celebrities without any previous party career. Yet in reality the recruitment of celebrities has remained relatively marginal. Few candidates without any previous political career have been elected. During the past decades some dozen former sportsmen and other nationally well-known persons have been

Table 4.2. *Previous candidacy of newcomers to the*
Eduskunta in 1991 and 1995 (%)

	1991	1995
No previous candidature	31.9	45.1
One previous candidature	42.0	25.6
Two previous candidatures	17.4	18.3
Three previous candidatures	8.7	11.0
Total	100.0	100.0
N	(69)	(82)

elected. Most of them have, however, been party members for several years; a successful career in some other sector has indeed helped to gain a parliamentary mandate.

By far the most important factor explaining electoral success is incumbency (Ranney 1981: 98–9). Incumbents have proved to be so victorious that they have been regarded as a threat to democracy in several countries (Somit et al. 1994). Yet parliamentary turnover in Finland is about average for advanced democracies, since about one-third of the deputies leave the Eduskunta every election (Matland and Studlar 1995). Most of them give up their seats voluntarily. It is relatively exceptional for an MP to be defeated by a party colleague (Noponen 1989).

To examine the political experience of newcomers to the Eduskunta this was measured by whether they had run in previous parliamentary elections. Two newcomer-cohorts were analysed, namely those elected in 1991 and in 1995. The results suggest that some could gain a seat without much experience in previous elections but many entered parliament after at least three contests. This kind of career requires persistent political activity at the constituency level (cf. Czudnowski 1975: 187). Many newcomers to the Eduskunta have previous experience in campaigning work. The sample of candidates included only a couple of celebrities who were nationally well known.

Based on the survey in Turku we can analyse candidates' activities in local politics and affiliation in associations. The results support the idea that most candidates for Parliament have had a career at the municipal level. Three-fifths of the candidates held seats in municipal councils; most of them also on influential municipal boards. Yet it is true that almost a third (29 per cent) of the candidates could be seen as 'political amateurs' with neither previous experience nor active engagement in municipal affairs as elected officers or salaried office-holders. Many of the political amateurs were recruited by those parties or electoral alliances which emerged during the last year before the election.

Activity in associations also constitutes a good base for success in politics. About a third of the respondents held a post in an association at the national level. Most of these were in trade unions, professional associations, or organisations of entrepreneurs, that is, in occupational associations. The other types of association of importance were those of social policy and culture, including sports.

Organisational resources were divided very unevenly among the candidates. Among those candidates who were either elected or placed in the first half of the list of successful candidates there was not anybody without a post either in a municipal council or in the leadership of a nation-wide association (cf. Czudnowski 1975: 187). This means, in practice, that experience either in local politics or in an associational sphere is a necessary condition to being elected.

The Finnish electoral system with personal votes counting has also brought with it certain phenomena which are quite unknown in the systems applying closed (or long) party lists. Active personal advertising in newspapers and on television has until now been the most conspicuous feature in this respect. Given the lack of accurate data it is difficult to estimate how much most candidates have invested in personal advertising, but a clear positive correlation exists between the size of advertising budgets and the probability of being elected. Advertising does not, however, constitute a guarantee of getting a seat. On the contrary; there are numerous examples of actively advertised candidates with only very marginal electoral success (see Sundberg 1995: 59–63).

Certain new facilities for campaigning have emerged, especially during the past decade. The most important is the establishment of personal electoral teams of supporters. These are usually established several months before election day. In many cases the teams have already begun to play an important role during the campaign for nomination. In those parties with party primaries the supporter teams usually activate themselves before the primaries. Because the results of the party primaries are usually published in the mass media the success in the primary is an important indicator for voters. The primaries often indicate whose career is rising or falling; a setback in the primary may indicate that the career is going downhill.

When asked in the survey, about 70 per cent of the candidates reported that they had a group of supporters. The size of these groups varies from a couple of persons to several hundreds. Only 11 per cent of the candidates reported a supporter team consisting of more than one hundred people. A clear difference between the parties exists. A majority of the candidates of the established non-socialist parties and the SDP reported having personal teams, while the candidates of the political left and the small bourgeois parties almost completely lacked such groups. A similar issue concerns also another novelty of the 1990s, a personal electoral office for campaign work. Only 16 per cent of the candidates reported having a personal campaign office, and all of these belonged to the established parties.

Two trends in Finnish campaigning are worth mentioning. One is a shift from a collective, party-based style to individual candidate-concentrated work, even on the political left. The other is that campaign work has become professionalised, with campaign plans usually made by the advertising offices, and implemented by extensive supporter teams (Sundberg 1995: 53–9). As a consequence control by the party leadership has been reduced, and parties have become more decentralised (Sundberg 1989: 56–7).

Motivational factors

As several scholars have stressed, it is important, but very difficult, to penetrate the motivational factors of politicians (Norris and Lovenduski 1993a: 402–3). The motives of the candidates were charted in the survey by an open-ended question: 'For what reason did you want to stand for candidacy in this election?' Even if the question was put at a general level, the main part of the answers were codable in a relatively unambiguous way. Eight categories covered the motives expressed by the respondents (see Table 4.3). Many expressed the desire to exert influence on societal affairs, which may be interpreted as a conventional motive for politicians to participate in politics at the top level. The socialist candidates in particular emphasised this collective goal. The desire to advance the goals of the party was put forward particularly by one group of respondents, the candidates of the newly established parties who wanted to raise the profile of their party. Among those striving to advance the goals of certain groups the most often mentioned categories were to represent women, the unemployed, and old age pensioners, but few mentioned clear interest organisations.

Respondents motivated by a desire to correct some evil or deficiency in society referred most often to the actual problems in Finnish society. Unemployment was mentioned as the most acute and most serious such issue. Unemployment and the problems of financing public expenditure were by far the most widely discussed issues during the electoral campaign. It is no wonder that the candidates of the opposition parties, in particular, as well as the non-partisans, presented this reason for their political activity. Almost a quarter of the candidates mentioned certain

Table 4.3. *Motives for candidacy by party affiliation*

	Socialist	Non-socialist	Non-partisan	Total
Continue as a deputy	4.4	5.6	0.0	4.5
Exert influence on societal affairs	34.8	22.2	12.5	23.4
Advance the party goals	0.0	9.7	0.0	6.3
Advance the goals of certain groups	13.0	6.9	12.5	9.0
Correct certain obvious societal evils	4.4	19.4	25.0	17.1
Change the direction of politics	8.7	9.7	6.3	9.0
Request by certain group(s)	26.1	22.2	25.0	23.4
Personal motive	8.7	4.2	18.8	6.3
No answer	0.0	0.0	6.3	0.9
Total	100.0	100.0	100.0	100.0
N	23	72	16	111

Source: Candidate Survey in Turku, 1995.

outside stimuli, such as a request by a group, for their candidacy. This reason includes a reference to activities by a collective actor; the person under consideration has proved to be active and skillful enough to be asked to stand for Parliament. The collective – usually a party branch – has requested the respondent's consent to the post. The candidates of the political left have traditionally been motivated by this reason.

Many of the motives categorised as *personal* ones include such reasons as the possession of personal capacity or resources. As one female candidate put it: 'In this political situation women are capable, and are needed in good balance to solve the problems of society. I feel that I am such a kind of person.' Some respondents referred also to their life-situation, which allows effective participation in politics at that point in time.

The candidates of the constituency of Turku were also asked their preferences concerning the representation of different kinds of communities or groups. The question was formulated as follows:
'A deputy usually has some kind of conception about the group or community he/she represents in the first place. In the event that you get elected, do you regard it as your principal goal to promote the goals and affairs of
(1) the whole country,
(2) your own constituency,
(3) your own party,
(4) certain organised group(s) or
(5) certain population group(s)?'

Table 4.4. *The preferences of representation among candidates*

	Socialist	Non-socialist	Non-partisan	Total
Whole country	20.8	52.8	31.3	42.9
Own constituency	12.5	4.2	0.0	5.4
Own party	29.2	9.8	0.0	12.5
Certain interest group(s)	0.0	1.4	0.0	0.9
Certain population group(s)	8.3	2.8	50.0	10.8
Whole country+constituency	8.3	5.6	6.3	6.3
Whole country+party	4.2	11.1	0.0	8.0
Other combinations	16.3	12.5	12.5	13.4
Total	100.0	100.0	100.0	100.0
N	24	72	16	112

Source: Candidate Survey in Turku, 1995.

The findings can be interpreted in a relatively unambiguous way. The Burkean style of representation, with the emphasis on the affairs of the whole country, proved by far the most favoured alternative among the respondents. It may also be regarded as an 'easy' selection; like several western constitutions the Finnish constitution formally presupposes the independent Burkean style of representation. Promotion of those goals which the party regards as important is also clearly important to the candidates. In contrast, the representation of interest organisations is extremely exceptional. This may be somewhat unexpected since one of the most characteristic features for the 1995 parliamentary election was the success of the delegates of interest groups, particularly those of the trade union movement. As far as the partisans and non-partisans are concerned the emphasis put on different foci was as expected. Hence, the non-socialist candidates in particular stress the whole country as their main focus of representation. The leftist candidates put more emphasis on their own party as their principal group of reference. Finally, one half of the non-partisans prefer to represent certain demographic groups.

Demand-side factors

Electoral alliances – a way out from smallness?

It has been pointed out that the Finnish electoral system with the d'Hondt method greatly favours the large parties (see Sundberg 1989:

72–3; Nurmi and Lagerspetz 1984). To avoid this bias the small parties usually try to establish electoral alliances. They regard electoral alliances as 'correcting' the final results which are biased by the adoption of the d'Hondt instead of the Sainte Lague method, but also by the smallness of the constituencies. Minor parties usually stress the technical character of an electoral alliance, and how the votes cast are not wasted.

From the viewpoint of the participants the system of electoral alliances has its disadvantages as well (see Valen 1994: 292–3). One reason why the large parties are reluctant to join electoral alliances with the small parties lies in the fact that the number of personal votes gained determines the ranking order in an electoral alliance. For this reason the procedure may result in a more or less random outcome. A party gaining the most votes may lose the seats to its allies which have more 'stars' getting to the top of the list. By concentrating their votes on one main candidate the small parties with one or a few candidates usually may succeed at the expense of the larger party (Kuusela 1995). For this reason the ability to establish an electoral alliance is an art with strategic calculations. To avoid a random outcome, and to level the gains and losses between the partners, the parties often strive to bring about an electoral alliance in as many constituencies as possible. Because the district party organisations decide about entering electoral alliances, nation-wide cooperation between parties is often sacrificed to strategic local calculations.

Among the big Finnish parties it is only the Center Party that has been relatively active in joining electoral alliances. The small parties of the political centre, the Liberals, the CL and the SPP, have been the most usual companions of the Center Party. The other big parties, the SDP, the NCP, the LWA and the GL, have traditionally been reluctant to establish electoral alliances. In the 1995 election this tradition seems to have been broken. The SDP was the only big party not allying with other parties.

It is true that the Center Party has gained directly only marginal benefits from electoral alliances. It may be noticed that the party has even lost a lot of votes because the allies have been ideologically too polarised. Voters have often chosen to stay home, or to vote for a candidate on another party list, rather than support a small party to which he or she feels a certain aversion. The technical advantage gained through an electoral alliance may erode the support of the party on the ideological scene. This also concerns the small parties (Sundberg 1989: 73). The cooperation with the small parties of the political centre has, however, benefited the Center Party in an indirect way. Even if the party has lost seats it may have counted on support from its small alliance parties in legislative work.

The number of electoral alliances has increased during the existence of the Electoral Act (Sundberg 1989: 72). The electoral alliances have actually become essential to the existence of the small parties. For the 1995 elections as many as twenty-six electoral alliances – on average two per constituency – were established. It can be calculated that the electoral alliances secured about five to ten members for the small parties in this election. The allied partners often emphasise that the alliances are purely technical ones. It is true that alliances with ideologically relatively remote parties were established in several constituencies.[3]

Party primaries or party conventions?

Although the provisions of the Electoral Act presuppose that the party primary constitutes the principal procedure for candidate selection the practice differs considerably from this ideal (see Sundberg and Gylling 1992). There is only one party, the SDP, that has consistently applied the party primary method in its selection procedures. It had already applied it before the enactment of the Electoral Act in 1975, and was actively supporting the reform.

The NCP has also widely applied the party primary procedure, and the party has continually increased the use of the method. The reason reported by the district party secretaries for not applying the primary method in certain constituencies was simply the lack of sufficient supply; no more than the number of aspirants that can be put forward was offered by the local branches.

The Center Party which is – as far as the number of members is concerned – the biggest party in the country, applied the primary method for selection of candidates only in nine of the fourteen constituencies. The other principal method applied by the Center Party has been to nominate the candidates in special areas by organised party conventions (cf. Valen 1988). In these conventions the local party branches are represented by branch delegates. It is true that the convention system is not as democratic as the party primaries as it may be more easily controlled by the constituency party elite. The procedure is not, however, a very elitist one; the conventions usually gather tens or hundreds of participants to vote on the names put forward by the delegates.

The convention method is applied in the Center Party on two grounds. First, it constitutes an effective device for balancing the list, especially the

---

[3] The most curious effort was under consideration in the Mikkeli constituency where such parties as the Liberals, the LWA (Left Socialists), the FRP (Populists) and the CL (Christians) planned electoral cooperation to exceed the electoral threshold of about 11 per cent factually valid in this constituency. The party leadership of the LWA with its critical stance torpedoed, however, the unique project before it was put into effect. The case may, however, be symptomatic for future developments.

Table 4.5. *The characteristics of the nomination process: major parties in Finland*

	LWA	SDP	CP	NCP
The average number of aspirants supplied by party branches	17	41	18	27
The share of party-branch supplied aspirants (%)	40	32	15	30
Party primaries held in constituencies (%)	50	100	56	82
The average turnout in the party primary (%)	49	63	20	43
The share of aspirants dropped from the final list (%)	6	4	7	12
Candidates/aspirants (%)	97	40	80	60

geographical representation of different parts of the constituency. The geographical aspect is important to the Center Party which gets most of its supporters from the rural areas. The convention system also allows the balancing of the party list in other respects as well. The second reason for the extensive application of the convention procedure is based on the fact that the Center Party has entered into electoral alliances with other parties. The convention method can allow the district party leadership to regulate the number of candidates and eliminate intra-party conflicts. The Center Party arranged a party primary in all those districts in which it did not enter into an electoral alliance with other parties. As far as the other parties are concerned, particularly the CL and FRP, party primaries are very exceptional. The LWA applied the party primaries in seven of fourteen districts. The main reason for not using the party-primary method reported by the party districts was simply the fact that there were no more aspirants than the party could put on its lists.

The activity of party cadres in the selection process seems to vary somewhat between parties. The local branches have been most active in putting up aspirants for the nomination process. Related to the total number of local branches the Center Party membership has been more passive than that of the SDP and the NCP. In fact only 15 per cent of the local Center Party branches have proposed aspirants. The share for the SDP and the NCP is twice as high.

The opportunity assigned to individual party members to put forward aspirants has not remained a mere formality. The district party survey indicated that in about one half of the constituencies the members of the big parties have applied this opportunity, in addition to the normal party branch supply of aspirants. The members of the socialist parties seem to have been more anxious to make use of this opportunity than the members of the non-socialist parties.

Seen from the viewpoint of intra-party democracy the mobilisation of members in party primaries is of great importance. If a party primary takes place the district party leadership usually sends a letter to all party members. The voting procedures varies greatly between parties, and in the 1995 election postal ballots were the most usually applied method. According to Timonen (1981: 25–7), in the 1979 parliamentary elections among the four big parties the participation rates in the primaries varied between 39–45 per cent. In 1995 participation rates in party primaries varied quite a lot between the parties. The SDP, which is the first party to apply the party primary method, was also in the recent election the most successful party to mobilise its members. The turnout rose at least to 60 per cent in all districts under consideration. The most active districts reached as high a share as 67 per cent, with the average percentage being about 63. The NCP reached a level of about 43 per cent for the whole country with the minimum for the constituencies being 35 per cent and the maximum 54 per cent. The membership of the CP proved to be by far the most passive. Only a fifth of the members participated in the party primaries, with one district showing as low a share as 11 per cent. Compared with several European countries the participation rate in Finland may be regarded as relatively high (Gallagher 1988: 245–7).

The great differences in membership activity between the big parties may partly be explained by the political situation. The poor result of the CP may be due to the party's position as the leading party in the cabinet which made great cuts in the state budget. Perhaps the most important situational factor was the intra-party dispute about membership of the European Union. A large proportion of the party membership was dissatisfied with the positive stance taken by the party leadership toward joining the EU. In the parliamentary election the dissatisfied party supporters voted for those candidates opposing EU membership.

It may, however, be stated that situational factors do not explain all differences between the parties. The long tradition within the SDP with arrangement of party primaries, and with high-grade participation in them, has been well documented in the literature (Timonen 1972; Timonen 1981). The party primaries quite well forecast the personal ups and downs in the election. Those at the top of the list after the primary can usually expect success in the election.

Manipulation of the lists

As the Electoral Act provides the district party organisation is entitled to remove from the list at most one quarter of the aspirants who gained enough votes in the party primary to be placed on the list. Evidence from the 1995 election suggests that about half of the district party organisations of the four biggest parties made use of the right to change the list produced by the party primary. The average number of changes was two per constituency. The reasons for the changes vary somewhat. The most commonly expressed reason was to bring about as balanced a list as possible (see also Gallagher 1988: 247–56) to correct certain biases due to gender, occupation and age. Women, entrepreneurs and the young were the categories most often mentioned as being under-represented on the final list. The other general reason reported by the district party officers was a refusal, evidently based on the poor result obtained in the party primary.

The district party officials reported only two cases in which the national party leadership had interfered in the nomination process. The mass media also reported a couple of cases where the national party leadership was anxious to drop names from the lists. These cases concerned aspirants with a suspicious past in business circles. In these cases the party leadership wanted to keep the party label as clean as possible.

Aspirants, candidates and deputies: the impact of supply and demand

In general the selection processes to parliament are more or less biased to the advantage of certain groups. The pathway from a rank-and-file party member to a deputy is paved with numerous hindrances resulting in highly elitist assemblies. In common with most democratic parliaments, compared with his/her party members, elected members as well as candidates are usually highly educated, are men rather than women, possess higher-status occupations, are usually of middle age, and come from large cities (Czudnowski 1975; Valen 1988: 225–8).

The strongly elitist traits have usually been explained by the role played by the party machinery. Demand-side factors have usually been regarded as decisive in this respect. It has been only recently that the importance of the supply-side factors have been stressed in the European context. As a result of a comprehensive study by Pippa Norris and Joni Lovenduski (1995) the supply-side factors have come under examination.

The Finnish electoral system, with party primaries and preferential voting, provides a good opportunity to assess the role played by party members and voters either as accelerators or as retarders of the process.

For an empirical test three groups were compared. The first was composed of those *aspirants* who did not succeed in the party primaries. The second group was composed of the *candidates* put on the lists. In addition to those aspirants who passed the party primaries this group included quite a few who did not participate in the primaries, but were put on the list by the district party organisations. The third group are the *elected deputies*. It may be noticed that the data cover only the four biggest parties (LWA, SDP, CP and NCP), and those constituencies in which these parties arranged a party primary.

The empirical findings support the idea that the outcome of the selection process is an elitist one. But it is striking that the supply of aspirants is relatively elitist and biased; those persons offered by the local party branches do not constitute a representative sample of the party members, still less of the electorate as a whole. The array of aspirants is biased in an elitist direction already at this stage.

The recruitment process seems to distort further the supply of the candidates in the elitist direction. The trends are not, however, linear. It may be stated that the first step from an aspirant to a candidate is usually shorter than the second step from a candidate to a deputy. In the party primary stage, party members have favoured female and young aspirants, thus balancing the list in relation to the aspirants. The voters have been more conservative, favouring older age cohorts and male candidates, hence greatly furthering elitist tendencies.

The age variable seems to have also certain curious tendencies. The strong grip on power taken by the so called baby-boom cohorts born in 1945–49 is clear in the data under analysis. With one-third of the seats, this cohort have a significant over-representation in the present Diet (Myrskylä 1995).

As far as the share of female candidates is concerned the results suggest that demands made by selectors are not the primary problem for women's representation. The original array of aspirants corresponds roughly to the situation after the election. If these findings hold true in general, the main change to alter the situation is to try to influence the supply of women aspirants.

The longitudinal trends confirm the findings made on the basis of the 1995 elections as far as the gender is concerned. The share of female deputies correlates quite highly with the share of female candidates, and the votes assigned to female candidates. The collapse of the female representation in the Finnish Eduskunta in the 1995 parliamentary elections, after a continuous rise over the past thirty years, seems to have had its origin in the limited supply of women candidates. The Finnish trend clearly supports the generalisations about the importance of supply-side

Table 4.6. *The social background of aspirants, candidates and legislators in Finland*

	Aspirants (558)	Candidates (393)	Legislators (113)
Men	65.4	57.0	67.3
Women	34.6	43.0	22.7
Non-graduates	56.2	49.5	37.0
Graduates	43.8	50.5	63.0
18–29 years	11.8	15.2	4.4
30–44	39.0	38.0	26.5
45–49	24.2	27.0	31.9
50+	25.0	19.8	37.2
Large city	43.5	36.1	60.7
Small city	32.4	38.4	27.7
Countryside	24.1	25.5	11.6

Note:
Includes only the four biggest parties with party primaries in 1995.

factors made in the British context (Norris and Lovenduski 1993a: 390).

The elitist nature of the selection process also becomes clearly apparent as regards education. In comparison with the whole population eligible to vote, 11 per cent, the share of the academics in our sample of aspirants, 44 per cent, is very high. The following steps, the party primaries, and the election greatly further the tendency (cf. Pesonen 1972: 223–4).

Conclusions

As far as the Finnish recruitment system is concerned it may be regarded as different from several other countries. The structural contrasts compared with countries using majority electoral systems are considerable. But certain features in the Finnish electoral system mean it also deviates from many countries with proportional representation systems. The divided, even if relatively stable, party system further accentuates the differences.

The Finnish electoral system, which emphasises such highly individual factors as the opportunity of a small local party branch or several party members to put forward aspirants for nomination, clearly favours, in principle, grassroots activity in candidate recruitment. It is also true that the national party leadership cannot apply a severe gatekeeper role in the selection process. Nor have the district party organisations any strong devices to put serious hindrances on the activities of the local party communities. From the viewpoint of both the formal rules and practical procedures the Finnish system of candidate recruitment seems to fulfil at least the minimum criteria of democracy quite well.

In spite of the decentralised nature of the Finnish electoral system the recruitment process results, however, in a relatively elitist parliament in terms of social background. The political culture with a strong contempt for parties and politicians has not been able to change the picture. The professional politicians with skills and other kind of resources constitute the pool from which the legislators are recruited.

The selection process in all its stages results in a more and more elitist outcome. The party members at the first step in the recruitment process are conservative: among the array of aspirants they usually prefer to select male, highly educated, urban persons with an adequate occupation for political activities. The voters are, if possible, even more conservative in electing to Parliament persons among whom these qualities are even more accentuated.

How are these findings to be interpreted? At first sight it looks as if the demand-side factors are important, seen from the viewpoint of the composition of parliament. Some kind of funnel phenomenon without doubt plays a certain role in the nomination process causing a highly elitist assembly. But the supply-side factors seem to be even more important than the demand-side factors for the composition of parliament. The standards for aspirants concerning such qualities as education, occupation and previous political experience are so high that even a randomised selection may result in a very elitist composition of parliament. The choices made by the voters can only very marginally correct the biased agenda at their disposal.

In spite of the fact that the Finnish recruitment system greatly differs from countries with different opportunity structures it generates an outcome that does not radically deviate from those in other countries. The empirical findings seem to give relatively strong support to the generalisations drawn in such countries as Britain. On the basis of these findings we may present a hypothesis that behavioural factors are more important than structural and legal factors. As far as the behavioural factors are concerned we may draw the general conclusion that overall the supply-side factors seem to be more important than the demand-side factors. If this holds true more widely it opens interesting views for comparative research in candidate recruitment.

5   Germany

Bernhard Wessels

Political recruitment is one of the main functions of every political system. It is one of the four central input functions (Almond and Coleman 1960: 47). The result of recruitment produced the political elite in most democracies. '*Legislative* recruitment refers specifically to the critical step as individuals move from lower levels into parliamentary careers' (Norris and Lovenduski 1995: 1). It refers to the mechanisms and processes that select from millions of politically motivated citizens those several thousands who reach positions in parliaments, whether on the regional, national or European level (Putnam 1976: 46).

Recruitment is closely related to the performance and functioning of democracy. In a normative sense it should be democratic, that is, it should be possible in principle for every citizen to run for office. However, in all advanced democracies it is obvious that legislatures are primarily drawn from particular segments of society: the better educated, more affluent, at least middle-aged, male, and politically experienced. More and more politicians are not only living *for* politics but also *from* politics, to use a formulation of Max Weber (Weber 1958). This distorting mirror of the social composition of society has been discussed along different approaches. From the perspective of a microcosmic concept of representation it has been regarded as a challenge to political representation assuming that 'just as portraits are representative if they look like the sitter, so legislatures are representative if they reflect the society from which they are drawn' (Norris and Lovenduski 1995: 94). System theory regards this development as one of the striking examples of functional differentiation (Luhmann 1984). Elite theory discusses it as a trend towards the professionalisation of politics (Herzog 1975).

In Germany, as in other advanced democracies, it has been observed that the availability of 'careerist' politicians for selection has made the members of parliament more homogeneous and thus reduced the chances for 'new blood' MPs (Roberts 1988: 113). This may have been a contributing factor to the phenomenon of *Politikerverdrossenheit*: the public's feeling that politicians pursue their own interests and have become unresponsive. This development also has raised some discussion about the emergence of a *political class* in Germany (Klingemann et al. 1991; Leif et al. 1992; Wessels 1992), whose prior interest is not to live for, but rather from, politics and collectively to ensure their own survival (Borchert and Golsch 1995: 614). While the term political elites refers to those with political power, who have a significant influence on the political agenda and political decisions, the definition of a political *class* is more narrow. Parts of the political elite can be regarded as belonging to a class *if* they meet four characteristics: (1) they have expressed an interest to live from politics; (2) they have experienced a political career which contributes to a common identity; (3) they actively pursue the monopolisation of chances of market exploitation (*Marktverwertung*) of their performance (which means they are the only ones to decide their income from politics and to select who becomes a politician); and (4) they possess political power (Wessels 1992: 544; see also Weber 1976).

In terms of the 'supply-and-demand' analytical framework proposed by Norris and Lovenduski (1995: 106–10), if the formation of a political class in Germany really is under way, this would imply that demand explanations become of more relevance for the selection of candidates than supply explanations. Selection of candidates under these conditions would be more and more influenced by those already in office in order to reproduce the political class. This would contradict the pronounced demands of German voters who give some priority to social representation. On average about one quarter of the voters regard it as essentially necessary for casting their vote for a particular candidate to the German Bundestag that she or he comes from the same region and the same social class, almost 20 per cent demand the same generation. A remarkable 40 per cent of the workers who do not feel represented by the government regard having a working-class background as an essential prerequisite for candidates to receive their votes (Rebenstorf and Wessels 1989: 417–22).

In elite research social background has often been regarded as insignificant for political representation, because its impact on attitudes and behaviour of political elites is rather weak (Edinger and Searing 1967; Schleth 1971; Matthews 1985: 42). It is well established that the impact of the social background of politicians on their attitudes and behaviour is modest, and far less significant than party affiliation. But more recent research has found that social background matters *within* parties. In German regional government it has been demonstrated that congruence in policy positions between voters and local politicians of the same party is higher between those of the two groups which share the same social background. This is true for social class, generation, gender, and particularly education (Wessels 1985: 50–72). The same seems to be the case in other democracies, too. A recent Swedish study (Esaiasson and Holmberg 1996: 31–48) reveals that the social background of MPs does have an impact on their attitudes. There is an even stronger relationship between this background and MPs' formal positions of power in parliament. As Esaiasson and Holmberg put it, results show that 'we are not talking revolution. The correlations are too weak for that.' However, 'it is conceivable that another kind of recruitment would be significant in a longer perspective' (Esaiasson and Holmberg 1996: 46). Thus, there it seems likely that political recruitment has a small but nevertheless significant effect on two central aspects of a democratic political system: its legitimacy and its outcomes.

Recruitment is not only affected by the *demand*-side mechanisms. Although in the debate about a political class it is usually suggested that the demand side of political recruitment is the more important process, one should not neglect the fact that there is a second side of the coin. As Norris and Lovenduski (1995: 108) have pointed out, recruitment opportunities are restricted by the *supply* of applicants who wish to pursue a political career. Not everyone is motivated and willing to enter politics. Typically this might be the case for social groups with limited resources in terms of time, money or experience. Moreover, as in the economic market-place, supply and demand interact. The supply of aspirants can be influenced by the mobilisation processes within political parties. They control some of the risks of a political career. Thus, it is difficult to separate the two dimensions of supply and demand since they influence each other.

This chapter is an attempt to answer the question of whether candidate recruitment has changed due to professionalisation or the emergence of a political class. If this is the case it should be reflected in changing recruitment patterns and in the changing relevance of specific selection criteria. The chapter focusses upon legislative recruitment to the national parliament, the *German Bundestag*.

The structure of opportunities

The electoral system

Voters in Germany cast two votes simultaneously during elections for the German Bundestag (the lower house), one for a candidate to be chosen by the plurality in single-member districts (*Wahlkreis*), and the other one for a party list to be awarded seats by proportional representation in a state-wide multi-member district (*Land*). There is a nation-wide five-percent/three seats threshold. The percentage of votes a party receives in the party list vote determines the final allocation of parliamentary seats. 'Each party then gets its plurality-won seats plus the number of seats won by the proportional rule less the number of plurality-won seats' (Riker 1986: 37). Half the seats are filled from single-member constituencies. The remainder are filled from party lists, irrespective of whether the seat vacated is from a constituency or a party list. The German electoral system has no by-elections. Seats becoming vacant during a term are filled by the next available non-elected candidate from the party list. This electoral regulation provides a specific opportunity structure for candidates: first, the possibility of running as a double candidate; second, the chance to fill vacancies between federal elections. The number of seats vacated between elections has ranged from thirty to fifty-nine, and the average is forty-two (or 16 per cent of list seats).

Reflecting the dual-voting process in federal election, there is candidate selection on the district and state (*Länder*) levels (regional lists). The Basic Law (constitution) requires internal democratic organisation for political parties, including for the selection of candidates. As in Finland, recruitment therefore occurs within a fairly rigorously defined legal context, more than in many other democracies (Roberts 1988: 97).

Candidate selection at *district level* is mainly in the hands of local party organisations. The state party executive has the greatest impact on who is put on the party list. Selection is done either by all party members of the local party branch (*Kreisverband, Unterbezirke*), or by a committee of delegates chosen by the members. The size of such election committees ranges from twenty-five to one hundred (Zeuner 1971; Porter 1995).

At the *state level* a meeting is held of 250–300 delegates representing the local party branches in proportion to their membership size. Usually the state party executive proposes a list of candidates, and the delegates vote on each proposed candidate, starting with the first position on the list. In order to win a position a candidate must receive an absolute majority of the votes.

The structure of competition between applicants differs somewhat between the district and state levels. In the perceptions of candidates and local party chairs there are clear differences with respect to the importance of candidate characteristics (Porter 1995). At both levels, candidates regard their political competence as the most important aspect for their nomination. But at the district level their ability to win votes and their performance in constituency service come second. In contrast their political position within the party and their experience of party work are more important at the state (*Land*) level (Table 5.1).

Interestingly enough, conflicts about candidate nomination occur much more often at the state level. This might indicate that a good posi-

Table 5.1. *The importance of candidate characteristics for district and regional list nomination*

	For district nomination	For regional list nomination
	(1=very important; 5=not important at all)	
My ability to win votes	1.89	2.92
My political position within the party	3.84	2.32
My performance at party work	2.44	2.52
My performance in constituency service	1.91	3.06
My competence in political matters	1.69	2.21

Note:
Number of candidates interviewed: 315.
Perception of candidates of SPD and CDU/CSU.
Source: Porter 1995: 84–6.

tion on the *Land* party list is a much more secure way to get a mandate than running in a district. Only 17 per cent of all districts can be regarded as safe (Schindler 1995: 553). At the district level conflict seems to be a rare event. However, comparing the importance of different conflicts, the structure is very similar. Political conflicts between party factions, and hierarchical conflicts between the party leadership and regulars, are much more infrequent than a conflict between old and new candidates (Table 5.2). This suggests that newcomers experience difficulties in establishing themselves.

Competition between candidates for good list positions may have even increased during the past decades, and in particular since 1990, due to rising numbers of candidates. From 1949 onwards the number of candidates in federal elections increased continuously from about 2,324 to 3,244 in 1976. The total dropped somewhat until 1983, then increased dramatically to 3,923 candidates in 1994 (Figure 5.1). Taking the fluctuations into account there is a net positive increase of 1,599 candidates. Yet the proportion of candidates elected has not changed very much, however, due to the increase of seats in the German Bundestag. The parliament expanded by a hundred seats in 1953 and, as a result of German unification, by another 143 seats in 1990. There are on average 5.4 candidates per seat, or, to put it the other way around, on average 18.6 of the candidates are elected. The huge increase in candidates in 1990 and 1994 has decreased the proportion of those elected to 17 per cent, despite the increase in the number of seats.

Table 5.2. *Conflicts at district-level and state-level candidate selection meetings as perceived by local party chairs of SPD and CDU/CSU*

Conflicts between:	At district level (1=applies fully; 5=does not apply)	At land level
Old and new candidates	4.06	2.80
Party factions	4.20	3.63
Party leadership and regulars	4.53	3.71

Note:
Number of party chairs (Kreisvorsitzende) interviewed: 350.
Source: own calculations from Porter 1995: 29, 32.

Trends in the social background of candidates and members

There is no parliament in the democratic world in which members reflect the social composition of the electorate. Germany is no exception in this respect, in terms of gender, age, education and class. One of the strongest disparities exists with respect to *gender*. Until the early 1990s the proportion of women MPs did not exceed 30 per cent in any of the OECD countries, except for the Scandinavian countries where it was between 30–40 per cent (Norris and Lovenduski 1995: 187). In Germany the new women's movement of the 1960s made this a salient issue in the discussion of political equality, and it has not left the agenda ever since. This is no accident, given the fact that women's representation in the German Bundestag is still far from reflecting the gender proportions in society. This dimension of social representation, however, is the only one in which the situation has significantly improved. In 1949 only 9 per cent of the candidates were female. Until 1969 the figure stayed below 10 per cent. Since then it has continuously increased to 30 per cent in 1994.

Although candidate figures do not fully reflect the supply side (for a full definition of supply see Norris and Lovenduski 1995: 108–10), they could serve as a yardstick as compared to demand expressed in the proportion elected. As the proportion of female candidates has grown, so has the proportion of women elected, starting with a time lag in 1972. Since then the share of female MPs has increased from below 10 per cent to 26 per cent. This is still anything else but equal representation. The chances for women to get elected do not fully reflect their proportion of candidates. In this respect Germany is back to the situation in the 1950s where the proportion of women elected was almost similar to the proportion of female candidates. The 'gender chance ratio', (that is, the proportion of

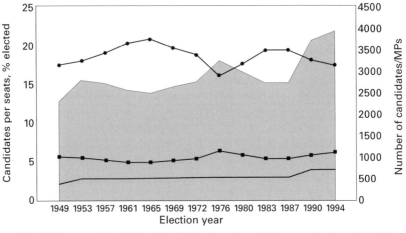

Figure 5.1. Electoral competition in German federal elections,
1949–94.
Sources: Own calculations from Schindler 1983: 188; 1994: 255–6;
1995: 553, 556.

male candidates who are elected divided by the proportion of female
candidates who are elected) was on average a little above one, i.e. in
favour of male candidates, in the 1950s. The ratio got much worse for
women in the period from 1961–80, when the relative chance for male
candidates to be elected was almost three times as high as that for women.
Since then the ratio has decreased again tremendously but did not con-
verge to a 1:1 chance until 1994 (Figure 5.2). In relative terms, as compared to the gender ratio among candidates and even more among voters,
women are still disadvantaged. In absolute terms, the situation has
become better since the late 1960s.

Another strong dissimilarity between the composition of parliament
and society exists with respect to *age groups*. In contrast to the development of the gender ratio, the situation for younger candidates has not
really improved. The mean age decreased from 50 to 46.6 between 1949
and 1972, but increased to 49 again after 1972. The proportion of MPs
under forty was never higher than about 15 per cent except for the years
from 1972 to 80, where it was atypically high. In 1994 the proportion
under forty was 11.6 per cent, one of the lowest in the history of the
German Bundestag. Except for the years 1972–80 the persisting pattern
is an average age of about fifty years, and the proportion of MPs under

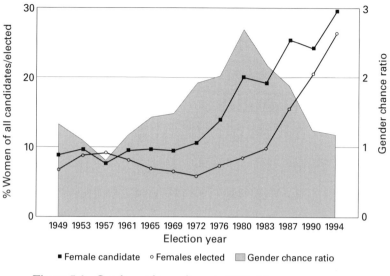

Figure 5.2. Gender and recruitment, 1949–94.
Gender chance ratio: % of elected male candidates divided by % of elected female candidates.
Sources: Own calculations from Schindler 1983: 188; 1994: 255–6; 1995: 553, 556.

forty has been less than 15 per cent of MPs. In contrast to this the proportion of the adult population under forty years was 40 per cent in 1950. Although the population gradually aged, the proportion of adults under forty is twice the proportion of MPs in this age group (34.4 per cent in 1992) (Statistisches Bundesamt 1995: 64).

The gap between the electorate and the elected is even larger with respect to *education*. Today, three-quarters (77 per cent) of MPs have higher education. This has not always been the case. There is no other social characteristic featuring such extensive and continuous changes in parliament as much as education. From 1949 to 1956 just over half of all MPs (55 per cent) lacked higher education. Since then the share of academics increased from election to election to almost 80 per cent now (Figure 5.3). These days the non-academic is the atypical MP. The 'educational revolution' (Allardt 1968) in Western democracies during the 1960s also increased the level of education of the population significantly, yet in the early 1990s only 13.5 per cent had an education which allowed them to enter university (Statistisches Bundesamt 1995: 401), while 8.9 per cent have a university degree (ALLBUS 1990: 141).

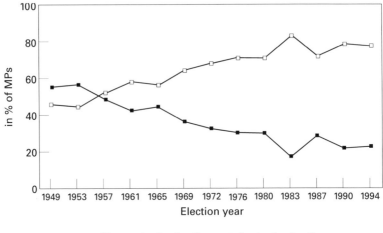

Figure 5.3. Education of MPs, 1949–94.
Sources: Own calculations from Schindler 1983: 195, 196; 1994: 268–9; Holzapfel 1995.

The proportion of academics in parliament exceeds the share of academics in the population by about a factor of eight. For no other social characteristic are the figures for social representation compared to the population so disproportional.

Beginning with the 1960s until the mid-1970s almost half the MPs with university degrees had studied law and administration. From 1976 to 1990 this proportion declined to 30 per cent, whereas the share of the whole range of social sciences, including economics and theology, increased to more than 40 per cent, and of natural and technical sciences to almost 30 per cent (Schindler 1986: 236; 1994: 270). With respect to academic disciplines, the German Bundestag has become more open. There is no monopoly of legal professionals any more, even though this was suspected for a long time.

Not much has changed as regards the occupational sectors the MPs come from. The public sector remains the main reservoir: on average 45 per cent of MPs come from this sphere. This is a quite constant pattern. What Max Weber called *Abkömmlichkeit* – an occupation which allows enough flexibility and security to start a career which is quite costly, at least at the beginning – is still one of the most important factors bringing people into politics. Self-employed and employers have a share of almost a quarter of the MPs, about 13 per cent are or have been employees of

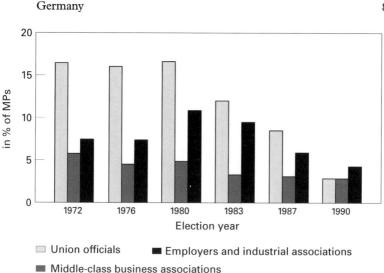

Figure 5.4. Interest-group officials in the German Bundestag.
Sources: Own calculations from Schindler 1986: 246; 1994: 283.

organisations like interest groups and parties, only a little more than 1 per cent are workers. This distribution has been quite constant throughout the past twenty-five years. These developments show that a 'sheltered' sector rather than functional specialisation, (i.e. a particular profession or discipline) provides the main avenues for a political career.

One might regard it as sufficient that a social group's spokesmen are represented in parliament. This has been argued in particular with respect to workers' representation. However, the number of union officials in the German Bundestag has rapidly declined since 1980. Between 1972 and 1980 about 16 per cent of the MPs were union officials. This portion sank continuously to less than 3 per cent in 1990. The figures for representatives of employers' and industrial associations have also declined, from 5.6 per cent in 1972 to 2.9 per cent in 1990. There has also been a decline during the past decade in the proportion of officials of middle-class business associations (Figure 5.4). The overall decrease in the number of interest-group officials in parliament might be an indicator of an ongoing functional differentiation of subsystems, and the professionalisation of politics.

Trends in the social composition of the German Bundestag clearly reveal some major changes, most of them indicating a widening gap between distributions in the population and in parliament. The situation

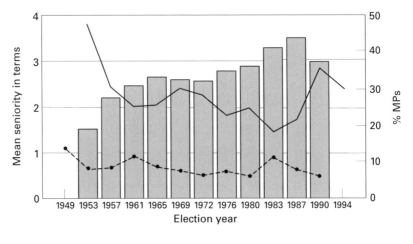

Figure 5.5. Turnover and seniority, 1949–94.
Sources: Own calculations from Schindler 1983: 178; 1994: 242;
1995: 554–5.

has only improved with respect to women's representation. In contrast, the situation has not changed as far as occupation and age are concerned, and it has even worsened as regards education. In summary the public sector is the main reservoir from which MPs are drawn, their mean age is still about fifty years, the number of interest group officials in parliament is declining, and the vast majority of MPs are well educated. These developments allow us to conclude that distortions between the Bundestag and the electorate are (except for gender) enduring, and in some respects even increasing. These developments can go along with professionalisation as well as an emerging political class.

Looking at the turnover in parliament and the seniority of MPs offers further insights in this respect. Turnover rates in the German Bundestag show a clear downward trend. Not taking into account the turnover between the first and second parliamentary term, which can be regarded as a period of consolidation of the new democracy after Nazism, turnover declined from 31 per cent in 1957 to 21 per cent in 1987. This is reflected in the seniority of MPs. From 1965, the fourth term of the German Bundestag, the mean number of re-elections of MPs increased from about 2.5 times to 3.5 times in 1987 (Figure 5.5). Assuming a regular term of four years means that on average MPs are in parliament for fourteen years. The 1990 turnover increased only because of the enlargement of the Parliament from 519 to 662 seats, due to German unification, and turnover fell again in 1994. The long-term decline in the turnover rate seems to be a universal characteristic of parliamentary systems (Blondel 1973: 85–7).

Falling turnover has significant implications. It takes on average about 10.5 years from a person's first local party office to first entering the German Bundestag (*German Representation Study* 1988/89). The average age of entry of an MP is forty-two. Adding an average of 3.5 parliamentary terms this brings a person close to the age of retirement in ordinary professions. This finding suggests that being a politician has become a real profession. The low turnover clearly shows that MPs mainly get into parliament because they are incumbents. This is an indication that politicians have monopolised the administration of political careers, although it is no proof. These results show that demand factors have become of more relevance for the explanation of recruitment and support arguments about a rising political class and the professionalisation of politics. To analyse this further, the characteristics influencing nomination and election will be analysed for candidates in the 1994 federal elections.

Pathways to the German Bundestag 1994

'If we wish to face facts squarely, we must recognize that, in modern democracies of any type other than the Swiss, politics will unavoidably be a career', wrote Schumpeter in 1942 (Schumpeter 1962: 285). In 1921 Max Weber argued for politics as a profession (Weber 1958). In the late 1960s, Kogon, an important thinker in Germany, made a proposal for a national foundation for the education of the coming generation of parliamentarians (Herzog 1975: 184). The reality in Germany today meets this demand for politics as a profession. Trends in recruitment clearly show some evidence that the pathway to parliament has become more narrow. What can at least be said is that those who get there show in social and career terms typically a particular profile: a sheltered occupation in non-political life, a university education, an age above forty, and political experience. Whether this is a matter of supply or demand cannot be answered by data about the elected alone. Therefore in this section the pool of candidates in the federal elections of 1994 will be compared with the elected. We will go on to analyse how social characteristics and political experience determine electoral prospects and electoral success.

The social background of candidates

One of the most striking trends in federal elections in Germany is the increase in the numbers of candidates. The supply side is not the dimension restricting recruitment. The reservoir of potential MPs has become greater and greater during the past decades. Today at least 4,000 people are willing to become an MP. However, the supply of candidates clearly does not represent the social structure of society. This is most obvious with respect to gender. But still, the number of women willing to run for office exceeds demand. If we compare the newly elected members, the incumbent MPs and the new candidates, the portion of women is largest in the group of new candidates (30 per cent), and exceeds the portion in the other two groups by about 4–6 percentage points. With respect to gender, demand clearly does not reach the limits of supply (Table 5.3). Age is another factor where there are some differences between new candidates, incumbents and newly elected members. Thus, supply does not impose limits to reduce the age gap between the public and MPs. The age differences again point to the fact that recruitment processes are almost always based on more or less long-standing political careers (Herzog 1975). Only after what is called a 'Ochsentour' in a political party, that is, taking responsibility for less attractive service positions in the party for longer periods and climbing the ladder in a toilsome way, are party members rewarded by becoming candidates for a more attractive office and are even later rewarded by a candidacy which opens the opportunity to get into parliament (see also McAllister chapter 2) (Table 5.3).

Looking at the most important complex of socio-demographic factors, it is obvious that candidates are mainly drawn from the pool of professionals, in particular from law, economics and education. However, some important differences appear between new, incumbent and elected candidates. In particular the relative number of legal and technical professionals is much greater in the group of incumbent MPs and newly elected members than in the group of new candidates. It is also striking that almost 25 per cent of the new candidates come from white-collar occupations, whereas this proportion is below 10 per cent in the other groups. There is a higher proportion of people who are not in the paid labour force (students, retired, homemakers) among candidates than the others. Looking at the Duncan index of dissimilarity, which is a summary measure of the differences between distributions, the candidates are clearly different from incumbent MPs and newly elected members in terms of profession. Speculating about the funnel of recruitment, one can clearly say that candidates are a selection of particular professions compared to voters. But the funnel becomes even more narrow: new candidates differ from established members quite strongly in their professional composition. Putting these results into the context of trends of parliamentary recruitment in the previous section, this suggests that recruitment has become more narrow, and is more influenced by demand than supply.

Table 5.3. *The social background of candidates and legislators; 1994 federal elections*

	Candidates	Incumbent	Legislators elected 1994
Mean age in years	44.3	51.0	49.3
Women	44.8	49.1	46.9
Men	44.1	51.6	50.1
Women (%)	30.0	24.4	26.3
Professions (%):			
Farmers	1.7	3.2	3.8
Workers/handicrafts	7.6	4.9	4.0
Technicians	2.7	0.2	0.2
White-collar general	12.1	4.4	4.7
Trade	3.7	1.2	1.2
Banking/insurance	2.3	1.2	1.0
Financial controlling	1.6	0.2	0.2
Social/medical services	4.9	2.0	2.3
Police/army	1.8	1.2	1.2
Public administration	4.0	4.2	3.8
Managers/employers	3.9	3.9	3.7
Professionals:			
Agriculture	0.8	0.5	0.3
Technical	8.9	13.8	13.3
Economic	8.0	6.1	7.9
Medical	2.8	3.2	2.3
Cultural	1.3	0.2	0.2
Media	2.3	3.2	3.7
Education	11.9	12.3	14.0
Lawyers, judges	3.3	15.5	14.3
Social, political scientists	0.0	2.5	1.6
Members of Government	0.0	10.1	8.6
High-ranking Politicians, not Gov., not MP	0.0	2.2	4.4
Miscellaneous	1.6	2.2	1.9
Students/in education	5.8	0.0	0.3
Not working/retired/homemaker (family members without renumeration)	6.9	1.5	1.0
N=100%	3.215	513	672

Notes:
Duncan Index of Dissimilarity for professions:
    between new and incumbent candidates: 35.9
    between new and elected candidates: 35.9
    between incumbent and elected candidates: 7.7.
(Duncan Index of Dissimilarity: sum of absolute percentage point differences between the proportions of each of the two distributions across each category, devided by two. Range: 0: identity; 100: totally different.)
Source: German Bundestag Candidate Data 1994.

90   *Bernhard Wessels*

Table 5.4. *Candidate characteristics and electoral prospects*

Chances of election*	No chance	Some chance	Strong chance
Mean age	43.6	46.0	50.0
Women	42.9	44.6	47.9
Men	43.9	46.7	50.9
Women (%)	66.3	16.5	17.3
Men (%)	67.5	14.0	18.5
Occupations (%)			
Workers, handicrafts	78.6	8.6	12.9
White collar general	82.6	9.8	7.6
Law professionals	52.1	18.6	29.3
Media professionals	61.5	13.5	25.0
Professionals in education	68.5	13.5	18.0
Technical professionals	69.7	13.9	16.3
Managers, employers	65.9	23.9	10.2
Types of candidates (%):			
Double candidates	42.8	25.0	32.2
Incumbent candidates	28.7	15.2	56.1
Seniority (mean number of terms)	0.2	0.6	2.0
Average (%)	67.2	14.7	18.1

Notes:
* Calculations are based on the 1990 figures of seats per party won by party lists in Länder (List position≤seats=good chance; list position seats×2=no chance; in between: some chance) and on district classification according to the following rule: some chance (safe district): a party won continuously more than 55 per cent of the votes in the districts 1983–90; good chance (stronghold): a party won continuously more than 60 per cent of the votes in the districts 1983–90.
Sources: German Bundestag Candidate Data 1994.

Determinants of electoral prospects and electoral success

To go further we need to analyse selection in the recruitment processes. If there is a specific *social* selectivity this should show up in the chances of particular groups of candidates winning office. If recruitment comes close to climbing a ladder then this should show up in the placement of experienced candidates. Candidates can be placed in a stronghold district for a party or in a safe rank in the state (*Land*) list of the party. In order to elaborate the question of placement, a simple scale of electoral prospects ranging from 'no chance' through 'some chance' to 'a strong chance' has been constructed (for construction see footnote to Table 5.4) for candidates of parliamentary parties.

Looking at the social characteristics first, the distribution of electoral prospects within different occupational groups reveals large differences. On average, 18.1 per cent of the candidates of parliamentary parties are placed either in a safe district or on a safe list place. Clearly, legal professionals are on average placed best. Almost 30 per cent are safely placed, while about half have at least some chance (Table 5.4). Only media professionals are equally safe, while professionals in education are about average. Technical professionals, white- and blue-collar workers and handicrafts are clearly disadvantaged with respect to electoral prospects. Women are placed slightly worse than men, however this is not a very significant difference.

Characteristics which can be related to political experience also show some interesting differences. Age reflects political experience only very indirectly; however the results fit the career argument well. The older the candidates the better they are placed on average. Even more interesting are variables which directly relate to political experience, i.e. incumbency and seniority. The figures show that incumbency does not fully guarantee a safe place but does so more than any other characteristic. Almost 30 per cent of incumbent candidates are placed with no chances. However, 56 per cent are safely placed, and another 15 per cent have some chance. Seniority also does not guarantee a safe place. But seniority is on average lowest in the group of candidates with no chance, and quite high in the group with strong chances.

With respect to type of candidate, i.e. district, party list or both, results shed an interesting light on the double candidates. Although in legal terms, the possibility of double candidacy is not allowed in most other electoral systems, and it opens new opportunities for candidates, this is only partially true in empirical terms. In total in the 1994 elections 419 of all candidates of parliamentary parties ran only in district, another 638 ran only on party lists, while 1,069 ran on both. Although there are 328 seats to fill from districts, only a very small portion can be regarded as safe. This is the case even though the district classification used here is less restrictive than is common in Germany. The classification here sets the threshold for quite safe districts as 50 per cent of the vote. For strongholds 60 per cent is the threshold. Only fifty-two (15.9 per cent) of the districts can be regarded as quite safe, and only eleven (or 3.5 per cent) as strongholds. Only 3 per cent or thirty-two of the double candidates run in quite safe districts or strongholds. But 30 per cent or 321 have safe places on the party lists. Only 6.9 per cent of the district candidates ran in quite safe districts or strongholds, only 9.1 per cent of the party list candidates have safe list positions. In other words, double candidates are clearly advantaged. But this advantage does not come from the double candidacy but from their safe positions on the party lists. Electoral outcomes in districts are not stable enough to increase their chances greatly. The competition between candidates is for the position on the party lists. This suggests why candidate selection at the district level is more consensual than at the land level for the party lists (see Table 5.2). The real fight is for the list position. This strengthens the role of party organisation and the party leaders in recruitment processes. The highest leaders have the best chances of determining the rules of the game, and thus who gets in.

The findings about the distribution of electoral prospects on the individual level confirm what has already been said: candidates with professions which allow some flexibility and who are connected with knowledge helpful in politics are in an advantaged position. Even more advantaged are those who can already point to a political career record. The electoral mechanism of party lists gives the party organisations, and particularly the higher ranks within the party, a strong influence. They control the party lists and therefore the only means of placing candidates safely. In other words, party organisations have the means, not to say the monopoly, to determine who gets into parliament. This comes close to what Max Weber regarded as a constitutive element of a class: the monopolisation of the chances of market exploitation (*Marktverwertung*) of achievements.

To analyse this further, a regression analysis of electoral prospects and success has been performed. Results show that electoral prospects as well as success can be quite well explained by the political characteristics we have discussed. The portion of explained variance is 41 per cent for electoral prospects, and 60 per cent for electoral success. Interestingly enough, most of the social characteristics reported so far show only insignificant effects if included in the analysis together with variables about political experience (Table 5.5). Only in a separate regression including social characteristics alone do they account for 7 per cent of the variance in electoral prospects, and for almost 10 per cent of the variance in electoral success, with the dummy variables of age, white-collar and legal professional showing a significant effect, while gender proves insignificant.

In order to give a picture not restricted to variables with significant effects only, gender, age, a white-collar dummy representing an occupational group with very low chances and a legal professional dummy representing an occupational group with very strong chances have been included in the equation together with incumbency, seniority and type of candidate. The results show that political experience (as measured by incumbency and seniority) together with the dummy for double candidates have the strongest and most significant impact on electoral prospects, and even more on electoral success. It is important to notice

Table 5.5. *Regression of social characteristics and type of candidacy on electoral prospects and success. Parliamentary parties, 1994.*

	Electoral prospects[a]		Electoral success[b]	
	beta	Sig. T	beta	Sig. T
Gender (women=1)	0.06	0.00	0.02	0.25
Age	0.02	0.20	0.01	0.39
White collar, general	−0.03	0.09	−0.02	0.15
Legal professional	0.04	0.03	0.03	0.01
Double candidate[c]	0.33	0.00	0.25	0.00
Incumbent candidate[d]	0.28	0.00	0.56	0.00
Seniority[e]	0.17	0.00	0.09	0.00
Adj. R^2	0.41		0.60	

Notes:
[a] Chance to become elected. Coded 0 'low', 1 'some', 3 'strong'.
[b] Being elected.
[c] List and district.
[d] MP in the term 1990–94.
[e] Number of terms in parliament. If MP in the previous term (1990–94), the value is 0, because the MP is already measured as an incumbent candidate. Starts with 2, range 2–9.
Number of cases: 2126.
Sources: German Bundestag Candidate Data 1994.

that the influence of double candidacy is not due to the fact that the chances greatly increase if a candidate is running at both levels. The explanation is due to the fact that those running only in districts have little chance because of the insecurity of districts, and those running only on party lists have little chance if they are not well placed. Double candidates are on average much better placed than others on the party lists, hence this has a strong influence on electoral prospects and success. The correlation of double candidacy with electoral prospects on the party list is .53, with being elected .56. It is about zero with electoral prospects in the district. Putting double candidacy aside, the major variable explaining who gets in and who does not is incumbency. This variable alone explains 30 per cent of the variance of electoral prospects and 54 per cent of the variance for electoral success. This is an extraordinarily high proportion for individual data. And almost nothing is left for social characteristics.

The analysis of the determinants of electoral prospects and electoral success carried out on an individual level produced results suggesting that variables related to political experience account for an almost complete explanation. What matters most is whether a candidate has already joined the 'crew' or not. Quite obviously this is the most important criterion for selection. The questions then are, who implements this criterion, and why?

Conclusions

The empirical results presented here will be reviewed in the light of the following three perspectives: which development indicates functional differentiation, which professionalisation, and which an emerging political class? In empirical terms this might be regarded as an artificial undertaking. The intermingling of the three processes makes it difficult to attribute empirical findings to one particular strand of interpretation. However, in theoretical terms this approach might open up new perspectives for the interpretation of legislative recruitment in Germany and elsewhere.

There are three clear hints that a process of *functional differentiation*, and therewith a separation of politics from other subsystems, is going on. One of them is the finding that becoming and being an MP is most likely to take a whole professional life-time. It takes on average ten years to get from one's first elected party office into parliament. The time period that MPs stay in parliament has increased since 1961 (the fourth term) from 2.5 terms to 3.5 terms in 1987. Given a regular term, MPs stay on average about fourteen years in parliament today. Together with the time it takes to get there, this sums up to some twenty years. Politics has become a profession in this respect. If one pursues a political career there is not much room left to do anything else. More specific with respect to functional differentiation is the decrease in the number of cross-overs from other sectors than politics into parliament (Wessels 1987). In line with this is the finding that the presence of interest-group representatives in parliament has gone down dramatically. This is particularly true with respect to unions but also with respect to business associations and other interest groups. Since the reason cannot be in the profile of interest-group officials given the fact that they are privileged in terms of resources and qualifications to enter politics, this development can most clearly be regarded as an indicator of functional differentiation.

Many of the findings point to a *professionalisation of politics*. These findings also mean that there are quite strong differences in the social composition of society and of candidates and to some extent between candidates and elected. MPs come from 'sheltered' occupations, which means that they have the flexibility and the time to invest in a political career. This is a general indication for professionalisation. Nonetheless, the figures for MPs coming from the public sector have not increased during the past twenty-five years. But the time span of about ten years between first party office and mandate point in the same direction. More specific are results concerning the education of MPs. There is no other social characteristic in which the composition of the Bundestag has changed so much. Today four out of five MPs have higher education. And legal professionals have the highest chances of getting into parliament of all professional groups. This may also be an effect of their privileged occupational situation. Legal professionals mostly are either self-employed or working in public administrations. But there are evident reasons as well to 'co-opt' people with legal qualifications into legislature.

Some other findings can be regarded as indications for an *emerging political class* although they are related to professionalisation too. Professionalisation and political class share many characteristics and the effects are confounding. This makes it difficult to attribute them distinctively to either one of the interpretations. However, merging separate findings into an overall picture, it can be justified to speak of an emerging political class. First of all turnover has decreased quite dramatically, discounting the enlargement of parliament in 1990 due to unification. Supply as measured here by the pool of candidates would allow a higher turnover in terms of professional characteristics. Thus, it is the demand side which limits turnover. On an individual level results for the 1994 elections show that incumbency and seniority have a very large impact on electoral prospects and the success of candidates whereas social characteristics are of minor relevance. The best predictor of who gets into parliament is knowing who is already there. This is because parties organise their selection in this way. The only relevant possibility to place candidates safely are party lists, because district outcomes are quite unstable. Positions on party lists are allocated by the higher party ranks. Thus, the latter set the rules of the game and the criteria for selection and thus largely decide which of the candidates has a good chance from the very beginning and who does not. Thus, the influence of voters on who gets in and who does not is very limited and more or less restricted to the overall distribution of their votes. This is why candidates perceive conflicts about candidate selection as being much stronger at the state level where party lists are composed. The struggle for safe places takes place at that level. And it is no accident that conflicts between newcomers and the established are regarded as the most important conflicts. For all these findings an interpretation in line with the professionalisation argument is also possible. However, since supply seems not to be the constraining factor and since the predictive power of incumbency for safe places and electoral success is so extraordinarily high (it accounts respectively for 30 and 54 per cent of the variance), one is inclined to speak of a monopolisation of chances by those already established. These findings are quite well in keeping with the criteria for a political class defined earlier. Becoming an MP is almost impossible without a long-standing career within a party. Being an MP is clearly connected with having political power. It is also connected with a life-time professional prospect given the long duration of office in parliament, thus most likely linked up to a (necessary) interest to make a living from politics. Last but not least, party elites have monopolised the chances for pursuing political careers and the criteria for how to embark on this. However, it would be clearly an exaggeration to say that all MPs belong to a political class, or maybe even to say that there is a considerable political class already. But there are no doubts that quite a few MPs already meet these criteria and that tendencies for a political class to emerge are present.

The central question is, however, how does this affect policies, political representation and democracy? Putnam (1976: 65–9) summarises the most important arguments with respect to the role and effect of turnover. On the one hand, a high turnover, that is less professionalisation and less political class, allows for greater innovativeness and flexibility of a system in terms of policies. It does not guarantee new policies but it provides favourable conditions. On the other hand, a high turnover is on average related to a lower level of experience which, although it makes new ideas more likely, involves difficulties for their implementation. Effective policy changes might be associated with the stability of experienced elites. Another matter is the relationship between turnover and democracy. It is obvious that the higher the turnover the more people can attain elite status. In some normative theories of democracy this is regarded as a prerequisite for democracy. It was, for example, part of the policies of the Greens in Germany to use a rotation principle for MPs of their party in parliament. It has also been argued in elite theory that a higher turnover prevents the build-up of frustrations of potential challengers and that political stability increases with smooth elite replacement instead of abrupt changes which become necessary if replacement does not take place continuously. Thus, everything depends on the balance of continuity and change. But there are more specific questions with respect to the German situation and the effects of the constraint structure of recruitment on policies. A crucial question is how career interests are combined with policy production (Borchert and Golsch 1995: 623). Since the power to decide the distribution of career chances and chances to stay in parliament is clearly with the parties, the role of parties as collective actors is strengthened also with respect to policies. They can reward MPs who act in line with the official party policy. Compliance with party positions thus seems to be an important factor. This is also reflected in the fact that the political position within a party is regarded as one of the most important factors for being nominated as a candidate on party lists. In other words, parties as collective actors have quite some power to select MPs who are in line with the policy positions of the party as collective actor for their parliamentary faction. Policies are therefore more dependent on parties than on persons. This has implications for the electoral process. It means a great deal of security for voters regarding their expectations of what policy positions will be put forward in parliament if they vote for a particular party. They can rely on the party's collective stand-points and programmes. Klingemann et al. (1994) have shown empirically that party platforms do translate into policies. This can be regarded as a positive effect of the monopolisation of career chances and selection criteria by political parties. Alongside the fact that all this is also related to professionalisation, the positive aspects of more constrained recruitment procedures might exceed the negative ones. However, it is a fine line for parties to tread between securing policy identities and professional politics on the one hand and fossilisation on the other.

6   Japan

Haruhiro Fukui

Japanese politics has been going through a process of transformation in recent years, following the end of the Liberal Democratic Party's predominance in the post-war era. The opportunities to enter the Diet used to be extremely limited, with a narrow pathway to power, and a highly centralised selection process within the LDP. Recent changes in the legal regulations of campaign finance, the fragmentation of the party system, and reform of the electoral system may have significant consequences for the process of legislative recruitment. Nevertheless it seems unlikely that these changes will radically affect the type of politicians who succeed in entering the Diet. The aim of this chapter is to outline the structure of opportunities for candidates in Japan, to examine who gets elected to the Diet, and to consider how this may change following the 1994 reform of the electoral law.

The structure of opportunities

The legal regulations

The formal rules of legislative elections in contemporary Japan constitute a structure of 'opportunity' only to a very limited extent from the average Japanese citizen's point of view. The post-World War II Japanese constitution does offer Japan's citizens a number of important political opportunities. For example, it guarantees them the right not only to vote but also to run as a candidate in a Diet (parliamentary), prefectural, or local election, regardless of their race, creed, gender, social status, family background, level of education, wealth or income (Constitution, Article 44). Thus, any Japanese citizen is eligible for election to either chamber of Japan's bicameral parliament, (that is, the upper house known as the House of Councillors and the lower house known as the House of Representatives) who is not judged as medically incompetent, is not currently serving a sentence given by a court of justice, is not currently employed by the national, prefectural or local government, and who meets the age requirements (Public Office Election Law [POEL], Article 10).

If one reads the fine print in the laws, however, the formal rules begin to look far more like a set of constraints, rather than of opportunities. To begin with, there is a great deal of bureaucratic red tape a potential candidate must contend with. One must, for example, register with the Central Election Management Committee by reporting in a written and hand-delivered statement his or her name, permanent address, current address, date of birth and occupation (POEL, Article 86). A political party that wishes to sponsor one or more candidates must likewise report similar particulars about itself to the same committee. Should one want to run as a candidate of a particular party, one must choose a party that has at least five current members in the house and that won at least 2 per cent of the total valid vote cast in the most recent election.

Under the new electoral system introduced in 1994, the 500 members of the lower house are elected by two different methods: 300 from single-seat districts and 200 from eleven regions by party-list proportional representation. A candidate running in a district must deposit ¥3 million (about $25,000 at the official $1 per ¥120 exchange rate in early 1997). This is subject to confiscation if the candidate fails to win at least 10 per cent of the total valid vote cast in the district (POEL, Article 92).

Once duly registered as either an independent candidate or a particular party's official candidate, one may not engage in any activity that can be interpreted as electioneering except during the officially defined campaign period, which has been progressively reduced over the years to twelve days in a lower-house election, and seventeen days in an upper-house election (POEL, Article 129). Besides, each candidate may set up only one campaign office in the entire election district (POEL, Article 131). His or her campaign staff may be provided with no more than forty-five meals, that is, three meals for one day for fifteen people or three meals per day for fifteen days for one person or some intermediate arrangement for more than one person but fewer than fifteen people (POEL, Article 139). Nor can a candidate use for campaigning purposes more than one vehicle or one vessel, each equipped with no more than one loudspeaker and bearing no more than four passengers besides a driver or a crew (POEL, Article 141).

The list of legal constraints does not stop here but goes on and on. A candidate may not use more than 35,000 postcards or more than 70,000 handbills (POEL, Article 142); nor display more than three posters, each no larger than 85 cm × 60 cm, per campaign office (POEL, Article 144); nor broadcast his or her views more than five times on the radio or television during an entire campaign period (POEL, Article 149); nor set up and maintain more than one fund-raising organisation (POEL, Articles 6, 19). Both a candidate and a political party are required to keep detailed and complete records of their income and expenditures and report them each year either to a prefectural election management committee or to the Minister of Home Affairs (Political Fund Control Law [PFCL], Article 12). A party may receive no more than ¥20 million per year in political contributions from one individual and no more than ¥30 million from one corporation, labour union or any other organisation (or less, depending on the size of the donor organisation) (PFCL, Article 21). An individual donor may give no more than ¥1.5 million, and a corporation or labour union no more than ¥500,000, to the same candidate in one year (PFCL, Article 22). A candidate or a party may not collect more than ¥1.5 million from one participant at a fund-raiser (PFCL, Article 22). Violators of any of the foregoing injunctions are subject to imprisonment and/or a fine and, depending on the seriousness of the case, loss of the right to vote or to run as a candidate in future elections (PFCL, Articles 26–28).

The electoral system

Today's Japan also has an extremely complicated and confusing electoral system (Fukui and Fukai 1996b: ch. 4). Members of the nation's 47 prefectural (provincial) and 3,250 or so local (city, town, village and ward) legislatures, called 'assemblies', are elected, uniformly for a four-year renewable term, under the so-called single nontransferable vote (SNTV) system. This uses multi-seat election districts in which each voter casts one nontransferable ballot for a particular candidate (POEL, Article 15; Local Autonomy Law [LAL], Article 93). The majority (152) of the 252 members of the House of Councillors are elected by the same SNTV plurality method from the 47 prefectures, while a minority (100) are elected by a proportional representation method (d'Hondt). All upper-house members serve a six-year renewable term. Under the new system adopted in 1994, a minority (200) of the 500 House of Representatives members are also elected by the d'Hondt variant of the proportional representation system, while the majority are elected from 300 single-seat districts by the 'first-past-the-post' method. The lower-house members' term is four years and renewable. Since this house, unlike the upper house, may be dissolved and a new general election called by the cabinet at almost any time, its members serve much shorter terms in practice. The first general election under the new system is expected to be held in 1996, with uncertain results for all parties.

Table 6.1. *Lineages of contemporary Japanese parties*

Name	Year founded	Antecedent parties (year founded)	Status in early 1996
LDP	1955	LP (1945); JDP (1945)	Governing
SDPJ	1945 (called JSP until 1991)		Governing
NPH	1993		Governing
NFP	1995	DSP (1960); CGP (1964); JNP (1992); JRP (1993); NPF (1993); LP (1994)	Opposition
JCP	1945	JCP (1922, but illegal before 1945)	Opposition

Abbreviations: LDP =Liberal Democratic Party
　　　　　　　LP　=Liberal Party
　　　　　　　JDP　=Japan Democratic Party
　　　　　　　SDPJ=Social Democratic Party of Japan
　　　　　　　JSP　=Japan Socialist Party
　　　　　　　NPH =New Party Harbinger
　　　　　　　NFP =New Frontier Party
　　　　　　　DSP =Democratic Socialist Party
　　　　　　　CGP =Clean Government Party
　　　　　　　JNP　=Japan New Party
　　　　　　　JRP　=Japan Renewal Party
　　　　　　　NPF =New Party Future
　　　　　　　JCP　=Japan Communist Party
Source: Fukui and Fukai, 1996b, Appendix.

The party system

Until a few years ago, Japan had a very stable party system in which five major national parties competed in national, prefectural and local elections, with some minor and invariably ineffectual parties running a few candidates each. Independents won a few seats in the Diet and a far more substantial number in local assemblies. As shown in Table 6.1, the Social Democrats (SDPJ) and Communist Party (JCP) had been around since 1945, the Liberal Democratic Party (LDP) since 1955, the Democratic Socialist Party (DSP) since 1960, and the Clean Government Party (CGP) since 1964. The Liberal Democrats (LDP) had won the majority or a substantial plurality of seats in every Diet election, and formed every government by itself. Since 1992, however, not only have several new parties been formed, then all but one of them have merged with each other and two of the older parties (DSP and CGP). All have participated in one or another of the three coalition governments formed since 1993. At the end of 1995, there are thus five major parties, three of which (LDP, SDPJ and NPH) form a governing coalition opposed by the other two (NFP and JCP).

The recruitment process within parties

The formal rules governing Japanese national, prefectural and local elections are thus varied and complex, while the Japanese party system is in great flux. Moreover, Japanese elections are also governed by a number of informal rules that further, and significantly, narrow the scope of opportunities for most Japanese citizens to enter the Diet.

A Japanese citizen who meets all the legal requirements for candidacy in a Diet election may run for a seat in either house of the Diet as an independent or as a candidate of a small local group. As shown in Table 6.2, 5 of 39 independents and 2 of 144 small-group candidates won in the district-based races of the 1992 upper-house election. In the 1993 lower-house general election 30 of 110 independents and 4 of 66 small-group candidates won. These winner-to-candidate ratios, however, were far lower than those of party-sponsored candidates, with the exception of the JCP's. Furthermore, the majority of independents in any Diet election are partisan candidates in disguise who are denied nomination by their party, usually due to the presence of a competing candidate, and who join the party if they win. Twenty, or two-thirds, of the thirty independent winners in the 1993 lower-house election belonged to this type. In other words, less than 10 per cent of bona fide independents won in that general election.

This pattern has been due to the extremely high costs of an election campaign under the SNTV system, which has been in effect since 1945 in district-based races in upper-house elections, and for seventy years (from 1925 to 1994) in lower-house general elections. Under SNTV, each of the nation's forty-seven prefectures constituted a multi-seat upper-house election district, each with nearly two million voters on average. Each of the 129 lower-house election districts in the 1993 general election had nearly three-quarters of a million voters on average.[1] The relatively large size of each district, and the correspondingly large number of voters in it, alone made an effective campaign very expensive (Horie 1993: 124). It

---

[1] The total numbers of registered voters at the time of the 1992 upper-house and 1993 lower-house elections were, respectively, about 93.3 million and 94.5 million. *Asahi nenkan*, 1995: 672–3.

Table 6.2. *Candidates and winners in Diet elections, 1992–3*

Party	1992 Upper house election (district races)		1993 Lower house election	
	Candidates	Winners (%)	Candidates	Winners (%)
LDP	55	49 (89.1)	285	223 (78.2)
SDPJ	18	12 (67.7)	142	70 (49.2)
CGP	6	6 (100.0)	54	51 (94.4)
DSP	3	1 (33.3)	28	15 (53.5)
JCP	44	2 (4.3)	128	15 (11.7)
JRP	–	– –	69	55 (79.7)
JNP	–	– –	57	35 (61.4)
NPH	–	– –	16	13 (81.2)
Other Parties	144	2 (1.4)	66	4 (6.0)
Independents	39	5 (12.8)	110	30 (27.0)
Total (mean)	309	77 (24.9)	955	511 (53.5)

Note:
Abbreviations: see table 6.1.
Source: Kokkai benran, 1994: 314–32.

cost a great deal just to maintain a large and active campaign organisation, known generically as *koenkai* (support association).

Moreover, the multi-seat district system forced the largest parties, especially the LDP, to run more than one candidate in each district in order to win a majority or a large plurality of seats in either house. Candidates of the same party could not fight each other on policy issues, as they were expected to be in agreement with each other by the party rules, and usually were in fact. As a result they competed by currying favour with, or even bribing, voters with small gifts and promise of more largess, such as hefty subsidies from the national government for local projects, to be delivered later in return for their votes (Fukui and Fukai 1996a). Even small gifts, such as cases of soap bars and hand towels, add up.

It is thus extremely expensive to run for a Diet seat. It is estimated to have cost a candidate at least ¥200 million to run an effective campaign in a lower-house election in the late 1980s, or about five times as much as in Israel, ten times as much as in Canada, and sixty times as much as in Britain or the Netherlands (Fukui and Fukai 1991: 60–3). A candidate running as a nominee of a major party has at least part, and often virtually all, of the campaign expenses paid by the party or organisations affiliated with it. JCP and CGP candidates have theirs paid almost entirely by the party treasury, while SDPJ and DSP candidates have theirs paid mainly by labour unions affiliated to the respective parties (Fukui and Fukai 1991: 59). LDP candidates have to raise the majority of their campaign funds by themselves, but they get at least some help from the party treasury: a flat ¥5 million 'nomination money' plus either ¥10 million, in the case of a veteran candidate with past service as a cabinet member, or ¥20 million, in the case of a novice without such a record, in the 1993 lower house election (*Mainichi shinbun* 1993a: 2). Moreover, they routinely receive comparable amounts from the intra-party faction to which they belong, or pledge to belong if elected.

Aspirants thus needed to run as an official candidate of one major party or another to have a fair chance of winning a Diet seat. It is, however, virtually impossible for most Japanese citizens to do so. This is because the major Japanese parties select their candidates according to three rules:
(1) approval by local and prefectural party organisations;
(2) a high probability of winning; and
(3) incumbency, where applicable.
Candidate nomination decisions are invariably made by a group of the highest-ranking national party officials in every major party. For example, such decisions are made in the LDP by its Election Policy Committee chaired by the party's president and composed of the four other highest-ranking officials – the vice president, secretary general, and chairs of the Executive Council and the Policy Research Council – plus ten other veteran LDP members of the Diet (Jiyuminshuto, 1994a; Motomiya, interview). The party's current guidelines for the nomination of candidates in Diet elections, however, explicitly state that such decisions are to be made on the basis of recommendations received from the party's prefectural (regional) branches. In a lower-house election, these recommendations are invariably based on the recommendations of, and usually consensus among, district-level party branches. The selection of the LDP-sponsored candidates in Diet elections is thus effectively controlled by the party's prefectural and local organisations. The other major Japanese parties all follow exactly the same rule (Nihon shakaito chuo honbu 1991: 14; Nihon shakaito 1995; Nihon shakaito senkyo taisaku iinkai 1995; Kishimoto, Kawashima, and Hashimoto, interviews).

Nearly all the major Japanese parties insist on selecting as their official candidates only those who are highly likely to win, although none says so officially. The JCP appears to be one exception, judging by the disproportionately low percentage of winners among the remarkably large number of candidates that party routinely runs in a Diet election, as shown in Table 6.2. But a party official insists that winnability is an important consideration even in the JCP's nomination decisions (Hashimoto, interview). The emphasis on winnability in turn leads all but the SDPJ to give preference to incumbents over new candidates.[2] For example, the current LDP 'criteria' for the selection of candidates in Diet elections explicitly stipulate that incumbents should be given preference (Jiyuminshuto 1994b; 1994c).

Who gets selected?

These rules that govern the selection of party-sponsored candidates in Diet elections favour certain groups in Japanese society over others as potential sources of viable candidates. The power of prefectural and local party branches gives distinct advantage to those who dominate those branches, namely prefectural and local politicians in all parties, prefectural and local party staffers in all but the LDP, and labour union leaders in the SDPJ, DSP and JCP. These groups have contributed three of the five largest pools of candidates in recent Diet, especially lower-house, elections (*Asahi shinbun* 1990a: 8; Asahi shinbun senkyo honbu 1990: 123; *Yomiuri shinbun* 1993c: 5). As in Germany (Wessels chapter 5) and Australia (McAllister chapter 2), a record of long party service therefore seems critical.

The emphasis on professional careers is also found in Japan. The other two groups favoured by the rules of candidate selection commonly used by the Japanese parties are Diet members' aides and national government bureaucrats. When a seat becomes available due to the retirement or death of an incumbent, either one or the other of these two groups is tapped as the most likely source of a 'winnable' new candidate, the first type by the LDP and, to a lesser extent, the SDPJ and the second nearly exclusively by the LDP. Many of the retired or deceased LDP incumbents' aides who have run as that party's new candidates in recent years have been those incumbents' close relatives, usually their sons. By simply taking over their relatives' *koenkai* machines, most of them – 140 (72 per cent) of 194 for all parties and 115 (84 per cent) of 137 for the LDP alone in the 1990 general election – have easily won (Asahi shinbun senkyo honbu, 1990: 130–2). In the 1993 general election, a quarter of the 511 winners and about 40 per cent of the LDP winners, were such 'hereditary' or *nisei* (second generation) candidates (*Imidas* 1995: 382).

[2] The SDPJ's maverick treatment of its incumbent Diet members no doubt reflects the deep concern of the party's leaders over the steady decline of its popularity and belief that a fast turnover of the party's contingent in the Diet is highly desirable, perhaps essential, for its survival as a viable parliamentary party in the coming decades. The party now enforces mandatory retirement at 70 for all its Diet members, probably for the same reason (Kishimoto, interview; Nihon shakaito, 1995).

Table 6.3. *Women members of Japanese prefectural and local assemblies,*
1975–93

	1975		1993	
	All	Women (%)	All	Women (%)
Prefectural	2,828	32 (1.1)	2,839	73 (2.6)
City	20,167	360 (1.8)	19,130	1,134 (5.9)
Town/village	48,220	217 (0.5)	41,944	910 (2.2)
Ward	1,088	72 (6.6)	1,004	121 (12.1)
Total (mean)	72,303	681 (0.9)	64,917	2,238 (3.4)

Source: Sorifu 1994: 46 (Table 3–1–5).

The same three common rules of candidate selection by the major
parties serve as effective barriers against certain groups. By far the largest
and the most obvious of such groups is women, very few of whom are
found in any of the favoured groups. As of the end of 1993, they
accounted for less than 4 per cent of the nearly 65,000 members of prefectural and local assemblies. They are found in far greater numbers
among the rank-and-file members of most major parties, except the DSP,
but not among their national officials, except in the JCP. The same applies
to labour unions and the government bureaucracy. The 8,930 officials
filling positions in the top three ranks of the national civil service in 1992
included 63 women, or 0.7 per cent of the total (Sorifu 1994: 50).

Women are nearly absent from either house of the Diet, since they are
found in such modest numbers in the pools of potential candidates commonly tapped by the major Japanese parties. In the 1992 upper-house
election, they accounted for only 18.6 per cent of all major party candidates and 9.0 per cent of winners in the district-based races, and 20.7 per
cent of major party candidates and 11.4 per cent of winners in the proportional representation races. In the 1993 lower-house general election,
they accounted for 7.3 per cent of all candidates and 2.9 per cent of the
winners. In the eleven preceding lower-house general elections held since
1960, their share of lower-house seats had ranged from 1.2 per cent in
1976 to 2.3 per cent in 1990 (Asahi shinbun senkyo honbu 1990: 320).

Both the formal and informal rules of electoral politics in Japan thus
distribute the opportunity to run and win a legislative seat, especially in
the Diet, very unevenly among groups of Japanese citizens. Some groups,
such as women, are virtually excluded from entering legislative politics.
Even for those who are privileged to do so, however, surviving more than

Table 6.4. *Women members and national officials in major parties, 1994*

	Rank and file			National party officials		
	All	Women (%) (in 1,000)		All	Women (%)	
LDP	2,496	948	(38.0)	321	9	(2.8)
SDPJ	128*	20*	(15.6)	39	3	(7.7)
CGP	216	96	(44.6)	35	3	(8.6)
JCP	400*	160*	(40.0)	205	39	(19.0)
DSP	109	6	(5.6)	69	3	(4.3)
Total (Mean)	3,349	1,230	(36.7)	669	57	(8.5)

Note:
* Indicates rough estimates. For abbreviations see table 6.1.
Source: Sorifu 1994: 48 (Table 3–1–6).

Table 6.5. *Women candidates and winners in 1992 upper-house election*

		District races			PR race		
		All	Women (%)		All	Women (%)	
LDP	Candidates	55	2	(3.6)	27	4	(14.8)
	Winners	49	2	(4.1)	19	1	(5.3)
SDPJ	Candidates	18	4	(22.2)	25	5	20.0)
	Winners	12	2	(16.6)	10	2	(20.0)
CGP	Candidates	6	1	(16.6)	17	4	(23.5)
	Winners	6	1	(16.6)	8	2	25.0)
JCP	Candidates	46	16	(34.8)	25	7	(28.0)
	Winners	2	1	(50.0)	4	0	(0.0)
DSP	Candidates	3	1	(33.3)	17	3	(17.6)
	Winners	1	0	(0.0)	3	0	(0.0)
Sub-total	Candidates	128	24	(18.8)	111	23	(20.7)
	Winners	70	6	(8.5)	44	5	(11.4)
Other parties	Candidates	144	30	(20.8)	219	42	(19.2)
	Winners	2	1	(50.0)	0	0	(–)
Independents	Candidates	39	4	(10.3)	0	0	(–)
	Winners	5	0	(0.0)	0	0	(–)
Total (mean)	Candidates	311	58	(18.6)	330	65	(19.7)
	Winners	77	7	(9.0)	44	5	(11.4)

Note:
Abbreviations: see table 6.1; PR: proportional representation.
Sources: *Asahi shinbun* 1992: 2; *Yomiuri shinbun* 1993: 2.

Table 6.6. *Women candidates and winners in 1993 lower-house election*

		All	Women (%)
LDP	Candidates	285	2 (0.7)
	Winners	223	1 (0.4)
SDPJ	Candidates	142	10 (7.0)
	Winners	70	3 (4.3)
CGP	Candidates	54	2 (0.4)
	Winners	51	2 (3.9)
JCP	Candidates	129	32 (24.8)
	Winners	15	2 (13.3)
DSP	Candidates	28	0 (0.0)
	Winners	15	0 (0.0)
JRP	Candidates	69	1 (1.4)
	Winners	55	0 (0.0)
JNP	Candidates	55	3 (5.4)
	Winners	35	2 (5.7)
NPH	Candidates	15	0 (0.0)
	Winners	13	0 (0.0)
Sub-total	Candidates	777	50 (6.4)
	Winners	477	10 (2.1)
Other parties	Candidates	66	10 (15.2)
	Winners	4	1 (50.0)
Independents	Candidates	112	10 (8.9)
	Winners	30	4 (13.3)
Total (mean)	Candidates	955	70 (7.3)
	Winners	511	15 (2.9)

Note:
Abbreviations: see table 6.1.
Sources: Mainichi shinbun 1993b: 3; 1993c: 1.

one election is not easy and requires lots of work and money. Much of what is required of an incumbent to retain his or her seat in a Japanese legislative, especially Diet, election is also due to informal, rather than formal, rules.

Incumbency turnover

Despite all the restrictions imposed by both the formal and informal rules, a seat in Japan's national legislature is obviously a very desirable thing to many citizens. The fierce competition that takes place in every Diet election attests to the validity of this observation. While incumbency is an important asset in a Diet election, the rate of Diet membership turn-over has been relatively high in recent elections and, more important, there has been a considerable amount of volatility and uncertainty about the performance of the major parties and their incumbents, obviously due to the SNTV system. As Table 6.7 shows, widely and unpredictably varying numbers of incumbents of the major parties lost their seats in recent Diet elections.

A good way to reduce the degree of uncertainty, particularly for LDP incumbents during the party's long rule, has been to become known as a skillful and successful player in the game of pork barrel politics. An LDP Diet member's political career is in fact made or broken largely by how good a player he or she is in this particular kind of game (Fukui and Fukai 1996a; Ike 1980; Richardson and Flanagan 1984; Hrebenar 1986; Curtis 1988). The preoccupation with pork barrel politics reflects the serious-ness of the economic plight in which many of Japan's local communities find themselves today. Despite the nation's reputation as one of the wealthiest in the world, many of its local communities suffer from griev-ously inadequate social capital and infrastructure, such as modern roads, sewage facilities and nursing homes. Most lack resources of their own to cope with local problems, and they depend on help from the national government. This is important because the national government collects as much as two-thirds of the tax monies collected annually (Fukui and Fukai 1996a). As a result, virtually all major public works undertaken at the regional, prefectural or local level are at least partially financed by the national treasury.

Under such a system Japan's prefectural and local governments devote an inordinate amount of their time and effort to earning their pet projects the attention and support of the national government. Local party organisations and politicians play a key role in fetching pork barrel to local communities from the national treasury. As suggested already, this is where a politician's worth to his or her constituents is tested, and his or her chances of re-election in the future are in large measure decided.

All Diet members are eager to prove themselves effective spokesmen for their constituents by helping their pet public works projects receive funding commitments from the national government. That is how they try to ensure their victory in future elections. Some politicians are, or are at least believed to be, more effective and skillful than others as intermedi-aries between their constituents and the national treasury, and thus are more likely to survive at future polls. An LDP Diet member's reputation as an effective and dependable spokesperson for his or her constituents is often built on his or her presumed influence on bureaucrats in one min-

Table 6.7. Loser : all incumbent candidate ratios for major parties

	Upper-house election (district races only)				Lower-house election			
	1989		1992		1990		1993	
	No./No.	%	No./No.	%	No./No.	%	No./No.	%
LDP	24/37	(64.9)	3/35	(8.6)	42/270	(15.5)	33/212	(15.7)
SDPJ	0/10	(0.0)	0/19	(0.0)	3/67	(4.5)	57/121	(47.1)
CGP	0/2	(0.0)	0/1	(0.0)	8/42	(19.0)	1/25	(4.0)
JCP	3/3	(100.0)	0/1	(0.0)	13/23	(56.5)	7/15	(46.7)
DSP	1/2	(50.0)	0/0	(–)	12/20	(60.0)	2/12	(16.7)
JRP	–	–	–	–	–	–	1/35	(2.9)
JNP	–	–	–	–	–	–	0/0	(–)
NPH	–	–	–	–	–	–	1/10	(10.0)
Other parties	0/2	(0.0)	1/1	(100.0)	0/5	(0.0)	1/5	(20.0)
Independents	3/7	(42.9)	0/1	(0.0)	1/5	(20.0)	3/14	(21.4)
Total (mean)	31/63	(49.2)	4/58	(8.3)	79/432	(18.3)	106/449	(23.6)

Notes:
Abbreviations: see table 6.1.
Sources: *Asahi shinbun* 1989: 1; 1990b: 1; 1990c: 1; *Yomiuri shinbun* 1989: 2; 1992: 1; 1993a: 1; 1993b: 1, 1993c: 1.

istry of the national government or another. This influence is in turn presumed to be based on his or her expertise in the area of public policy under that ministry's jurisdiction. A group of such politicians is known as a 'tribe' (*zoku*). There are thus a construction tribe, a transportation tribe, an agriculture tribe, a trade and industry tribe, and so forth (Inoguchi and Iwai 1988; McCubbins and Rosenbluth 1995: 50; McCubbins and Noble 1995: 61). Aware of the significant electoral advantage that reputation as an influential member of an important policy tribe gives a candidate in a Diet election, many Diet members, especially LDP members, specialise in a particular policy area or areas.

An incumbent with a reputation as an effective intermediary between his or her constituents and the national treasury attracts a large number of supporters among prefectural and local government officials and politicians who form an electoral coalition known as *keiretsu*, or 'line' (Fukui and Fukai 1994). For a Diet member, a line serves as a valuable means to reach and mobilise many, if not all, of the affiliated local politicians' constituents. For the local politicians, it serves as a valuable 'pipeline' between them and the national treasury. In short, a line is a coalition of a Diet member, on the one hand, and local officials and politicians, on the other, formed for mutual benefit.

An incumbent Diet member's line resembles, and is related to, his or her *koenkai* machine. Both are formed to help re-elect the incumbent, so that he or she may continue to serve the interests of his or her local constituents in the highly competitive game of pork barrel politics, as it is played in contemporary Japan. Nearly all prefectural and local government officials and politicians affiliated with a Diet member's line serve as officials of his or her *koenkai* organisation as well. The larger and the more active these organisations are, ceteris paribus, the more useful they are. It takes, however, much effort and, usually, much money to build a large, strong and active line or *koenkai*.

Once formed and developed into a viable organisation, a line or *koenkai* is often maintained even after the retirement or death of the Diet member for whom it was originally formed and, as mentioned earlier, is inherited by his or her relative or aide. A new candidate who runs in a Diet election with the support of an inherited line and *koenkai* poses a serious challenge to all incumbents running in the same district and forces them to work harder on their own reputation as influential members of an important policy tribe and on their own lines and *koenkai* organisations as vote-mobilising machines. An incumbent's struggle for survival thus goes on without a let-up and ensures that the opportunity for a new candidate, even for one with an inherited campaign machine, not to mention for one without such a machine, remains ever so narrowly limited.

The potential impact of the 1994 electoral reform

The foregoing discussion has been concerned mainly with the recent Diet elections under the upper-house election system, which remains unchanged, and the lower-house election system, which underwent a significant change in 1994. As mentioned in the first section of this chapter, the change involved the replacement of the multi-seat SNTV system, which had been in place since the mid-1920s, with a hybrid or mixed system that combines a single-seat district plurality vote system and a proportional representation system, for lower-house elections. The new system is, however, yet to be tested and its actual effects remain unknown at this point. The observations that follow therefore remain speculative.

First, the major parties are likely to remain committed to the same old rules in the selection of their candidates, that is, the acceptance of recommendations made by their prefectural and local branches, respect for incumbency, and the importance attached to winnability. It is therefore unlikely that they will choose to sponsor in future elections any types of candidate very different from those they had chosen under the old system. In other words, prefectural and local politicians, party staffers, labour union leaders, national government bureaucrats and Diet members' aides will continue to dominate both the pool of candidates officially sponsored by the major parties and, therefore, the Diet itself. Other groups, particularly women, will continue to be effectively denied the opportunity to compete with those in the privileged groups.

Second, a Diet member's role as an intermediary between his or her local constituents and the national treasury is unlikely to be significantly affected by the change in the formal election system. As long as so many of Japan's towns and villages continue to suffer from as numerous and as serious economic problems as they do, while the national government controls the lion's share of the tax revenue, Diet members will continue to be called upon to act as intermediaries between the hard-pressed local constituents and the national treasury.

Third, the role of individual Diet members' *koenkai* and electoral lines may significantly change under the new lower-house election law, as the national and local party organisations will play central roles not only in the compilation of candidate lists for proportional representation races but also both in the selection of candidates and in the management of their campaigns in district races. This assumes, however, that local party organisations will have sufficient financial and technical resources to run successful campaigns for their candidates against their partisan competitors similarly supported by other parties. If local party organisations prove incapable of mastering and deploying sufficient resources, some, if not all, *koenkai* machines will probably still survive for a long time to come.

Fourth, and last, the 1994 political reform was a result of a campaign to purge Japanese politics of the corrosive influence of money, which was blamed for a series of political scandals and the LDP's defeat in the 1989 upper-house election and, particularly, the 1993 lower-house election. Whether the reform will achieve its purpose is far from certain, however. If money ceases to be an important factor in future Diet elections, or prefectural and local elections for that matter, it will be because of a change in voters' values and attitudes rather than the reform of the electoral system. This view is consistent with the victory of the thirty-five little known and deliberately thrifty candidates of the brand new JNP in the 1993 general election. As suggested above, however, 'money politics' in the sense of pork barrel politics is likely to remain an outstanding feature of Japanese elections for a long time to come, if not forever.

INTERVIEWS

Hashimoto, Eiichi. Member of Staff, Election and Local Government Bureau, Japan Communist Party. 7 December, 1995.

Kawashima, Nobuo. Chief of Staff, Election Policy Committee, Clean Government Party. 7 December, 1995.

Kishimoto, Yasuo. Deputy Director of the Secretariat, Election Policy Committee, Central Headquarters, Social Democratic Party of Japan. 7 December, 1995.

Motomiya, Kaoru. Member of Staff, Election Policy Committee, Liberal Democratic Party. 7 December, 1995.

7   The Netherlands

Monique Leijenaar and Kees Niemöller

Research on legislative recruitment in the Netherlands used to focus on party politics. If one pursues a career as a MP one first has to become a member of a political party, preferably one of the larger parties. Within the party one not only has to pay his or her dues, but also become politically active: go to the meetings of the local or regional branches, become a delegate to the national party congress, and subsequently chair a local or regional branch, and be nominated for the national party board. After five to ten years of party activities there is a high probability of being asked to stand on the party list for parliament. Then whether candidates are nominated for a safe place or not, and hence will be elected to the Parliament, depends on other features like gender, ethnic background, regional descent, professional occupation and local councillor experience. Therefore party service and activism used to be the primary factors facilitating legislative recruitment (Hillebrand 1992:290; Koole 1992: 306; Thomassen et al. 1992:34; Leijenaar 1993:223–4).

During the early 1990s recruitment into parliament became less predictable. Recent developments, such as the declining strength of old community and group identities (depillarisation and individualisation), have caused the crumbling of the 'partitocratie'. Voters have turned their backs on traditional parties, and on politics in general. Consequently party membership is declining rapidly. The proportion of the electorate who carry a party membership card has fallen from 9 per cent in 1963 to less than 3 per cent. The party leadership has reacted to all of this with a demand for a higher quality of parliamentary members, and more MPs with close ties to large groups of citizens. Hence, the criteria for selecting candidates are changing, as well as the selection procedures within the parties.

Many studies of recruitment for the legislature have been carried out to assess the Dutch representative democratic system. The quality of a representative democracy is assumed to depend on the degree of correspondence between the opinions of the electorate and the legislative behaviour of the representatives (Thomassen 1993:350). The three models explaining the mechanisms by which this correspondence can be reached – focussing on roles, representation, and the responsible party model – are often used as a framework for analysing legislative recruitment. The early literature reflects the traditional split between the study of the selection procedures within parties (the institutional approach), and the analysis of individual candidates and MPs (the individual approach). Helped by the availability of personal data about MPs most studies look at the composition of parliament, asking whether the representative legislature is 'an exact portrait, in miniature, of the people at large, as it should think, feel, reason and act like them' (John Adams cited in Pitkin 1967:60). In common with most parliaments, this is not the case in the Netherlands: Dutch MPs have been, and are still, recruited from the highest layers of society in terms of social class, education and income (van den Berg 1983:259).

In the 1970s the composition of parliament changed drastically: from the representation of organised interests into a 'workroom for professionals' (see also Wessels chapter 5). Van den Berg (1983) explains this by referring to depillarisation and democratisation: both had their impact on the nomination processes within parties. Depillarisation caused a looser tie between candidates and interest groups, while democratisation produced increased consultations within parties. Political careers only became possible for people with flexible jobs and time on their hands: mainly people working in the public sector in high level jobs (van den Berg 1983:194; see also Thomassen 1993:351).

Another recent development is the research on the representativeness and responsiveness of *local* government. After the local elections of 1990 when turnout in the larger cities declined drastically (under 50 per cent) surveys among citizens and representatives of seven large cities have been carried out and the results have been extensively reported. Again at this level representativeness in terms of social background and policy preferences is weak. There is a high level of public cynicism and distrust of politicians, while citizens also stated that differences between parties at the local level were hardly visible (Tops et al. 1991; Denters and van der Kolk, eds. 1993).

This chapter focusses on how the composition of parliament has altered under the pressure of changes in the opportunity structure, and changes in the rules and procedures of parties for selecting their representatives. The first section gives a short overview of the opportunity structure, notably how the electoral and party systems influence the recruitment process in the Netherlands. The chapter goes on to analyse the demand side of the recruitment process, including the selection process within Dutch parties, focussing on the recent party reforms. Here we draw on data from the survey of candidates in the 1994 parliamentary election.[1] The third part considers the supply side of legislative recruitment, including the background characteristics of MPs and the motives of people entering the political arena. Lastly we discuss attitudes towards the affirmative action policies that most parties use to select more women.

The opportunity structure in the Netherlands

The electoral system

The Constitution states the legal eligibility criteria for candidacy: citizenship, a minimum age of eighteen years, and no exclusion from the right to vote. The current electoral system goes back to the end of the First World War when the system of proportional representation was introduced together with universal suffrage. There is an election every four years for the Second Chamber, after which the leader of the largest party is asked by the Queen to form a majority cabinet together with other parties. Parliament controls the activities and decisions of the cabinet. The seventy-five representatives of the First Chamber are elected indirectly by members of the provincial councils.

In the current electoral system the whole of the country is one large constituency. For pragmatic reasons, the country is divided in eighteen electoral districts, and the votes for each party list in these district are added up. This system is one of the most proportional in the world, because there is a very low threshold for participation: 0.67 per cent of votes are needed for parliamentary representation. The absence of constituencies means that candidates do not have to compete for the votes in a particular district. Therefore there is no constituency work to be done, nor is there any need for service responsiveness or symbolic responsive behaviour. Strangely enough, the absence of constituencies does not mean that territorial backing is of no importance at all. Most parties in the Netherlands are structured by region and it used to be that each regional branch was allowed a certain number of candidates for the parliamentary party. Therefore each candidate had to be nominated by a regional branch. In the past this meant a lot of moving around for candidates (Koole and Leijenaar 1988). Recently in most parties selection has become centralised and the regional factor has lost some of its relevance (Koole 1992; Leijenaar 1992).

---

[1] In 1994 before the elections for the Dutch Parliament all candidates on the final lists of the parties were approached with a questionnaire. The analyses in this chapter are all based on these data.

Although the electoral system functions well in terms of turnout at parliamentary elections – between 70 and 90 per cent – the system always meets with criticism. In the 1960s the debate about institutional reform reached its first peak. Some politicians pointed out that the Dutch political system did not even meet the minimal definition of democracy as formulated by Schumpeter (1942): the electorate deciding who was going to be in power. Because of the necessity of forming a governing coalition more than once the party which won the election with the largest number of seats, was kept out of government. This led to a plea for 'polarisation': that parties should form a coalition *before the election* so that the electorate would not only vote for a party, but also for a certain government coalition (van Thijn 1967; Den Uyl et al. 1967; Dittrich and Andeweg 1982). Other points of discussion at that time were the direct election of the prime minister, and the introduction of referendums. Since then several parliamentary or expert committees have studied possible reforms of the system without much success.

The 1990s have revived the debate on institutional reform in reaction to the negative public image of politicians. When at the local elections in 1990 turnout in the large cities decreased to 45–50 per cent, politicians started to worry about the large gap between voters and representatives, and the possible lack of legitimacy of the current local political system. The chair of the Second Chamber established several reform committees. They were to advise parliament on such matters as changing the system of proportional representation into, for example, the German mixed system; the possibility of a directly elected mayor instead of the current nomination by the cabinet; and the possible introduction of referendums. Although the recommendations from these committees were rather conservative, in the parliamentary debate in 1993 it became clear that a large majority was unwilling to embrace the proposals for change. The only reform that gained some sympathy was an increase in the weight of preference votes for candidates in general elections. However the debate was not ended. The 1994 election produced the so-called 'purple cabinet' consisting of three parties, PvdA (the Labour party), D66 (the Left Liberal party) and VVD (the Conservative Liberal party). The Christian Democrats (CDA) who are ideologically positioned between D66 and VVD were kept out of government, something which had not happened since 1917. During the strained coalition negotiations D66, which had always promoted a radical reform of the political system, insisted on the introduction of institutional reforms in the cabinet agreement. In 1995 the cabinet kept its promise: it submitted a proposal to parliament for a radical change in the system of proportional representation, as well as the introduction of a corrective referendum. The cabinet proposal in 1995 for institutional renewal suggests a dual electoral system: half of the members of the Second Chamber would be elected by means of proportional representation and a party list system while the other half should be elected through five districts. Within these districts parties would still submit lists but with fewer candidates since in each district only a total of fifteen seats could be gained. This proposal hoped for closer ties between the electorate and its representatives by decreasing the physical distance. In 1996 the proposal was defeated by the parliament.

Under the new purple cabinet a wave of reform swept through politics affecting parliamentary behaviour. Before the 1994 election the relationship between cabinet and parliament could be described as static: a monistic relationship between government and the governmental parties. Governmental parties were very disciplined as far as voting in parliament was concerned. Bills submitted by the cabinet were sometimes amended, but almost always passed parliament. Under the purple cabinet parliamentary behaviour changed. The VVD parliamentary party, and less often the PvdA and D66 parliamentary parties, do not automatically follow their own cabinet members, and several times the cabinet failed to gain a majority for its plans. Much more often than it used to be, roll calls are necessary.

This does not mean that individual MPs have become more, and political parties have become less, important. The impact of parties on the behaviour of MPs is still very visible, especially where voting behaviour is concerned, but the traditional split between governmental and opposition parties is not so clear cut any more. These days the overall impact of parties on the decision-making process is difficult to estimate. Some believe that their power within cabinet and parliament has increased in the recent years (Koole 1992). Yet parties as organisations are losing ground. Membership is gradually declining, parties are losing their intermediary function between politicians and citizens. These days the mass media inform the public about the ideas and policies of politicians, and opinion polls inform the politicians about the wishes and demands of the public. The electoral-level party is also in trouble: party choice is highly unpredictable, and the background characteristics of voters (such as their education, social-economic status, income and age), party ideology and party identification, have lost some of their predictive value. Consequently the vote is highly volatile and short-term factors such as the personality of candidates and issues are becoming more important in predicting party choice.

The ongoing debate about the reform of the electoral system, the negative image of politics and politicians, and the unstable voting behaviour, undoubtedly have had an impact on the demand side as well as on the supply side of legislative recruitment. Parties are looking for different qualities in their candidates than they did a decade ago, and standing for parliament is not a guarantee of professional success any more.

Demand side: selection within parties

The selection procedures of the main Dutch parties have been reported extensively elsewhere (Koole and Leijenaar 1988; Leijenaar 1992). Koole and Leijenaar looked at the theory and practice of selection processes and describe the changes in these procedures since the 1960s. They conclude that party control over the representatives grew in this period and selection procedures became more rigid (1988:206). The influence of regional and local party branches over selection declined drastically within the large parties. In contrast the central leadership, as well as individual members, gained in influence over the selection process (Koole 1992:305; see also Hillebrand 1992). Here we will focus on recent changes in the main features of candidate selection in the Netherlands in the 1990s.

In the Netherlands political parties are legally free to organise the selection of candidates as they consider appropriate. Since there are no laws or regulations prescribing how parties recruit their representatives, the procedures differ among the parties. In all parties local, regional and national party bodies are involved and the whole process takes about a year. In most parties the regional party branches used to initiate the process of candidate selection by suggesting names of candidates. On the basis of these suggestions an advisory list of candidates was constructed by the national party board. This list was discussed again by local party groups, and an adapted list was finally decided upon by the national party congress, consisting of delegates from all over the country.

This influential role of the local and regional branches was a leftover from the 1960s. As a result of the democratisation wave of this decennium, the organisational structure of parties also had to democratise. The wishes of the rank and file had to be taken into account by including them in the selection process of MPs. Some parties, such as the PvdA and D66, even introduced membership referendums: all members could make their preferences known by filling in postal ballots. The Labour Party abolished this procedure not so long afterwards, but it is still in use with D66. In the late 1980s parties started to feel uneasy with their selection procedures and their outcome: the composition of their parliamentary party. Since then the parties have been changing the procedures roused by the debate on institutional reform.

Parties were dissatisfied with the selection process for various reasons.

It was felt that the parliamentary party consisted of too many white, highly educated males of whom the majority came from the public sector (civil service). Moreover many believed that more effort should be put into the recruitment of young candidates. It was felt that criteria such as certain professional experience, ties with interest groups and debating skills, should be valued more highly than simply a long party career. Lastly it was argued that it happened too often that the national party leaders had to 'beg' for a place on a 'regional list' for one of its own candidates (Koole and Leijenaar 1988; Hillebrand 1992). The pressure for greater leadership involvement came not only from inside the parties. Women's groups (inside and outside the parties) were also demanding fairer representation in terms of gender (van de Velde 1994). The national parties were also aware that parliamentary parties were facing increasing public scrutiny given the growing dissatisfaction with politics and politicians.

Accordingly, the four main parties altered their recruitment practices, providing the national party organisation with a more dominant role. The PvdA introduced a quota for the number of women candidates, and the other large parties explicitly announced their aims of looking for more women and younger candidates. Long and faithful party service was less of a relevant resource, and there seemed to be more room for political amateurs. Ties with interest organisations or specific professional experience became more important attributes for office-seeking candidates.

The survey of candidates for the parliamentary election of 1994 provides some insight into their experience of the selection processes within their parties. Our respondents differed in terms of 'eligibility': how far they would be willing to enter parliament if elected. The lists contain many names of people who come forward to help attract voters to the party list but who do not ever expect to be elected. One third of the respondents indicated that they were not eligible on their own request, some 25 per cent label their position on the final shortlist as 'eligible', and the remainder were not sure about their position. The distribution of candidates who do not consider themselves as 'willing' is highly skewed towards the smaller parties. Therefore, in the remainder of this chapter we will concentrate mainly on the group of respondents who, irrespective of their chances, wanted to become a MP. We will label them as 'candidates'; all other respondents are referred to as 'pseudo-candidates'.

In order to examine how the candidates viewed the selection process of their own party, we asked them whether it was *democratic, efficient, complicated, supportive for women* and *fair* on a four-point scale. The lower the score the more positively the process is evaluated. The mean scores indicate that the majority of candidates tend to have a positive evaluation of

Table 7.1. *Evaluation of selection procedure*

	Green-Left	PvdA	D66	CDA	VVD	Small Right
Democratic	3.1	3.8	1.2	3.1	3.9	2.3
Efficient	4.0	2.9	3.9	2.9	3.2	2.6
Complicated	4.8	5.7	3.6	5.0	4.4	5.5
Supportive for women	2.4	3.9	2.6	2.7	3.0	3.7
Fair	2.8	3.9	1.5	3.0	3.5	1.7

Notes:
Mean scores calculated from an ordinal scale from 1 to 7. A score of 1 means 'very democratic', a score of 7 means 'not democratic at all' (candidates only).

the process (see Table 7.1). The candidates of D66 view their selection process as very democratic and fair. This reflected the use of a members' postal referendum in D66, contrary to the practice in the other parties where only members who visit the relevant party meetings take part in the selection. The candidates from the Labour Party consider, on average, that their selection process is less supportive for women than the candidates from the other parties do. This is an interesting result, since Labour is the only party with a 33 per cent quota for women.

To examine the experience of candidates we asked whether they had run before, and their experience of the selection process (see Table 7.2). Again, there are significant differences between the parties, but most of these seem not to be associated with differences between parties like 'old–new', 'small–big', 'left–right' and 'incumbent–not incumbent'. The results confirm that candidates of the party with the shortest parliamentary history – GreenLeft, a recent merger of left-wing parties – are by far the least experienced. Compared to the other parties very few have previous candidate-experience. Looking at the difference in ranking from the beginning to the end of the selection process, the parties show quite different patterns: many candidates of GreenLeft and VVD report 'lower ranking' while candidates of the PvdA and of the small religious parties are more often upgraded. Not many candidates were subject to any preferential action in their favour: only 12 per cent of all candidates. Candidates of GreenLeft and D66 have a much higher percentage of preferential treatment than candidates from PvdA and CDA. Controlling for sex does not alter this pattern: there is no significant gender difference.

To determine the degree of internal party democracy, we asked respondents about the influence of specific people and groups over the selection

Table 7.2. *The political experience of candidates*

	Green-Left	PvdA	D66	CDA	VVD	Small Right	All
Ran for parliament before	13	68	52	46	35	68	46
Been elected in previous elections	4	59	26	42	28	9	28
Elected in 1994	4	55	44	19	39	24	30
Position at list changed							
higher	9	36	35	42	8	25	25
lower	35	18	35	31	48	9	30
Preferential action in candidate's favour	21	5	22	8	15	0	12

Note:
(percentages; candidates only).

of Parliamentary candidates. Altogether we presented eighteen different actors, all of whom were rated on a seven-point scale ranging from 'little' to 'much' influence. Factor analysis[2] yields a structure of five underlying factors explaining 69 per cent of the variance. These factors are as follows:

civic society: ethnic groups, issue groups, organisations for the aged, women's groups, civic organisations, youth groups, community groups

work: employers, business associates, trade unions

family: spouse/partner, other family

party national: national party leaders, party members, former fraction in Parliament, party officials

party local: local/regional party leaders

The differences between candidates and pseudo-candidates, as well as between parties, can be found by analysing the factor scores of the respondents on the five factors. The influence of family and the national party is the same for candidates and pseudo-candidates. However, the influence of civic organisations, regional leaders and local party leaders is much higher in the eyes of the pseudo-candidates, whereas candidates allocate more influence to employers, business associates and trade unions.

The differences for the candidates of the various parties can be seen from Table 7.3, where for each party the mean score on each of the five

[2] Principal Component Analyses, factors with eigenvalue > 1 and varimax rotation.

Table 7.3. *Influence structure underlying the selection process of Parliamentary candidates*

	Green-Left	PvdA	D66	CDA	VVD	Small Right	All
Civic society	0.65	−0.19	0.29	−0.03	−0.50	−0.97	−0.15
Work	−0.16	0.20	−0.31	1.17	0.49	−0.43	0.15
Family	0.08	−0.31	0.18	−0.38	0.10	0.22	−0.01
Party: national	0.20	0.38	−1.10	0.10	0.40	0.17	0.00
Party: local/regional	−0.51	−0.89	−0.69	0.45	0.37	0.66	−0.13

Note:
(candidates only).

factors is tabulated. The main conclusions are that the influence of civic society on the selection process is very high for the farthest left party, GreenLeft. The further to the right on the left–right dimension, the less the influence of civic groups on the process. This phenomenon is well known from other research: members of the board of civic organisations are disproportionately adherents of left-wing parties. The influence attributed to the national party is considerable for every party except D66. There exists a marked difference between left-wing and right-wing parties on the local and regional level. Those on the left of the political spectrum rate the influence of local and regional party officials clearly below average, while those on the right indicate a high level of influence. Lastly the influence of associations of employers and employees is concentrated in the parties with the highest level of political power; the Labour party (PvdA), the Christian Democratic party (CDA) and the Liberal party (VVD).

Besides our questions about the influence of all kind of people and groups on the selection process, we invited the pseudo-candidates to rate the importance of a number of personal qualities with respect to their final ranking on the list of candidates. Factor analysis[3] of nineteen of these qualities yields a structure of six underlying factors explaining 62 per cent of the variance. These factors and the qualities loading high on them are as follows:

acquired characteristics: good speaker, specific expertise, personal energy and enthusiasm, knowledgeable on issues

inherited characteristics: sex, age, ethnic descent, good personal appearance

[3] Principal Component Analyses, factors with eigenvalue >1 and varimax rotation.

Table 7.4. *Dimensions of personal qualities and their importance for the final ranking on the lists of candidates*

	Green-Left	PvdA	D66	CDA	VVD	Small Right	All
Personal qualities:							
aquired	0.14	−0.11	−0.13	−0.12	0.01	−0.07	−0.05
inherited	0.14	−1.25	−0.61	−0.59	0.12	−0.06	−0.23
Local orientation	0.0	0.69	0.16	−0.49	−0.28	0.61	0.10
Religion/values	0.47	0.73	0.83	−0.97	0.28	−1.42	0.06
Political experience	0.18	0.97	−0.60	0.48	−0.32	−0.13	0.09
Miscellaneous	−0.57	0.03	0.5	0.09	−0.47	0.14	−0.12

local orientation:	committed to district, well known locally, connections with party support and civic organisations
religion, norms, values:	religion, stable home life
political experience:	political experience, experienced party worker
miscellaneous:	support group's views, well known nationally

The difference between candidates and pseudo-candidates on most dimensions is not very remarkable, with the exception of inherited personal characteristics, which in the eyes of the pseudo-candidates are clearly more important than for the candidates.

The differences for the candidates of the various parties are summarised in Table 7.4, where mean factor scores lead us to the following main conclusions. First, inherited characteristics are not very important for most parties: only VVD and GreenLeft candidates rank them above average. Acquired qualities seem to be of even less importance: they played a positive role only in the selection process of the GreenLeft party. In the incumbent parties, PvdA and CDA, special importance is attached to political experience. For the other parties, this factor seems to be (far) less relevant. Not surprisingly, the religious parties CDA, and the orthodox parties of the right favour candidates on the basis of their religion and support of the family norm.

On the demand side we can conclude that the composition of the parliamentary parties has always been a topic for heated debates about the representativeness and responsiveness of the legislature. Consequently, selection procedures and criteria have been changed many times in order to meet the criticism. First there was the demand for a more decentralised procedure, then party leadership wanted a larger say in the selection. In the 1990s in the grip of institutional reform a different profile is wanted: assets are being under forty years old, being a woman, being very communicative, and coming from the private sector. Candidates themselves, especially from the structural parties PvdA and CDA, still view party experience as very important.

Supply-side factors: who are the candidates?

Who are the candidates and why do they wish to pursue a political career? According to some rational-choice theorists the decision to run for office derives from a clear desire for high political office. Lovenduski and Norris point to the popularity of this approach in the United States where candidates can be seen as 'strategic political entrepreneurs, developing their own resources and support networks, managing their own primary and general election campaigns, balancing the estimated costs against the potential rewards of office' (1994a:22). In the Netherlands, however, given the prominent role of parties, there are other reasons for pursuing a political career. It does not have to be a rational process, it often happens that, after becoming a party member, one more or less accidentally ends up in the next party function. Looking at the motives for becoming a party member strengthens this view. Less than 10 per cent of the candidates interviewed for the parliamentary elections of 1986 answered that a career perspective was an important reason to join. The most often mentioned motives were showing their sympathy for the party (90 per cent); viewing it as a duty as a citizen (75 per cent) and because it enables them to influence decision-making (73 per cent) (Niemöller 1991:32).

Before we look at the motives of the candidates for the 1994 parliamentary election, we can analyse some background statistics of MPs and candidates. Does the supply already mirror the changes in orientations of parties about the 'ideal' composition of the parliamentary party? Many studies of the composition of parliaments show that all over the world the chances to penetrate the political elite are unequally divided among groups (Matthews 1984:548). The background data on Dutch MPs, systematically recorded since 1848 by the *Parliamentarian Documentation Center*, support Matthews' conclusion. Before 1970 the majority of MPs came from a high-/middle class background, they lived in cities, and a large proportion had a university degree. Many of them were civil servants often working in an educational institution, and the average age was over sixty. Women were hardly represented (van den Berg 1983:230). Under the influence of the democratisation wave and the ongoing process of depillarisation the composition of parliament changed rapidly starting in the 1960s. After 1963 the elderly MPs were replaced by very young MPs, some of them in their twenties (van den Berg 1983: 167). Between

Table 7.5. *The social background of Dutch MPs: 1918–86 (in percentages)*

	1918–46		1947–67		1968–77		1978–86		Total %		Total N	
	M	F	M	F	M	F	M	F	M	F	M	F
Highest social class	48	77	51	70	50	82	46	90	47	79	632	73
With university degree	45	54	52	45	59	54	64	53	52	50	756	98
Age by entry (mean in years)	46	47	45	45	42	41	41	41	44	43	771	91
With children	100	17	100	44	93	41	61	61	92	52	148	52
Marital status: married	100	50	96	47	92	63	93	77	93	56	225	77

Source: Leijenaar 1989: chapter 5.

1968 and 1979 the number of MPs descending from a 'political family' diminished. In contrast the number of MPs with party experience, and with experience as a local or provincial councillor, increased (van den Berg 1981:55). In the 1980s the over-representation of MPs from the large cities was corrected, while the percentage with a university degree stabilised and was around 60 per cent, most of them having studied law. The majority of MPs were between forty and fifty years of age (van den Berg 1989:191–211).

In Table 7.5 some background statistics are shown for MPs represented in parliament from 1918 to 1986.[4] In this period 100 different women MPs and 774 male MPs were seated in the Second Chamber. The results are distinguished by period and by sex. Social class is measured by grading the profession of the father of the MP. It appears from Table 7.5 that over the whole period the percentage of MPs coming from a high social class background stays high: about half of the male MPs, and even more for women MPs. The university educated are highly over-represented, and there is hardly any difference in education between men and women. The age at entering parliament is in the early forties with hardly any gender difference. Most MPs are married and have children but when we make a distinction between men and women, a striking difference turns up. Almost all male MPs are married while, especially in the earlier periods, half of the women MPs are unmarried. About half of all women MPs, but only 8 per cent of male MPs, did not have children.

[4] The data were collected by the Parliamentary Documentation Center in The Hague.

Table 7.6. *Age and gender of Dutch MPs, 1990–4*
(percentages)

	1990	1994		
		All	Female	Male
<40 years	17	19	25	16
40–49 years	47	47	47	47
50–60 years	34	26	24	27
>60 years	2	8	4	10

Especially in the early periods married women were not likely to run for parliament, nor were the selectors keen on asking them to stand. Later the problem shifted to the difficult combination of being a mother and working outside the home, partly caused by the lack of child-care facilities in that period.

What has changed over time? In the 1994 parliament 48 of the 150 MPs are women. The average age is forty-five years for women and forty-eight for men. A majority have a university degree. Has the composition of the 1994 parliament changed as a result of the changes in the demand side of recruitment? Earlier we mentioned a perceived change in the outlook of selectors with greater demand for more women and young candidates, and less emphasis on party activism. In the 1994 parliament there are about 5 per cent more women than in the previous election. The average age is also somewhat younger (see Table 7.6).

Of the 150 MPs 19 per cent are under forty years of age, in 1990 this was 17 per cent (Daalder 1992:22). Breaking down these figures for gender, we can see that the two criteria, youth and more women, were combined in the selection process: 25 per cent of the women MPs are younger than forty. On the other hand we find more elderly members in the parliament of 1994, which can be explained by the entry of a new, one-issue party, the AOV, a party for the elderly. Of the 150 MPs elected in 1994, 71 were elected for the first time, including 54 per cent of the women and 45 per cent of the men, which also reflects the changes in the demand side.

Hillebrand (1992) discusses in which phase of the recruitment process the under- or over-representation of certain groups occurs. He distinguishes three phases: becoming a *member* of a party, becoming a *candidate*, and being *elected* in a representative position. He compares the background statistics of voters, party members, candidates and representatives in 1986 for the four main parties, PvdA, CDA, D66 and VVD. With regard to education there is a linear relationship: voters are less educated than members, who are less educated than candidates, while the representatives have the highest educational level. Unemployed people can only be found among the voters and party members, and no candidates came forward from this group. Not many housewives become a member of a party, and hence almost no housewives are found among the group of candidates. Looking at age, party members are on average older than voters. Although the group of over-sixty year olds is over-represented in the membership of the larger parties, not many of them find their way to the candidate list or representative bodies. A final background characteristic Hillebrand looks at is party experience and previous experience in a representative body. In all four parties more than half of the candidates have been a member of a local party board, and this percentage was even higher within the Labour Party and Christian Democratic Party. About one third of candidates and representatives had been a councillor or member of the provincial elected bodies, and many of them took part in local government as well (Hillebrand 1992: ch. 9).

We can conclude with an analysis of the most important reasons why the candidates of the 1994 elections ran for parliament. Respondents were offered five possible reasons: to support their own party; because they were asked to be a candidate; to promote their own political career; to become an MP; and because they were an incumbent. Respondents were asked to indicate their first, second and third most important reasons. As in 1986, for few pseudo-candidates a career perspective is important: only 2 per cent chose this reason as the most important one. On the other hand, for 42 per cent the main reason is the fact that they were *asked* to run for Parliament. If we take into account first, second and third choices, however, party support is the most important reason.

When we weight the responses (a first choice with three points, a second choice with two points and a third choice with one point), we can calculate the mean scores for the candidates for each of the parties to find out whether or not there are inter-party differences (see Table 7.7). On this basis the most important reasons were 'to be asked to be a candidate', 'to become an MP' and 'to support my party'. Promotion of a political career is relatively unimportant; this reason is even less important than 'being an MP already'. The breakdown of the mean score for the various parties shows, however, more variation. Especially in the religious parties (CDA and Small Right) and the extreme GreenLeft party, candidates run for Parliament because they were asked to. For candidates of the liberal democrats (D66) on the other hand, this reason was very unimportant. Support for their own party seems to be related to the size of the party:

Table 7.7. *Most important reason to run for Parliament (candidates only)*

	Green-Left	PvdA	D66	CDA	VVD	Small Right	All
Asked to be a candidate	1.9	1.2	0.4	2.0	1.3	2.1	1.5
To become an MP	1.4	1.2	2.1	1.2	1.6	0.9	1.4
Support my party	1.9	1.3	1.4	0.9	1.2	2.0	1.4
Was reelectable as an MP	0.2	1.8	0.4	0.9	0.7	0.4	0.7
To promote political career	0.4	0.1	0.4	0.3	0.8	0.6	0.5

candidates of the smaller parties rank this reason higher than their colleagues of the main parties. Political career opportunities are a consideration for slightly more liberal candidates (VVD) than others.

In the previous section we found a clear shift in the selection procedures, does this also meant a shift in the supply side? We can conclude that the elections of 1994 did bring many new faces into the legislature: more women, more younger people and many more of the politically inexperienced. This change in composition does mirror the changes in the demand side. With regard to the motives of the candidates to stand for office, career motives seem not to be so important. Standing to support a party is still seen as the most crucial factor.

The recruitment of women

One of the most remarkable changes in the composition of the Netherlands parliament is the increase in the number of women legislators. Parliament has got much more colour these days. In the 1990s the modern (cadre) party cannot allow itself to have just a small number of women in its ranks and in the representative bodies. In the Netherlands this simply is 'not done'. During the late 1980s attitudes of the party cadre shifted in favour of a greater political involvement of women. This is certainly true for the Netherlands where practically all political parties are engaged in one way or another in affirmative action policy-making.

Because political parties dominate the selection process for elected bodies, as well as the appointment of members of the cabinet, mayors and regional commissioners, the political representation of women is entirely dependent on the parties' attitudes towards the political involvement of women. It is interesting to see how these attitudes have changed over the years. For example the Anti-Revolutionary Party prohibited women from standing for election until 1956. Its successor, however, the Christian Democratic Party, launched in 1992 a very elaborate plan to mobilise women party members.

Compared with the past, this is a striking change. After the granting of women's suffrage in 1919 political parties were mainly interested in women as voters. They addressed them as mothers and housewives, explaining what politics could do for them. Mobilising women was mainly the task of the separate women's wings within the parties. These days, however, party *executives* take responsibility for the formulation and implementation of positive action strategies. As a consequence the women's wing of the Labour Party decided in 1995 to discard the organisation.

Lovenduski and Norris mention a shift in the 1980s agenda of political parties, the fact that gender became an explicit issue for many political parties. As possible explanations for this shift they put forward the continuous pressure of women activists within the party, and the increased party competition via the entry of new parties and altered party-state relationships (1993: 1,2). Several other factors can be added. For example, now that citizens are showing a certain dissatisfaction with the traditional political parties, some politicians view the campaign to promote a better representation of half of the population as a way to reaffirm their democratic credentials. Moreover there remains the concern of parties for the female vote. Research on women's voting patterns, for example in Germany, gave cause for worry: young women and women in their thirties and forties expressed a deep frustration with the large, traditional parties such as the CDU (Christian Democrats) and the SPD (Social Democrats).

Electoral considerations are important driving forces behind the current activities of parties to appoint more women. The fact that women candidates get relatively more preferential votes than their male col-leagues will certainly stimulate this process. There is some evidence that, when a party starts paying attention to its women, it becomes more attractive to women voters. For example after the SPD introduced quotas for women party members, the party gained female members. Another example is the Italian Communist Party, the PCI. While going through an identity crisis and a sharp decline in membership, it started to promote women and women's issues. The increasing support for women's causes can be seen as 'an attempt to capture women's electoral support and membership, which for many years belonged to conservative groups' (Guadagnini 1993:178).

Van de Velde has written an extensive study about the role of gender in parties in the Netherlands. She shows for the period from 1919 (enfranchisement of women) until 1990 how the parties' perceptions of women's political representation have changed under the spell of *historical developments* such as the struggle for the right to vote and the 'emancipation-waves' of the 1960s and 1970s. Both occasions forced the parties to form an opinion on the political participation of women. Another example is the occupation by the Germans and the active role of women in the resistance. Especially in the Protestant parties this caused some doubts about their ideas about the 'right' place for women. Another motor of change is the continuous *external pressure* by autonomous women's organisations demanding a more active role of parties and by governments in increasing the political power of women. An increase in the political participation of women became in the 1980s one of the objectives of governmental 'emancipation-policy' and was very vigorously pursued. One example is the subsidising by the government of parties to hire someone for three years in charge of formulating affirmative action strategies. As a result of these grants the main parties have so-called 'Positive Action Plans' which carry facts and figures about the participation of women in the party, as well as many concrete recommendations to increase this participation (van de Velde, 1994: 314–22).

Analysis of the impact of selection procedures on the likelihood that women will be selected has shown three factors to be of importance: the selectors; the selection criteria and whether there are any special policies to strengthen the position of women candidates (Leijenaar 1989: ch. 5). In the past decade all three aspects have changed in favour of the selection of women candidates. First, as described above, in the main parties the selection has become more centralised. Consequently, since national party leaders are more concerned about a female–male balance than are local or regional selectors, the participation of women in the parliamentary parties increased. With regard to the criteria used in the selection process, the condition of a long-term party career had a negative impact on women's chances to be selected. The recent focus on people with less party or political experience but with strong ties to interest groups or with a specific professional experience has definitely resulted in the selection of more women to the parliamentary party. Finally, referring to specific policies of parties to stimulate the selection of women, most parties practise, since the end of the 1980s, some kind of affirmative action policy for women. The PvdA (Labour Party) uses a quota of 33 per cent, the CDA (Christian Democratic Party) has set up a so-called 'Human Resource Data Base' of names, background characteristics and career intentions of women party members. In these two parties as well as in the VVD (liberal party with conservative overtones) cadre-training

Table 7.8. *Opinion about parliamentary representation of women*

		Green-Left	PvdA	D66	CDA	VVD	Small Right	All
Many more	W	88	83	67	70	57	–	69
	M	81	13	31	6	24	6	26
A few more	W	12	17	33	30	43	–	26
	M	19	73	31	63	35	22	40
About the	W	–	–	–	–	–	100	5
same as now	M	–	13	39	31	35	33	25
Fewer	W	–	–	–	–	–	–	–
	M	–	–	–	–	–	39	8

Note:
Question: Do you feel that there should be many more women in Parliament; a few more; about the same as now; or fewer women in Parliament? (candidates only).

courses for women have been introduced. All these changes in the selection procedures of parties have resulted in a parliamentary representation of women of one-third.

Let us see whether these positive attitudes and behaviour also reflect the opinions of the parliamentary candidates. In our survey we included several questions regarding the recruitment of women. When we conducted this survey 28 per cent of the MPs were women. To find out the opinion of the candidates about the representation of women in Parliament we asked: 'should there be many more, a few more, about the same as now or fewer women?' With the exception of the candidates of the small orthodox religious parties, the majority of candidates believe that there should be more women in Parliament. Women candidates of GreenLeft and the Labour Party are very explicit, while men candidates are a bit more reserved: about one third of the male candidates of D66, CDA and the VVD are satisfied with the 28 per cent representation of women.

The three Orthodox parties, SGP, RPF and GPV play an interesting role on the Dutch party stage. Each of these parties has a stable membership and electorate, winning every election between two or three seats. They are one of the most stable factors in Dutch politics. Referring to the Bible's view on women's role in society, they show a rather negative attitude towards the integration of women in politics. The most reluctant party is the small orthodox Calvinist party, SGP. They do not allow women to become members of the party. In the summer of 1994 this was brought to court with reference to the Netherlands constitution as well as to the penal law which forbids people to discriminate on the bases of race, gender, colour or sexuality. The courts' decision was favourable for the party. The argument was that the party is an organisation and the right to free organisation (autonomy) was seen as a 'higher' right than the issue of non-discrimination.

Why are there so few women in Parliament according to the candidates? The possible explanations can be categorised as individual and institutional barriers. The first category addresses the extent to which *individual* characteristics favour the attainment of a representative position. For example, a high level of educational or professional experience, or coming from a 'politicised' family are advantages when pursuing a political career. On the other hand being married and having small children is a disadvantage to women who are striving to achieve a representative position. *Institutional* factors affecting the achievement of representation by women relate to the organisation of society as well as to the political system itself (Leijenaar 1989). In most EU countries, and certainly in the Netherlands, recent changes in the gender division of political resources have meant that women have caught up with men since the 1970s with regard to their education and occupational status and individual factors have become less important. However, the number of women in party offices and representative bodies has not increased at the same speed, which reveals the importance of institutional barriers, such as the selection procedures of political parties.

The candidates were asked to give their view on the importance of several explanations for the under-representation of women in Parliament. Not many believed that women *do not belong* in politics. Only very few male candidates think that women are not suited to the job or don't fit into Parliament. The same is true for the statement that women tend to lose votes. With regard to individual barriers such as a lack of education and professional experience about 20 per cent, both men and women candidates, point these out as a likely explanation. Interestingly enough, more women than men are of the opinion that women have not enough confidence and therefore do not participate in parliamentary decision making. About 70 per cent of women candidates and 60 per cent of men view the strict division of labour between men and women as an important reason why women do not become candidates for parliament. The gender gap is larger with regard to possible institutional barriers: 40 per cent of women candidates agree with the statement that women are not given the opportunities by parties against 26 per cent of the male candidates. Consequently men candidates are also less in favour of policies directed to changing the institutions, to increase the number of women in Parliament. They are more in favour of training programmes than of quota setting or changing the hours of Parliamentary sittings.

Table 7.9. *Reasons for the under-representation of women in Parliament (candidates only)*

Explanations	Women candidates					Men candidates				
	Agree strongly	Agree	Disagree	Disagree strongly	Don't know	Agree strongly	Agree	Disagree	Disagree strongly	Don't know
Women don't come forward	14	40	19	5	7	15	51	15	3	5
Women lose votes	–	–	23	54	16	–	2	25	50	17
Women are not given the opportunity by parties	14	26	28	9	2	7	19	24	26	6
Women put their families above a career in Parliament	9	35	14	5	5	8	29	20	8	10
Women don't have the right experience and education	–	9	33	42	5	–	11	39	36	2
Women are not suited to the job	–	–	16	81	2	1	1	23	66	4
Women don't have the confidence	7	30	23	12	2	–	10	39	33	4
Women don't fit into Parliament	–	–	5	93	2	4	–	17	79	3
Women are not interested in politics	–	7	14	67	2	–	4	22	55	5

Women, on the contrary, approve strongly of the quota setting: 73 per cent against 25 per cent of the male candidates; and of more adaptable working hours: 42 per cent against 33 per cent. A majority of male and female candidates would like to see more and better child-care facilities: 85 per cent of the women; 60 per cent of the men. Improving the financial conditions will not increase the representation of women according to the candidates. In the Netherlands parties campaign, not individuals. The only reason to increase the salary of MPs is to make the job more attractive to top-level employees in the private sector. Those women candidates who agree with financial support for women candidates probably think of the extra costs they have for childminders and housekeepers.

The general attitude towards political integration of women is much more positive. Only very few hold the opinion that women do not belong in politics. The growing trend of more women in the parliamentary parties is undoubtedly a result of this change in attitude of the party cadre. The fact that these days many more women have the same educational level as men do, as well as the same professional experience, has also helped to redress some of the imbalance. Men and women candidates, however, still differ in their explanations for the under-representation, as well as in the solutions. Women more often point their finger to the parties, and a considerably number of men are still inclined to 'blame the victim'. Consequently women are more in favour of quota setting for example as an instrument to reach a gender balance in political decision making.

Conclusions

The Netherlands at this moment seems to be an interesting case for research by political scientists. The formation of a purple coalition refuted an important rule from coalition theory: the minimal (ideological) range. The present coalition consists of two parties to the left on the spectrum and one party to the right on the spectrum, while the party with the middle position (the Christian Democrats) has been left out. At the same time the country is in the grip of institutional reform. Politicians are worried about the growing lack of interest for (party) politics, the decline in party membership and the decline in turnout. By changing the electoral system into a German-type system of two votes, they hoped to restore some of the belief in politics and democracy. Parties too react to the 'crisis in politics'. By adapting the selection procedures and criteria they want to increase the democratic character of parliament and the legitimacy of decision-making. They hope to regain their importance as an intermediary between government and citizens.

Since the 1960s three main shifts in the selection of parliamentary candidates can be distinguished. First, in the 1960s under pressure of the strong demand for more participation there is a shift towards more decentralised procedures. To reduce the influence of regional and local party branches in order to acquire some more flexibility, in the 1980s selection procedures are to become more centralised again. Party leadership wants to be able to balance its parliamentary party according to sex, age, occupational status and, very importantly, knowledge in certain fields. In the 1990s, under the spell of political renewal, traditional selection criteria such as long party experience and previous experience in representative bodies have disappeared. These days the focus is on: being young and a woman with good communication skills and ties with civic groups and preferably with job experience in the private sector. The introduction of television coverage in parliament has also put much more emphasis on looks and performance as a debater.

These changes in the profile of an 'ideal MP' are already noticeable in the composition of the current parliament as well as in the background and opinions of the candidates. One third of the members of parliament are women, the average age is 46 years, and almost half of them are newcomers.

Another composition has already had an impact on parliamentary behaviour: the traditional pact between the government and members of the governmental parties is much weaker. It happens now and then that a cabinet's proposal does not pass the vote in the parliament, although the current cabinet has a comfortable majority. Restoring the dualistic practice is easier now that so many of the MPs are newcomers, without any burdens of past parliamentary experience. Whether the livelier debates in parliament, and the younger and more representative appearance of the parliament, will also restore some of the faith in politics of the citizens and eventually will lead to a higher turnout, has yet to be seen.

8   New Zealand

Helena Catt

Politics in New Zealand is in the throes of unparalleled change which will alter the opportunity structure for legislative recruitment. The 1993 referendum produced a majority for electoral reform. At the next election the First-Past-the-Post electoral system will be replaced by a form of proportional representation modelled on that used in the Federal Republic of Germany since 1949, but referred to in New Zealand as Mixed Member Proportional (MMP) (Vowles et al. 1995: 175). In anticipation of this change new political parties are being formed and wide cracks are appearing in the established major parties.

The outcome of these changes remains unknown at present so this chapter focusses upon legislative recruitment under the old electoral system. The aim of this chapter is to outline the institutional context of the recruitment structure in New Zealand, including the party system, and the costs and rewards of office. The chapter goes on to consider the 'demand' side of legislative recruitment including the selection process used by different parties, and the criteria used by selectors when reviewing applicants. Data is drawn from the 1993 *New Zealand Election Survey* of parliamentary candidates and party conference delegates.[1] The last section analyses the 'supply side', and the characteristics of the candidates who succeed in gaining a seat.

The structure of opportunities in New Zealand

The structure of opportunities in New Zealand is relatively narrow: with one house in the New Zealand legislature aspiring politicians have no

[1] The New Zealand Election Survey 1993 was sent to all candidates from National, Labour, the Alliance and New Zealand First parties and to delegates who attended the 1993 National Conferences of each party. Two reminders were sent to those who had not replied. The study received 697 replies, a response rate of 67 per cent. The New Zealand Election Survey was conducted by Peter Aimer, Helena Catt, Raymond Miller, Jack Vowles and Jim Lamare, and it was funded by the Foundation for Research, Science and Technology.

other national elections. Local councils and city mayors have limited power, and elections at this level arouse little interest and a low turnout (Mulgan 1994: 176). Parliament contains ninety-nine MPs. This includes the four Maori electorates which cover the entire country. The other 95 constituencies have an average population of 33,500 people. This small electorate has contributed to a strong belief in accessible MPs (Mulgan 1994: 123–5) and it is not uncommon to come across an MP when going about one's normal business. New Zealand has long exemplified a combination of plurality elections and a two-party system (Lijphart 1984: 16). Although at the 1993 election four minor party MPs were elected there have been only ten minor party MPs in the past fifty years. Single-party government has been the norm, although the elections of 1981 and 1993 resulted in governments with a wafer-thin parliamentary majority. The two-party system notwithstanding, New Zealand elections typically are contested by a range of minor parties, including the irrepressible Social Credit Party, formed in 1953, and the more transient Values and New Zealand Parties (Miller 1992). In the elections of 1978, 1981 and 1984 over a fifth of voters chose a third-party candidate, rising to 30 per cent of the vote in 1990 and 1993.

National is the major party of the right and has been in government for thirty-two of the past forty-five years. While in the past it was a pragmatic, centrist party the government of 1990–3 was dominated by strong monetarists. The party now favours a reduced welfare state acting as a safety net and follows a low inflation economic agenda designed to improve the international competitiveness of New Zealand exports and reduce the national debt. The 1993 manifesto, entitled 'Spirit of Recovery', stressed the need to build on the economic recovery. Other strong themes were the traditional ones of family, community and crime. The party has its strongest appeal in richer city electorates, small towns and the countryside. Voters are concentrated amongst those Europeans who have rural occupations, are self-employed, educated, on high incomes and non-unionised (Vowles et al. 1995: 24–7).

Labour was the major party of the left, a description which lost all relevance when a Labour government led by David Lange and Roger Douglas introduced strongly monetarist policies in the 1980s. The party has since been trying to retrieve its position on the centre-left of the spectrum. The 1993 campaign slogan of 'jobs, growth and health' epitomises the emphasis upon economic prosperity plus good welfare provision. Most of the party's MPs come from the cities, and before losing Northern Maori in 1993 Labour held the four Maori seats. Labour voters once came from the ranks of trade unionists, the poor, and manual workers, as well as from the Maori and Pacific Island communities, but many voters from this traditional base left the party over its monetarist policies. They were fleetingly replaced by some younger, middle-class voters who had benefited most from the 'boom years' of the mid-1980s. In 1993 the traditional voter base was still important (Vowles et al. 1995: 24–8) but Labour can no longer rely upon those voters.

The *Alliance* was formed in 1991 to enhance the electoral opportunities of the minor parties under the existing plurality electoral system. The constituent parties are NewLabour, the Greens, the Democrats, the Liberals and Mana Motuhake. NewLabour was created by Jim Anderton, an MP and former Labour Party president, who left Labour in protest at its monetarist policies, in particular the sale of such state owned assets as post offices and the Bank of New Zealand. He was joined by many of Labour's most active members. NewLabour upholds traditional social democratic principles of support for the needs of the poor, a mixed economy and a comprehensive welfare state. The Greens were formed out of another environmentalist party, the Values Party. The Greens place a strong emphasis on post-materialist values and the need for a sustainable economy. The Democrats were formed from the old Social Credit Party and still adhere to the unorthodox monetary reform ideas of the movement's founder. However, they now place a greater emphasis on 'representation' policies such as electoral reform and citizens' initiated referendums. The Liberals were formed by two first-term MPs who left the National Party in 1991 in protest over its monetarist policies, notably an increase in the claw-back provisions of New Zealand's national pension scheme. Their name is rather misleading since, on a range of social issues, they are far more conservative than 'liberal' in outlook. Mana Motuhake is a Maori party formed by a former Labour MP and Minister of Maori Affairs who alleged that Labour had failed to meet the needs of its Maori voters. In 1993 the five parties which made up the Alliance agreed on a combined election manifesto with the slogan 'Together we can make a difference'. Their guiding principles included a fairer and more egalitarian future, emphasis on the welfare state and the environment, and the need for honesty in politics. The coalition stood one candidate in each electorate and gained two seats in 1993. Their voters largely resemble Labour's (Vowles et al. 1995: 25–31).

New Zealand First also resulted from a split within a major party, in this case National. The party was formed only months before the election and was consequently heavily centred around the charismatic personality of its leader, Winston Peters. It won two seats, the leader's plus Northern Maori. Although both MPs are Maori this is not a Maori party and in fact has a strong following amongst conservative, religious and elderly voters (Vowles et al. 1995: 26–32). The party's policy thrust is pragmatic and centrist, in the tradition of the old National Party, with an emphasis on a small private enterprise, generous welfare provisions, and an active and interventionist state. They also stress 'representation' and the idea that the MP is answerable to the electorate rather than the party.

The job of an MP has strong incentives attached to it in New Zealand, not least the financial rewards. A normal MP's pay is NZ$67,000 per annum, a level earned by less than five per cent of the working population. On top of this basic pay there are payments to meet electorate office costs and accommodation in the capital. MPs also receive free travel within New Zealand, a perk that is retained when they are no longer an MP if they have served for two terms. MPs also have a pension scheme that is far better than the normal state provision. Ministers fare even better, receiving a significantly higher salary, a house in Wellington and a car. Due to the small size of parliament and a normal cabinet size of twenty or approximately a fifth of all MPs (Mulgan 1994: 109) most incumbent members in the governing party have a good chance of holding some kind of ministerial office. For instance in 1990, after two terms in power, only a fifth of the Labour MPs had not held a government post. Security of tenure is also good, with relatively few seats changing hands at each election. In the landslide National victory of 1990 Labour lost twenty-eight seats but a more normal rate of change would be about half that size (Vowles et al. 1995: 162–3; Mulgan 1994: 220).

Yet there are also costs involved in running for the New Zealand parliament. The pay may be high but public respect is low. In an annual opinion poll that asks for a 'trust' rating of certain professions, politicians have rated 4 per cent for the past four years and last topped 10 per cent in 1987. This low rating compares with a high of 73 per cent for firefighters and 48 per cent for the police. No group included in the survey question has a lower rating than that for MPs. The second lowest ranking group (civil servants) scores 9 per cent. There is also much discussion of governments breaking promises and the general dishonesty of politicians. In 1993 only a quarter of the voters trusted the Alliance and all other parties scored less well (Vowles et al 1995: 132). Hence the stress by the Alliance and New Zealand First on personal integrity and accountability.

In terms of individuals' resources, the strong party-based system means that few costs are met by the individual. The deposit of NZ$300 levied on each candidate is generally paid by the party, although minor party candidates often bear this cost themselves. The money needed for campaign material is also usually raised by the party. These costs are limited to NZ$10,000 in the three months prior to polling day. Time may be a more pressing resource for the candidates. The 1993 election was announced 52 days before the poll and the previous campaign was 78 days long. Almost a quarter of the candidates in the survey said they had started to campaign more than six months before polling day.

Demand-side factors: the selection process

Generally local party members choose their candidate for the election, although the exact process differs from party to party (Mulgan 1994: 233–5). National Party selection is done by a committee made up of local representatives, although the National Executive vets all of the nominees. Aspiring candidates have to attend informal 'meet the candidate' gatherings, present a short speech at the selection meeting and provide impromptu answers to questions put by the chair, one of which is provided by the party leader. Alliance selection is also done by a committee of locals, in this case comprising two representatives from each of the constituent parties. Nominees make a speech and answer questions at an open meeting. In some electorates those attending the meeting are polled but the result is only used for information. The central New Zealand Council of the Labour Party has a direct input into the selection process, providing three members of the selection committee. Local members provide between two and four committee members, depending on membership size, and a poll of those members at the meeting counts as a further vote. As a result head office has the power to decide who the candidate will be in a significant number of electorates. Nominees make a speech and answer questions from the floor. The selection process used by New Zealand First differs markedly from the others, in part due to the newness of the party and hence its small membership. In 1993 aspiring candidates had to submit a curriculum vitae and indicate an ability to provide funds and campaign workers. The final choice was made by a central committee of the party, with the leader playing a prominent, and in some cases decisive, role in the process. Survey respondents were asked to assess their party's selection process and the majority found it fair, efficient, not complicated and very democratic. However Labour delegates were out of step with the others as less than half thought it democratic, fewer than a quarter said it was fair and a third said it was complicated.

Whether the selectors represent the party locally or nationally, they are making decisions about nominees based on a subjective evaluation of the person. Many selectors will not know the aspiring candidates personally, so selection must be made on the basic information gleaned from a CV, a speech and possibly discussion at a 'meet the candidate' gathering. The choice of criteria used by selectors has a big impact on the type of people who become MPs. The general perception amongst party activists as to

Table 8.1. *The importance of qualities in choosing a candidate*

	% who think it is very important				
N	Labour 187	National 242	Alliance 197	NZ1st 51	Total 677
Qualities detectable in a CV					
Committed to electorate	75	75	67	90	74
Helps balance the caucus	40	44	30	28	38
Well known locally	37	36	42	37	38
Stable home life	21	42	27	30	31
Well educated	23	36	21	20	27
Political experience	30	22	25	12	24
Party worker	20	16	15	8	17
Well known nationally	6	5	7	9	6
Qualities detectable at a public meeting					
Conscientious	79	81	82	78	81
Enthusiastic	85	80	79	78	81
Knowledge on issues	71	66	76	64	70
Likely to win votes	63	66	49	55	60
Good speaker	61	58	59	74	60
Attractive personality	39	34	39	47	38
Personal appearance	26	37	30	55	33

Source: New Zealand Election Study.

the criteria used in selection also becomes important in determining who will put themselves forward. The qualities that selectors might value in a candidate range from proven political ability to how they perform in a political situation to aspects of their personal life. In the survey of activists, respondents were asked how important they thought a series of qualities were in aspiring candidates and what type of experience was relevant. Being well known nationally was the only one which less than half thought was important. Many of the qualities were deemed important by 99 per cent of the respondents. With such high levels of agreement on the desirability of these qualities, it is more useful to look at the percentage saying each is very important (see Table 8.1).

Proven political ability and views, along with aspects of an individual's life situation, can be recorded in a CV. Selectors will also have some idea about how 'well known' the individual is before they arrive at the meeting. So there is a range of factors 'known' about the nominee in advance of any meeting. Commitment to the electorate (constituency) is the only one of these factors that is seen as very important by the majority (74 per cent).

Next come political position within the party and being well known locally. Measures of personal standing come next: having a stable home life and being well educated are seen as vital by just under a third of respondents. Perhaps surprisingly, political experience and work for the party are only seen as very important by less than a quarter of respondents. This seems to be in marked contrast to the importance of party service in Australia (see McAllister chapter 2). Lastly comes being well known nationally which is very important for only one in twenty of the respondents. Overall the favoured nominee would be an educated local with an approved political stance.

There is some difference between the way that the parties order these qualities. Labour respondents put more value on political experience and are less concerned about a stable home life. Political experience is also more important for Alliance respondents while education is less so. In contrast National respondents are more concerned about home life and level of education. The qualities preferred by New Zealand First delegates differ from the foregoing in a number of respects. Not surprisingly, considering the newness of the party, political experience and being a party worker are not viewed as important. On the other hand a commitment to the local community is seen as vital by almost all of the New Zealand First respondents, reflecting the party's emphasis upon the MP as electorate spokesperson.

Subjective qualities which could be gauged at a selection meeting are recognised as being important by a high proportion of the delegates. Whereas the ephemeral qualities of 'attractive personality' and 'personal appearance' are esteemed by less than half the respondents, conscientiousness and enthusiasm top the list, with well over three-quarters of delegates regarding them as very important. A knowledge of the issues is valued more than the ability to win votes and speak well in public. Drive, commitment and knowledge are also valued qualities. In contrast to the other parties, New Zealand First respondents emphasise oratory, personality and appearance.

Respondents were asked how important they thought it was that candidates had experience in a range of activities and job types. In general specific types of work were not as highly valued as specific activities (see Table 8.2). Over half of the activists value business experience but this comes largely from the two 'right wing' parties. Not surprisingly, trade union experience is valued by Labour far more than the other parties. Despite the high number of MPs with teaching or legal backgrounds, these two professions are not seen as important by the respondents. However it may be that such occupations enhance desired qualities such as public speaking and so affect selection indirectly. Community experi-

Table 8.2. *Type of experience seen as important in candidates*

	% who think it is important				
N	Labour 187	National 242	Alliance 197	NZ1st 51	Total 677
Experience relating to the job of MP					
Community	92	90	92	84	90
Public life	74	78	79	72	77
Party work	72	65	61	33	63
Parliament	22	18	10	16	17
Work experience					
Business	35	80	28	61	52
Social services	50	23	42	53	38
Trade union	39	5	16	8	18
Legal	10	9	5	16	8
Teaching	12	3	8	4	8

ence was seen as important by the vast majority (90 per cent). In contrast, less than a fifth valued experience of parliament, although this was valued more by Labour than by the other parties. In general, however, there seems to be a desire for candidates to have some prior experience in aspects of the job of an MP outside of parliament itself. Over a third of respondents say social service experience is important but again National is out of step with a much lower percentage valuing this type of experience.

Comparing the views of the candidates and delegates within each party, eight qualities are desired by a significantly higher proportion of delegates. National delegates value a stable home life, commitment to the electorate and balancing the caucus more than the candidates do. Within Labour the difference is over enthusiasm, personal appearance, commitment to the electorate, being well known locally and being an experienced party worker. Candidates and delegates also differed over how much importance they attached to nominees' experience. Within Labour, National and the Alliance a smaller proportion of the candidates than delegates thought that previous party work was important. Labour delegates showed a greater interest in community experience and National delegates in experience of public life. Alliance candidates were more likely than the delegates to see trade union experience as important. Such differences may be because successful nominees do not realise which of their attributes won them selection or because they think they were selected for the wrong reasons. Whatever the explanation, the fact that those who are selected have a different perception of desirable qualities from the other activists raises questions about the effect of perceived norms and assumptions about what selectors are looking for.

In summary, there is general agreement on the qualities that are looked for in a candidate, with little party difference. How the nominees perform at the selection meeting is vital, since this is the only occasion when many of the key qualities are on display. Previous experience is not regarded as being of vital importance, although what candidates and delegates may be overlooking is that many of the desired qualities are first recognised and nurtured in the workplace and community or party organisation. From this information chances of selection would be greatest for a hard-working, well-informed local with community experience who has drive and shows promise of winning votes.

Supply-side factors: who becomes a candidate?

The parties differ in the type of people who join them and there is also evidence that those who become politically active differ in certain ways from those who do not (Vowles 1985). To go one stage further, it is useful to consider those characteristics that distinguish candidates from other activists, party affiliation notwithstanding. Some factors are important because of the characteristics demanded by selection meetings while others affect the supply of nominees. Without data on aspiring candidates the difference between supply and demand factors cannot be measured. However, by comparing *candidates* with *delegates* to party conference it is possible to find those characteristics which distinguish the two groups.[2]

Selectors may be prejudiced in the type of people they prefer: taking membership of a group as signalling that certain characteristics will be present in that person (Norris and Lovenduski 1993a: 377). Perceptions of such prejudices may also deter some people from considering selection as a candidate because of the feeling that defeat is inevitable so trying for selection would be a waste of time (Norris and Lovenduski 1993a: 381). For instance a young person may be selected because the selectors doubt an older person can do the job or because no older people sought nomination due to a perception that the selectors would want a young candidate. In either case it is the way that such background factors are

---

[2] In the following tables the Cramer's V figure is given for each of the personal characteristic variables in relation to the two dependant variables of party and candidacy. Where no figure is reported there was not a significant relationship at the .05 level. The values that are reported indicate the strength of the significant relationship with larger numbers showing a stronger effect. The percentage within each group that has the relevant characteristic is also reported to show the direction and strength of difference.

Table 8.3. *The effects of social background*

	Candidacy	Party	Candidacy – within each party*		
			Labour	National	Alliance
Age finished education		0.114	0.183		
Graduate	0.106		0.224		
Self-perceivded class		0.212	0.245		
Born NZ or not	0.081	0.174			
Ethnicity	0.081	0.124			
Religion	0.087	0.317			
Age	0.216	0.141			0.292

Notes:
Cramer's V only reported where relationship is significant at .05 confidence level.
Variable not listed because none had a significant relationship: gender.
* Values for New Zealand First are not included due to the small number of delegates who are not candidates which is a result of the party being very new.

perceived as affecting candidacy that cause the differences. In the survey respondents were asked about their gender, race, age, education, ethnicity, country of birth, religion and self-perceived class.

Background variables do distinguish candidates from delegates (see Table 8.3). For most of the variables there is also a significant difference between parties. In general the relationship with the party variable is stronger indicating a more distinct difference in the social make-up of the different parties than between all candidates and all delegates. Only for gender is there no significant difference between either candidates and delegates or parties. Education is a strong factor, in terms of both when it was completed and highest qualification. Candidates are more likely than delegates to have a tertiary qualification and, consequently, to have stayed in education for longer (see Table 8.4). However there is also a higher percentage of candidates than delegates who left school before they were sixteen. Within the political parties education is only significant for Labour where the tendency for candidates to have a tertiary qualification is particularly strong. Educational differences are born out when looking at subjective class. Overall this is not a significant factor but within Labour there is a strong tendency for candidates to see themselves as middle class, while the delegates profess to being working class.

Both ethnicity and country of birth distinguish the candidates from the other delegates. These variables are also significantly related to party. Candidates are more likely than delegates to have been born in Britain

Table 8.4. The social background of candidates (percentage)

	All		Labour		National		Alliance	
	Candidate	Rest	Candidate	Rest	Candidate	Rest	Candidate	Rest
N	216	461	79	132	39	203	79	118
Age finished education								
<16	28	23	35	44	23	33	39	31
>18	52	45	60	42	52	44	52	51
Graduate	72	62	83	61	74	61	73	64
Middle class	48	45	60	35	54	56	42	38
Born in NZ	85	90	82	86	97	95	78	85
Polynesian	7	3	4	5	3	2	8	3
Not Christian	39	30	44	45	13	15	54	41
Age <30	10	5	5	8	10	3	8	4
>50	9	26	35	38	36	60	35	63

Table 8.5. *The effects of life circumstances*

	Candidacy	Party	Candidacy – within each party		
			Labour	National	Alliance
Work status – pay	0.127	0.165	0.165	0.138	0.187
Housing – money	0.172	0.141		0.171	0.176
Time in district	0.103	0.134			

Notes:
Cramer's V only reported where relationship is significant at 0.5 confidence level.
Variables not listed because none had a significant relationship: work status – time;
housing – stability; household income; marital status; have children.

rather than New Zealand, indicating either an absence of bias towards born-and-bred New Zealanders or confirmation of the notion that 'poms' are more pushy. This pattern is particularly strong within Labour and the Alliance. A higher proportion of candidates are Maori than are the other delegates. Religious belief is also significantly related to candidacy and, more strongly, party. Non-believers and followers of non-Christian teachings form a higher proportion of the candidates than the other delegates. The difference is particularly strong within the Alliance, possibly due to the Green candidates who have a wider range of religious beliefs. Age differences occur between parties and also between levels of activism. For the group as a whole, and also within National and the Alliance, candidates are more likely to be younger (in their twenties, thirties or forties). Other delegates dominate in the over-fifty age groups. It seems that youth rather than 'experience of life' is important for gaining candidacy.

Other personal circumstances may influence the time and money available to an individual and so affect the likelihood of standing and/or chances of selection as a candidate. Work, housing tenure, income, children and marital status can affect the availability of time and money to devote to seeking candidacy and fighting the subsequent election. These factors, along with the length of time spent in the district, may also be taken as important indicators of suitability by the selectors. Only housing tenure, work status and length of residency in the area significantly distinguish the candidates from the other delegates and the parties from each other (see Table 8.5).

Household income, the easiest measure of finance, is not significantly related to the candidacy variable in any context. The likelihood of having a disposable income can also be gauged by looking at work status and

Table 8.6. *The life circumstances of candidates (percentage)*

	All		Labour		National		Alliance	
	Candidate	Rest	Candidate	Rest	Candidate	Rest	Candidate	Rest
N	216	461	55	132	39	203	79	118
Have paid work	85	74	92	78	94	80	77	58
Free housing	30	49	22	37	29	52	38	56
Owner occupier	87	90	93	87	87	91	86	90
In district for								
<4 years	12	9	11	17	11	6	12	6
10+years	59	70	63	61	68	78	50	66

housing tenure as these represent the largest sources of income and expenditure. Candidates are more likely than other delegates to have a regular income and delegates are more likely to have paid off their mortgage. However these factors are probably related to the age and education differences between candidates and delegates rather than showing that money has an effect on candidacy. Two factors that may affect the availability of time can be measured by looking at work status and number of children. In no instance does lack of a full-time job affect candidacy, so extra time is not a factor. Children at home is also not significant, except with the Alliance where candidates are more likely to have one or two children. The length of time spent in one place may also affect the availability of time in that support networks can be created. However, length of residency could equally be an important pointer for selectors in gauging stability or commitment to the community. Looking at the figures suggests that long residency in the area is not crucial. A higher proportion of candidates than delegates have lived where they are for three years or less but again this could be a function of the age difference. This pattern holds within both National and the Alliance, but the reverse is true for Labour. The evidence on the importance of available money and time is rather inconclusive.

Previous political experience may be a supply and a demand factor. Certain kinds of experience in politics may be taken by selectors to indicate a person capable of doing the job, or to suggest a 'successful campaigner' or a 'safe bet'. At the same time wide political experience may provide valuable stimuli for those considering seeking candidacy. Involvement in political activity may build confidence or increase the level of drive. There is also the likelihood that political activity will give access to support networks which can provide information or encouragement or advice. A political background could impress selectors due to the kudos attached to a 'political name'. On the supply side, coming from a politically active family may improve confidence or familiarity with the process. Three distinct aspects of political experience apply: involvement in the party; involvement in wider groups; and coming from a politically conscious and active family.

Measures of political experience are more often significantly related to party label than to the candidate variable (see Table 8.7) emphasising the importance of looking at the different party cultures. However, there are some instances where candidates as a whole differ from the other delegates. All but one of the measures of party experience show a significant relationship with candidacy. Previous experience as a candidate and time in the party have the highest Cramer's V values. However, a word of caution is needed as these significant relationships do not all point to can-

Table 8.7. *The effect of political experience*

	Candidacy	Party	Candidacy – within each party		
			Labour	National	Alliance
Time in party	0.332	0.508			
Held party office					
Local	0.233	0.355	0.154		
Regional		0.114			
National	0.106	0.189			
Previously been candidate in					
Local government	0.103				
General election	0.362	0.289			
Held office in					
Local interest group	0.144	0.133	0.175		0.276
Student organisation	0.209		0.190		0.276
Trade union		0.382			
Ethnic group		0.113			
Number of groups active in	0.144	0.092	0.221		
Aware of parents' party membership		0.173			
Family held office in					
The party	0.094	0.127			
Parliament	0.077	0.132			

Notes:
Cramer's V only reported where relationship is significant at 0.5 confidence level.
Variables not listed because none had a significant relationship: family in local government; held office in interest group nationally; held office in community group; held office in professional body; held office in women's organisation; aware of parents' vote.

didates having greater political experience. For instance, candidates are more likely than the rest of the activists to have been a party member for less than four years (see Table 8.8), suggesting that, contrary to McAllister (chapter 2), long commitment is not a vital condition in New Zealand. Likewise, candidates are less likely to have held local party office. The picture is of delegates being long-term party members and running the party locally, whereas candidates have been in the party for less time but have been active both as candidates and in the national offices of the party. It seems that those with MP potential are being fast-tracked.

Wider political activity is also important. There is a significant relationship between candidacy and both the number of groups in which individ-

Table 8.8. The political experience of candidates (percentage)

	All		Labour		National		Alliance	
	Candidates	Rest	Candidates	Rest	Candidates	Rest	Candidates	Rest
N	216	461	55	132	39	203	79	118
In party								
<4 years	45	18	16	14	10	8	53	32
>15 years	47	33	31	26	28	47	9	18
Held party office								
Locally	68	87	75	87	85	93	75	80
Regionally	44	46	45	48	54	43	51	51
Nationally	31	21	31	23	23	13	39	31
Been candidate in								
Local elections	37	27	40	26	26	20	54	42
General election	46	13	56	6	56	4	51	36
Held office in								
Local interest group	62	47	65	46	59	47	76	48
Student organisation	23	8	25	11	23	7	25	6
Trade union	24	21	42	45	8	5	37	32
Ethnic group	8	5	4	5	5	3	10	8
Mean number of groups active in	3.8	3.3	4.1	3.4	3.7	3.3	3.6	3.1
Both parents party members	28	28	38	23	36	41	20	14
Family members								
Held party office	23	32	30	27	28	37	18	31
In local government	20	18	21	16	23	21	24	15
MP	9	5	16	8	8	3	6	3

uals are involved and in which they have held office. Holding office in a student organisation is particularly prominent, but this is probably in part a consequence of the higher number of graduates amongst the candidates. Over the range of groups included in the survey a higher proportion of candidates than delegates had held office for all except women's groups. Perhaps this is tapping a general willingness or desire to stand for office. Candidates were also active members of a larger number of groups, significantly more so for professional associations plus environmental and peace groups. Such high levels of activity would have implications for available time, although they might also signal a life style that is organised to allow for much time spent on political activity. Membership may provide useful networks of supportive people who can be tapped during the campaign. Just over half of the candidates (53 per cent) said that they had received support from members of community groups and 45 per cent said women's groups had helped but in both cases the figures were much higher for the left-wing parties than for the right-wing ones. Overall the picture is of candidates as people who are generally active in a wide range of organisations.

Some aspects of awareness of a political family are also significantly related to candidacy, but again there is more often a difference between parties. Over three-quarters of candidates and delegates know how their parents voted (80 per cent) which is very high compared to voters (63 per cent know father's vote; 59 per cent know mother's vote). Awareness of parental membership of a political party is also high with over a third knowing that at least one parent was a member. Having parents from a political party is particularly high for Labour and the Alliance. Overall there is the picture of activists coming from political households. Candidates are also more likely to have a family member who has been in local government or parliament, hopefully suggesting wide discussion of politics rather than nepotism.

For political experience there is a greater difference between parties than has been the case for the personal variables. Amongst Labour delegates only a few types of political experience distinguish the candidates from the rest. Candidates are more likely to have been involved in student organisations and the local organisation of interest groups. They are also more likely to be active in a larger number of political groups and less likely not to be involved in any group. In particular, candidates are far more likely to be active in professional associations, probably again reflecting the high number of graduates. Alliance candidates are significantly different from the other delegates. They are more likely to have held office in local authorities, quangos, local bodies of interest groups, community groups, student organisations and professional groups. Reflecting the coalition's social democratic tradition and hetero-geneity, candidates are more likely to have been active in women's or environmental groups. Adding to this picture of involvement outside of the party, candidates are more likely than the rest to have been a party member for less than a year. National candidates differ from the other delegates far less than within the other parties with none of the variables showing a significant relationship. So the egalitarian parties of the left have more signs of a political elite.

So far several different types of personal factors that distinguish candi-dates from delegates have been separately considered. However, we do not know how these different factors work in combination. To this end ordinary least squared regression has been used with the dependent vari-able of candidate or not (see Table 8.9). Variables relating to social back-ground, life circumstance and political experience were included, however the expectation was that few would show a large effect. The R^2 value (at the bottom of the table) indicates the extent to which all the vari-ables in the model taken together can predict the likelihood of that person being a candidate or not. Comparing the values across the three parties, the R^2 is greater for Labour and National than for the Alliance or the group as a whole. However, even the highest value is not very impressive, indicating that there are other factors that more clearly distinguish between candidates and delegates.

The reported coefficients indicate the extent to which each factor can predict if a person will be a candidate, net of other factors, and taking account of the number of people with that characteristic. Most of the vari-ables have a low beta value and are not significant (at the .05 confidence level), indicating a minimal predictive power. Across the four groups the variable measuring previous candidacy has the greatest impact (beta range .28 to .57). However, this finding does not advance understanding of what makes a candidate, as we still need to know why they first became a candidate and what distinguished them then. Overall it is the measures of political experience that have an impact, rather than those for social background or life circumstances, although party differences do exist. Within Labour the only significant value other than previous candidacy is holding party office, but the negative value indicates that candidates are less likely to have held office. National candidates are more likely to have children but no other variable is significant. Alliance candidates are more likely to have held office in a number of groups and less likely to have been party members for a long time. Age is also a significant predictor for Alliance candidates.

Even if a person fits all of the characteristics most prized by selection committees and most likely to help selection, there is still an important

Table 8.9. *Demand-side model predicting whether respondents were candidates or not – beta values*

N	All 677	Lab. 187	Nat. 242	Ali. 197	Coding
Social background					
Social class	0.05	0.09	0.00	0.04	middle class/other
Education	0.07*	0.07	0.00	0.07	graduate/not
Ethnicity	0.05	0.00	0.00	0.02	Maori/all non-Maori
Place of birth	-0.07*	-0.09	-0.01	-0.06	NZ born/born elsewhere
Religion	-0.02	0.00	-0.00	-0.04	Christian/atheist+non-Christian
Age	-0.12*	-0.09	-0.09	-0.19*	years
Gender	0.00	-0.02	0.05	0.03	male/female
Life circumstances					
Work status	0.01	0.00	-0.00	-0.00	in paid work/not
Housing tenure	0.01	0.07	-0.02	-0.02	owner-occupier/not
Time in district	0.03	0.07	0.00	0.00	years
Marital status	0.00	-0.07	-0.07	0.13	married or living as married/not
Children	0.03	0.04	0.13*	0.03	have children at home/not
Political experience					
Membership	-0.18*	-0.04	-0.01	-0.16*	years
Candidacy	0.42*	0.55*	0.57*	0.28*	been candidate before/not
Held party office	-0.18*	-0.16*	0.03	-0.14	index[a]
Local government	-0.02	0.04	-0.07	-0.08	index[b]
Held office	0.13*	0.08	0.09	0.24*	number of groups held office in
Parents members	0.00	-0.01	-0.01	0.05	index[c]
Elected family	0.04	0.09	0.06	0.00	index[d]
R2	0.29	0.41	0.41	0.24	

Notes:

[a] Held regional or national office 1; held local office .5; held no office 0.

[b] Elected local government 1; candidate in local election .5; rest 0.

[c] Both parents members 1; one parent member .5; neither 0.

[d] Family member an MP 1; In local government or party office .5; rest 0.

* p ≤ .05

motivational element. The data set did not include personality trait measures so we cannot look at deep psychological factors. However, it did ask a series of questions about wider political motivation and about the level of support candidates experienced. Respondents were asked why they first became interested in politics and why they joined their present party. The open questions produced a vast range of replies that have been grouped into broad categories.

Looking at what first triggered an interest in politics the most popular reply (16 per cent) mentioned aspects of the social milieu when growing up, such as family or teachers. Next came two political events: an election campaign (7 per cent) and Vietnam (6 per cent). Grouping the replies into broad categories, candidates are much more likely than delegates to have been moved by an issue or philosophy. New Zealand First differs from the other parties the most with its respondents being much more influenced by issues and much less by specific events. Turning to reasons for joining their party the most common replies were that they agreed with the policies of the party (24 per cent); dislike of another party (12 per cent); then a number of specific issues such as 'environmental issues', 'social justice' and 'monetary reform'. Candidates were more likely to have joined due to issues or philosophy. The newer parties had more on the issue side and the older parties more in the 'take action' category. Candidates were also asked why they sought selection. The most popular replies were to have an influence (16 per cent); because they could do a good job (8 per cent); and to represent people (7 per cent). Alliance candidates tended to be motivated by issues, Labour and National candidates by the desire to be active and New Zealand First candidates did not know.

Conclusions

To what extent do the candidates display the aspects of political experience or personal attributes that respondents had earlier identified as important? Some of the qualities that respondents valued, such as enthusiasm or being well known locally were not measured in the survey. However, there are some qualities that were included in both sets of questions and it is interesting to see if the qualities that were described as important are the ones that distinguish the candidates from the delegates.

When asked about the importance of certain qualities in a candidate, commitment to the electorate was given the third highest score. The time a person has lived in the area could be taken as a measure of commitment to the electorate, and this variable did distinguish candidates from delegates in the cross-tabulation tables. However, it was the delegates rather than the candidates who tended to have lived in the area for a long time, and the beta values are both small and not significant. A stable home life and good education were desired by over a quarter of respondents. Graduates were significantly more prominent amongst candidates and this factor was significant in the regression analysis, although with a very small beta value. Measuring stable home life is rather more difficult, but being married and having children may go some way to tapping this quality. Marital status was not significantly related to candidacy in any of the analyses. Having children only showed as a significant factor in the multiple regression for National, where it has the second biggest beta value.

Although having political experience and being a party worker were seen as being very important by less than a quarter of the respondents, specific types of experience were, in fact, seen as being valuable. The majority thought that experience in the community, public life and the party were helpful. Various measures of political experience figured in the analysis which compared candidates with delegates. Having held office in a number of organisations was a significant factor in the multiple regression analysis and the second largest beta value for the Alliance. Candidates were active in more groups and were more likely to have held office, suggesting that broad political experience is valued. However, candidates did not score well as party workers, tending to have been members for a shorter period and not to have held local or regional office. In the multiple regression, candidates are significantly less likely to have held party office, both within the group as a whole and within Labour. Broad rather than party-based political credentials seem to be important.

Where we have measures of supply and demand there is not a consistent story. Education stands out as one factor that was seen as important in a candidate and did distinguish candidates from delegates. Various kinds of experience gained from involvement in political groups also figure as both desired qualities and distinguishing variables. This analysis has eliminated a great range of variables as possible predictors of candidacy. The challenge now is to look at other factors. Political experience is the most important factor, but we still need to determine why some people gain that experience while others do not. Gaining candidacy is the end point in a long hierarchy of political involvement. We need to know why people start on that ladder and why some stop on the way.

9 United Kingdom

Pippa Norris and Joni Lovenduski

It is well established that most parliaments are strikingly unrepresentative of society: legislators in Western political elites tend to be drawn from a privileged background. In terms of occupational class, gender, race and education, the British Parliament is no exception. Far from representing a microcosm of the nation, the 'chattering classes' with professional occupations fill backbenches on both sides of the aisle. Although the number of old Etonians and Harrovians has decreased over time, many new MPs continue to follow the traditional path of public school+Oxbridge. In the 1992 election sixty women were returned (9.2 per cent), and six Asian and Afro-Caribbean MPs (1 per cent). Concern about gender and racial membership of Parliament has increased over time although the general social bias has been familiar for years. As W.L. Guttsman (1968) noted:

If we ascend the political hierarchy, from the voters upwards, we find that at each level – the membership of political parties, party activists, local political leaders, M.P.s, National Leaders – the social character of the group is slightly less 'representative' and slightly more tilted in favour of those who belong to the middle and upper reaches of our society.

Two decades later, despite numerous studies counting the number of old Etonians or Oxbridge blues in the House, we seem little nearer to understanding the reasons for this phenomenon. It remains a long-standing puzzle which prompts the question: why the social imbalance?

Previous research has often focussed too much attention on analysing MPs. Because the Commons contains many public school and Oxbridge trained lawyers, journalists and company directors, many assume this must reflect the preferences of selectors. From public sources it is easier to count, rather than explain, the number of barristers or miners in the House. But winners are only the tip of the iceberg. Nor is it appropriate to explain the outcome by comparing MPs and candidates, the next strata down. We would expect significant differences in social background and political experience because MPs represent an older generation. The outcome of the process can only be understood if we know the total pool:

MPs, candidates, applicants, party members and voters. By comparing strata we can see whether the outcome of the selection process reflects the supply of those willing to stand for Parliament or the demands of party activists when adopting candidates for local constituencies.

The *British Candidate Study, 1992* collected data on the experience, background and attitudes of applicants and party selectors in the run-up to the 1992 general election (for details see Norris and Lovenduski 1995). On the supply side this chapter draws on the survey of 1,681 respondents including incumbent MPs, prospective Parliamentary candidates (PPCs), and applicants on party lists who had failed to be adopted in the 1992 general election (with a 69 per cent response rate). On the demand side this chapter uses the survey of 1,634 Labour and Conservative party members administered at 26 selection meetings throughout Britain (with a 74 per cent response rate to part 1 and 43 per cent to part 2). Information about voters was derived from the *British Election Study, 1987* (N.3,826).

The process of getting into Parliament can be conceptualised as a multi-step ladder, illustrated in Figure 9.1. This analysis compares the characteristics of different groups on the ladder in the Labour and Conservative parties. *Party voters* are those who supported the party in the 1987 general election. *Party members* are the grassroots card-carrying activists at selection meetings. In the next step up the ladder, *applicants* are those on the party list, the 'pool of talent' who failed to be selected by a constituency in the 1992 election. Lastly at the top of the ladder are non-incumbent Parliamentary *candidates* (PPCs) adopted for a seat and incumbent *Members of Parliament* (MPs) returned in the 1987 election. The term *'party elite'* will be used to refer to the combined group of applicants, candidates and MPs.

The supply and demand model

The model in the introduction to this book provides the analytical framework. On the *demand-side* selectors choose candidates depending upon their perceptions of how far the applicants' abilities, qualifications and experience fit their ideas of the role of an MP. Since candidates are rarely well known to most selectors, these perceptions may be coloured by direct and indirect discrimination about certain types of applicant. The term *discrimination* is used here in a neutral sense, since it can be for or against certain groups, whether lawyers, farmers, trade unionists, southerners, women or Asians.

What we mean by *direct discrimination* is that people are judged positively or negatively on the basis of characteristics seen as common to their

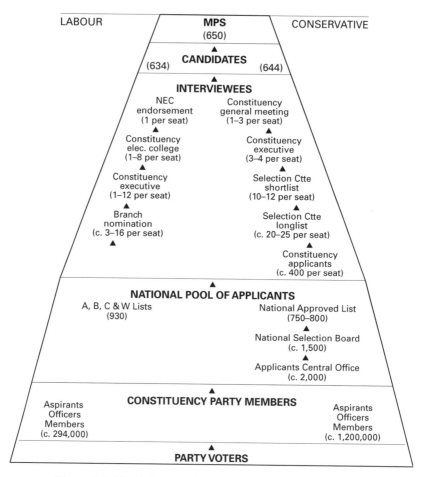

Figure 9.1 The Labour and Conservative ladder of recruitment.

group, rather than as individuals. Irrespective of their interview performance, political interests or personal abilities, a barrister may be perceived as more articulate than a trade unionist; a local businessman may be seen as better informed about employment problems in the constituency than an outsider; a woman may be expected to be more knowledgeable about childcare policy than a man. Party selectors, faced with non-local candidates, often have only minimal information on which to make their decisions. The curriculum vitae gives the bare bones. There may be hundreds of application forms. The interview process is relatively short and formal. Accordingly members may rely upon background characteristics as a proxy measure of abilities and character, and prejudice functions as an information short-cut. As a result individuals are judged by their group characteristics.

Indirect discrimination is different. Here party members may personally favour a certain category of candidate ('I'd like to vote for a woman', 'We need more blacks in Parliament'), or an individual applicant ('The Asian was the best prepared speaker'). But members may be unwilling to choose such a candidate because they expect they would lose votes among the electorate ('But, she'd never get in', 'There aren't enough black voters in Cheltenham'). Demand-side explanations suggest the social bias in Parliament reflects the direct and indirect prejudices of party selectors.

In interviews many expressed the belief that party members prefer well-educated, professional men in early middle age, the 'right sort' of candidates who will fit into the local party, serve the constituency and appeal strongly to local voters. What do party members look for? An experienced Conservative central office official summarised the position thirty years ago:

> What most associations want is a man of solid character. Not necessarily a brilliant man, you understand; in fact they may distrust a chap who seems too brilliant or flashy or glib. They want someone with the right sort of background, someone who looks and sounds right. They want someone they can count on to do the right thing, whether as a campaigner or a leader in association affairs or a Member of Parliament. They want someone who, by his business career or his war record or his party service or his social standing, has proved he is this kind of man. (quoted in Ranney 1965)

The search for the 'right chap' has broadened somewhat in the Conservative party in recent years, at least from army majors to merchant bankers, but similar echoes can be heard today in many of those we interviewed. Conservative MPs and candidates explained, in different ways, how some groups are ruled in while others are ruled out:

> Conservative committees..look for candidates in their own image. They look for candidates who will have a fair bit of money, preferably a county background, connections, and if he happens to be a barrister, or something important in the City of London, then they think he's an ideal chap!

> You're much more likely to go for the same options – to pick the merchant bankers, the solicitors, and the people from Eton and Harrow and Cambridge and Oxford, because they've been through the system and know what to expect.

> People start with prejudices about the candidates. In the old days, they used to band them and say 'We're not having anybody under 40, nobody over 50, or we're not having a lawyer, or we're not having somebody from the south-east', or whatever it might be. Whatever prejudice they decided to start with knocked out a whole lot of people many of whom might have been exactly what they really wanted.

But the obvious cause of the social bias in Parliament – discrimination by party members – is not necessarily the most significant one. This popular explanation may be based on inferences from the outcome, rather than any good evidence. In a plea of mitigation party members frequently claim their hands were tied: they would like to short-list more well-qualified women, Asians from the local community or experienced working-class candidates, they say, but few come forward.

Supply side explanations suggest the outcome reflects the supply of applicants wishing to pursue a political career. Constraints on resources (such as time, money and experience) and motivational factors (such as drive, ambition and interest) determine who aspires to Westminster. Legally most citizens, other than lunatics, traitors and peers, and a few other categories, are qualified to stand. Few do so. The narrow path leading to a political career is usually risky, gruelling and unglamorous. Nursing a hopeless seat for a couple of years – slogging up to the constituency every weekend, banging on unfriendly doors to drum up support, about as welcome as a Jehovah's Witness or brush salesman, attending poorly attended party committees in draughty halls, helping fundraise with whist drives, raffles and jumble sales, juggling work, party committees and constituency demands – requires stamina, optimism and dedication. The resources and motivation applicants bring to the role will vary according to their social background. Younger teachers from the Midlands, well-established middle-aged lawyers, self-employed company directors, experienced Scottish trade unionists, and London women social workers will bring different skills, qualifications and assets to political life. Many emphasised the difficulties of a political career, and the need for hard work, time, energy and dedication:

> You've got to be committed to it. If you're in doubt whether you really want to do it, I would say don't do it, because if you're going for a safe seat it is going to be a total commitment.
>
> I would say be single-minded, you'll have to sacrifice careers, families, relationships, all that sort of stuff, which can be quite tough.

Accordingly supply-side explanations suggest the outcome reflects the pool of applicants seeking a political career.

In practice supply-side and demand-side factors interact. Perceived discrimination by party activists, complex application procedures, or anticipated failure may discourage potential candidates from coming forward. The concept of hidden unemployment ('Why apply? I won't get the job') is a perfect analogy for the 'discouraged political aspirant'. The assumptions in this model suffer from certain limitations. Nevertheless despite these qualifications there remains an important distinction between the factors holding individuals back from applying for a position,

('I'm not interested', 'I don't have the right experience', 'I can't afford to move') and the factors which mean that, if they apply, they are not accepted by selectors ('He's not locally known', 'She's not got the right speaking skills', 'He would not prove popular with voters'). The supply-side and demand-side distinction therefore provides a useful analytical framework to explore alternative explanations.

The relative importance of supply and demand factors are tested throughout this chapter controlling for party, given important differences in the Labour and Conservative selection process and outcome. At constituency level party selectors are choosing from among the pool of list applicants. If members favour certain groups over others, the contrast would therefore be evident in differences between applicants and candidates. On the other hand if some members lack the resources or motivation to stand, this would be apparent in differences between members and list applicants. The two basic hypotheses, derived from this understanding of the process, are as follows:

(i) If demand-side factors are important, we would expect a significant difference in the characteristics of applicants and candidates.

(ii) If supply-side factors are important, we would expect a significant difference in the characteristics of party members and applicants.

This argument needs certain qualifications. First, some apply for individual constituencies who are not on the national lists, for example some local applicants. But these cases tend to be exceptional, particularly in the Conservative party. Second, some rejected aspirants never get on the list. In the Labour party trade unions screen who goes onto the 'A' list of aspirants, while constituencies nominate people for the 'B' list. All nominees are added to the list after formal rubber-stamping by Labour Party headquarters. In the Conservative party all aspirants are interviewed by Central Office and put through a rigorous weekend national selection board. Only 40 per cent of those who aspire are put on the Approved List. Accordingly there is a hidden pool of rejected aspirants not counted in our sample of those on the national lists. We can make no claims about this group although observation of the Conservative Party Selection Boards leads us to believe those involved make every effort not to discriminate against any particular social groups. Screening the Approved Lists does not invalidate the test of demand-side factors at constituency level.

Third, there is probably a group of 'discouraged aspirants' who never put their name forward for consideration, since they anticipate being unsuccessful. Again we make no claims to be able to analyse the characteristics of all groups in the process. There are many steps up the ladder from party member to MP. The comparison of applicants and candidates tells us a great deal about the process, but not everything about all stages.

Lastly 'supply and demand' factors operate within a broader context of the political system and the recruitment processes within parties, which cannot be dealt with adequately within the limited scope of this chapter (see Norris and Lovenduski 1995). The selection process works differently within each party, under certain guidelines and procedures. And in turn the parties operate within a broader political system, where opportunities to become a candidate are influenced by the legal system, the electoral system, legislative turnover and the wider political culture. Accordingly we start by briefly sketching the institutional context for all British candidates before focussing on supply and demand explanations.

Context of the political system

In the British political system opportunities to stand for Parliament are determined by four specific factors. First, the *legal process* presents few barriers. Almost any British citizen willing to risk £500 can become a candidate, with minor exceptions like criminals and Peers. There were 2,617 names on the ballot in the 1992 general election. But the British parliament remains dominated by the *two-party system*, and there are few chances of winning outside of these. Despite the growth of the center and regional parties since the late 1960s, over 90 per cent of seats continue to be won by Labour and the Conservatives.

Moreover, opportunities for good seats in these parties are restricted due to the rate of *incumbency turnover*. In the post-war period 91 per cent of all MPs who chose to stand again were returned. There are two routes for new MPs: candidates can inherit open seats where the previous MPs retired, or challengers can defeat incumbents. In the post-war period, in general and by-elections, this has produced about 140 new members per Parliament. Therefore even in the major parties most new candidates face inevitable disappointment unless there is a massive electoral landslide, such as in 1945.

Lastly, in the British *electoral system*, of first-past-the-post in single member constituencies, candidates can do little to change these odds. There is a modest personal vote but in Britain the strength of party voting, and the focus of attention on the national campaign, leadership and platform, means that individual candidates, by their own efforts, can rarely improve their party's share of the vote (Norris, Vallance and Lovenduski 1992). The electoral system has also influenced the way Labour and Conservative candidates are nominated by party members in local constituencies. The power of Conservative Central Office and the

Labour Party's National Executive Committee to influence the process in individual constituencies is very restricted. Therefore the key decision about who gets the good seats, hence who gets elected into Parliament – and ultimately into government – lies in the hands of the local Labour and Conservative gatekeepers. About two-thirds of constituencies are conventionally judged safe; in these selection for the incumbent party is tantamount to election.

The social background of candidates

We can start by considering differences between party strata in the social characteristics commonly included in previous research on the British political elite including occupational class, education, age, gender, ethnicity, children and marital status.

Occupational class

The most important and complex of the background factors is occupation. It is well established that over time Parliament has become more socially homogeneous on both sides of the aisle, with a decline in Conservative landed gentry and Labour's ex-miners and engineers. Today, in common with other legislatures, the British Parliament contains a disproportionate number of those drawn from the 'talking professions', notably law, journalism, lecturing and teaching. Nevertheless the reasons for this are not well understood. Previous research provides various demand-side explanations: Ranney (1965) suggests that party members, even in the Labour party, fail to choose working-class candidates because of social deference. Bochel and Denver (1983) found that manual workers were seen by party members as less able and articulate. Greenwood (1988) argues that attempts by Conservative Central Office to increase the number of working-class trade union candidates failed due to local party resistance.

On the supply-side, previous research by Ranney (1965) explained the class bias in Parliament by the resources that middle-class professional occupations provide for a political career: flexible working hours, useful political skills, social status and political contacts. The most illuminating supply-side explanation uses the concept of 'brokerage occupations'. This suggests that Parliamentary careers are facilitated by jobs which combine flexibility over time, generous vacations, interrupted career-paths, professional independence, financial security, public networks, social status, policy experience and technical skills useful in political life. Brokerage jobs – barristers, teachers, trade union officials, journalists, political researchers – are complimentary to politics. They minimise the costs and risks of horizontal mobility from the economic to the political market-place, and vice versa, since being a member of Parliament is an uncertain life.

Interviews found some with early political ambitions who consciously chose a brokerage career which they knew could be combined with pursuit of a seat. Some faced hostile employers, even the sack, while others worked for companies who encouraged employees with parliamentary ambitions, since they recognised the political advantages of contacts in Westminster. The importance of flexible brokerage jobs and sympathetic employers was stressed by many applicants, some referred to it as the need for suitable 'jumping off' points into politics.

Being active in politics mucks up your career like nobody's business. I mean, it really causes havoc...and if you've been an MP and then lose your seat, it again causes havoc, so you've got to say to yourself, I'm interested in politics, and I'm prepared to forego lots of career opportunities for the sake of what I believe in politics.

Certain employers are quite keen to encourage their employees to do things, and I have to say that I think that unless you're lucky – the silver spoon touch – you've either got to be self-employed or work for such a company.

What I thought, rightly or wrongly, was that as a solicitor in London I could earn my living there and be an MP, because my work is basically in court in the morning, whereas if you're a barrister you have all-day cases – so it would've fitted in.

The brokerage explanation helps illuminate not just the class disparity, but also why women and ethnic minorities are under-represented in Parliament, since they are often concentrated in low-paying skilled and semi-skilled occupations, or in family small businesses, with inflexible schedules and long hours, in sectors which do not provide traditional routes to political life.

In order to examine the importance of *occupational class* on a systematic basis party strata are compared using the respondents' occupational socioeconomic group, summarised into manual/non-manual categories. Work status is included, distinguishing those in paid work from others, and trade union membership since it was anticipated this might prove significant in the Labour party.

The analysis in Table 9.1 confirms the familiar observation that MPs are drawn overwhelmingly from professional and managerial occupations. The Parliamentary Labour Party is dominated by public-sector employees: lecturers, teachers, journalists, local government managers, political researchers, trade union officials and welfare officers. In contrast in the Conservatives there are more private sector managers, company directors, financial advisers and barristers.

Table 9.1. Social class, work status and Union membership

		Conservative					Labour				
		MPs	PPCs	List	Members	Voters	MPs	PPCs	List	Members	Voters
Class	Professional/Technical	44	46	41	33	20	61	66	56	46	13
	Manager/Administrator	54	46	56	39	16	24	24	23	19	4
	Clerical/Sales	1	6	1	22	30	1	5	11	14	19
	Skilled manual	0	1	1	4	15	11	5	6	12	19
	Semi-skilled manual	0	1	1	2	19	3	1	3	9	4
Class summary	Non-manual	99	98	98	94	66	87	94	90	79	36
	Manual	1	2	2	6	34	14	6	10	21	64
Work status	In paid work	100	98	92	39	59	100	94	95	65	52
	Retired	0	0	1	30	20	0	1	2	20	14
	Homemaker	0	1	3	22	16	0	1	2	6	15
	Other	0	1	3	10	6	0	4	1	8	19
Union member	Union/SA member	8	14	17	14	19	99	97	91	78	34
	Not Union member	91	86	83	87	81	1	3	9	22	65
Housing tenure	Owner occupier	99	93	96	92	83	98	91	86	82	52
	Not owner	1	7	4	8	17	2	9	14	18	48
N		142	222	225	601	1405	97	318	127	885	1000

Note:
PPC = Prospective Parliamentary Candidate: List = Applicant on the National List.
Source: BCS 1992; BES 1987.

But, more importantly, the results indicate the explanation for this phenomenon: *the class bias of Parliament is the product of supply rather than demand.* Within each party, the socioeconomic status of MPs, candidates and applicants is almost identical. If, for argument's sake, all incumbents resigned and all applicants took their place, the social composition of the Commons would be largely unaffected. Within each party the elite has higher social status than members, while members have higher status than voters. Parliament is dominated by the professional 'chattering classes' because journalists, lawyers, self-employed businessmen, financial consultants and university lecturers have sufficient security, flexibility and income to gamble on a political career.

Education

In terms of education, it is well known that Parliament contains far more graduates, especially from Oxford and Cambridge, and far more from public school, than the general electorate. Despite the extensive attention given to this phenomenon, the reasons for it are not well established. Ranney (1965) suggests that the explanation rests with demand: party members select the better educated because this is a sign of ability and social status, and they wish to 'choose their betters'. Rush (1969) suggests that Conservative selectors have an overwhelming preference for Oxbridge and public school products. Many Conservative candidates shared this perception:

A seat which is either winnable or safe looks for two things. I fear they do still go for the Old Guard – the old Etonian and the son of an MP...if you come in that way they don't look for anything, you can go straight in.

Yet, equally plausibly, on the supply side education may influence recruitment through motivation and resources. In European elections Holland (1986) found that selectors could not be blamed for favouring those of higher status; there was a greater public school/Oxbridge and socioeconomic bias among the total pool of applicants than among those chosen. The body of literature on political participation has consistently found education to be one of the best predictors of activism; increasing political knowledge, interest, confidence and skills. The influence of education continues even after controlling for income, although its effect on campaign activism is less clear-cut than other modes of participation (Parry, Moyser and Day 1992).

Table 9.2 confirms that MPs are drawn disproportionately from the better educated; 70 per cent of MPs are graduates compared with 6 per cent of voters. But, more interestingly, the results indicate that education affects recruitment primarily through supply rather than demand. In the

Table 9.2. *Education*

		Conservative					Labour				
		MPs	PPCs	List	Members	Voters	MPs	PPCs	List	Members	Voters
Education	More than 18 years	70	65	74	40	13	54	66	55	51	10
	16 to 18 years	29	28	22	44	42	27	23	33	25	36
	Less than 16 years	1	7	4	16	45	19	10	12	24	54
	Mean Years education	21	20	20	18	17	20	20	20	19	16
	Graduate	69	66	70	28	6	71	72	62	44	6
	Non-graduate	31	33	30	72	94	29	28	38	56	94
	Oxbridge+Public school	26	13	15	–	–	3	2	2	–	–
N		142	222	225	601	1405	97	318	127	885	1000

Source: BCS 1992; BES 1987.

Conservative Party MPs, candidates and applicants are equally well qualified. But there is a precipitous fall in the proportion of university graduates from the party elite to members, and another decline from members to voters. In the Labour Party there is a similar pattern, although the graduate gap is less between applicants and members, and greater between members and voters. Nor can the selectors be blamed for favouring those who have followed the traditional public school plus Oxbridge route; again this reflects the proportion of applicants who fall into this category. As with brokerage occupations, higher education influences the supply of volunteers willing to risk a political career.

Gender

The influence of gender on recruitment can be treated as a product of demand, if the selectors employ direct or indirect prejudice against women. Vallance (1984) has argued that parties have been reluctant to nominate women in winnable seats because selectors are directly prejudiced against women candidates, or because, indirectly, they fear women may lose votes. Many of those we interviewed believed men and women party members, particularly the older generation, discriminated against women candidates.

The basic problem is that selectors are not enthusiastic about women candidates. They believe the electorate does not want them. They do not see women as having the same commitment as men. They do not know how to categorise them in the same way as they can men. They fear that women might be unpredictable...in short, they apply different standards.

There was always the assumption that if you were selecting a woman you were taking a risk.

Alternatively gender can be seen as a supply-side effect; due to the conventional division of labour in the family, segregation in the labour market, and traditional patterns of socialisation, we would expect many women to have lower resources of time and money, and lower levels of political ambition and confidence. Bochel and Denver (1983) stress supply-side factors for the dearth of women politicians; if more women came forward to pursue a Parliamentary career, the study suggests, more would be nominated. An earlier study by Rush (1969) found that supply-side factors were most important: in the Conservative party women were the majority of grassroots members but only 10 per cent of those on the Approved List. Some believed that many women were underconfident and reluctant to stand:

Those talents and skills that women have are so undervalued, and usually women'll say, 'Oh well, I'm only this'...'but all I've ever done is...' and, 'this is all I can do...', and that sort of thing.

Gender could also interact with the effects of marital status and children. On balance married candidates would be expected to be advantaged over those who were single, since constituencies often look for a 'team', although given traditional attitudes marriage and children may prove an advantage for a man but a disadvantage for a woman. As some saw it:

If you're a man, they think that if they are also getting a wife, they're getting two for the price of one, essentially. But with a woman it's the other way around. Because she is married they see her as the support to her husband.

In terms of gender, supply seems more important for Conservative women while demand plays a greater role in the Labour Party (see Table 9.3). In 1992 Parliament included twenty Conservative and thirty-seven Labour women MPs. Given this situation, some believe Conservative party selectors, with traditional family values, must be prejudiced against women. But we found about the same proportion of women Conservative candidates and applicants, which suggests women party members are reluctant to pursue a Westminster career. Conservative women are the majority of the grassroots party, the backbone of the organisation in terms of constituency officeholders, the participants at party conference, but they are not coming forward in equal numbers to stand for Parliament. The most plausible explanation is that many women members tend to be middle-aged with traditional roles in the home, or elderly pensioners, with few formal educational qualifications. This generational difference was well expressed by a Conservative woman MP:

There was an older generation than us, who didn't approve of us being political. They thought we should do the coffee mornings and the committees and all that sort of thing. And I think we, and I would say most of us in our forties and thirties, when we came along and were stridently political, this was a shock to them.

In the Labour Party women have made considerable progress in Parliament, almost doubling their numbers in the last general election, to represent 13.6 per cent of Labour MPs. Yet, contrary to popular assumptions, women face greater problems from Labour than Conservative Party selectors. In the Labour Party women were 40 per cent of individual members, and about the same proportion (37 per cent) of applicants, but only 26 per cent of candidates. Therefore more Labour women are coming forward than are being selected. The main reason for this, our interviewees suggested, was that more men had trade union connections which helped in terms of sponsorship and informal constituency contacts.

Table 9.3. Gender, family and race

Voters		Conservative					Labour				
		MPs	PPCs	List	Members	Voters	MPs	PPCs	List	Members	Voters
Gender	Male	94	85	87	48	48	91	74	63	60	48
	Female	6	15	13	52	52	9	26	37	40	52
Marital status	Married	88	68	73	71	69	78	64	70	77	63
	Not married	12	32	27	29	31	22	36	30	23	37
Family	Children under 16	37	30	46	15	31	35	48	42	34	35
	None	63	70	54	85	69	65	52	58	66	65
Ethnicity	White	100	99	98	–	99	98	99	96	96	93
	Non-white	0	1	2	–	1	2	1	4	4	7
N		142	222	225	601	1405	97	318	127	885	1000

Source: BCS 1992; BES 1987.

Race

Ethnic minorities represent only about 4.8 per cent of the adult British population, and the population is clustered in certain constituencies, which causes problems for any conventional election survey. Some suggest direct racism by party activists may have influenced some recent selections.

A lot of people were very suspicious about black people – stereotypes – there were wrong things said about black people in the Labour party, and quite often by people who we regarded as our representatives and our leaders who should set standards.

Although the evidence that non-white candidates suffer an electoral penalty is mixed (Norris, Vallance and Lovenduski 1992), indirect prejudice may count against them.

Yet comparison of the characteristics of party strata confirms that in the Conservative Party the main problem is probably supply-side: very few non-whites are active within the party at any level. Among those who do come forward, non-whites are relatively successful at getting on the approved list of applicants, and becoming candidates. The first non-white Conservative MP this century was elected in the 1992 election. In the Labour Party the problems of supply and demand are combined. In absolute terms there are more non-white candidates and MPs in the Labour Party. But in relative terms, there are probably fewer non-white Labour candidates than applicants.

Age

Lastly, in terms of age, younger candidates might be most motivated to ascend the greasy pole of political office. Age could also affect demand: those looking for seats in their mid- to late thirties might be best placed, since they would have had time to establish a record of political activity, experience of public service, and good party networks. In contrast, as some of our respondents stressed, those over fifty might be considered over the hill by selectorates.

A comparison of party strata suggests age affects supply and demand (see Table 9.4). There were notable differences within the elite: 90 per cent of MPs, and two thirds of applicants, were over forty, while the majority of candidates were younger. Those in their late thirties and early forties may be seen as most energetic, enthusiastic and committed to the constituency, qualities seen as paramount by party selectors, as well as being sufficiently mature and experienced. In the Labour Party, the age

Table 9.4. *Age groups*

		Conservative					Labour				
		MPs	PPCs	List	Member	Voters	MPs	PPCs	List	Members	Voters
Age group	Over 60	17	0	1	44	14	14	3	2	21	22
	Fifties	33	9	16	23	17	34	11	12	16	19
	Forties	43	28	47	17	20	43	39	49	24	17
	Thirties	6	43	32	7	17	8	40	31	24	16
	Under 30	1	20	5	9	33	0	6	6	15	26
	Mean age	53	40	44	58	49	52	43	44	50	45
N		142	222	225	601	1405	97	318	127	885	1000

Source: BCS 1992; BES 1987.

profile of members and voters was fairly similar but in contrast Conservatives members were far more elderly than supporters.

To summarise, the influence of supply-side factors can be assessed by comparing the social characteristics of members and applicants. In both parties the most striking supply-side contrasts were by age, class and education. Members least likely to come forward as Conservative applicants included the elderly, women, the lower middle-class, and the less educated. In the Labour Party there was a similar but not identical pattern; those least likely to seek office included members who were elderly, less educated, manual workers and non-trade unionists.

The influence of demand is shown by differences between applicants and candidates. As in other careers, age proved important: selectors preferred younger applicants. In addition, women, and perhaps ethnic minorities, seemed disadvantaged by the Labour selectorate. But the most striking finding was that, in most respects, candidates were very similar to the total pool of applicants. Contrary to previous studies, there is no evidence in this analysis for discrimination by party selectors on the grounds of education or class. Parliament includes a social bias towards better educated and middle-class, because this reflects the pool of applicants. This mirrors the well-established socioeconomic bias in political participation in other forms of political activity. If other types of applicants came forward, this suggests, probably more would be selected.

Resources: time

On this basis we can test for direct differences in the resources of applicants and candidates. Resources are defined as assets which can be employed to advantage in pursuing a political career, including time, money, political experience and social networks. Among resources time may be among the most important, since standing for office is a demanding activity requiring attendance at regular constituency meetings, social and fund-raising events, local 'surgeries', public speaking engagements, door-to-door leafletting, canvassing and campaigning in local as well as general elections. Applicants need to invest time in the selection process, in nursing a seat and in the final general election campaign. In the Conservative Party, where applicants trail around the country for any vacancy, the interview process can be gruelling. Preparation for an interview, finding out about the constituency, also required time.

Every time I went for an interview, the research took an enormous amount of time. I went round to everyone from headteachers to the police...Four interviews, four rounds, and each time I went back and back seeing more people...the time it takes, you've no idea.

Once they get a seat, even a hopeless one, candidates then need to spend years campaigning, as one stressed:

If one's working full-time, the stress and strain that it puts candidates under – travelling and commitments...I mean, they spend a good two-and-a-half, maybe three years, all their free time.

Flexibility over scheduling may be important; paid leave of absence from work and/or child-care during the month-long formal campaign may be more indispensable than free evenings and weekends. Candidates need to anticipate being dedicated to the job, once elected: MPs claimed to spend almost twice the average workload, 66 hours per week, on their work at Westminster and in their constituencies. Therefore, applicants with more time to invest in a political career can be expected to move up the ladder of recruitment.

In this analysis *time* is measured by the number of hours devoted to party activities, in categories ranging from less than five hours, to more than twenty hours, in the average month. The results indicate a substantial difference in the time invested in party work by these groups (see Table 9.5). In the Conservative Party 87 per cent of candidates, but only 35 per cent of applicants, were in the most active group, devoting over twenty hours per month to party activities. In the Labour Party 83 per cent of candidates, compared with 53 per cent of applicants, fell into this category. In contrast the least active category included almost no candidates, but quite a few Labour and Conservative applicants (12 and 18 per cent, respectively). This confirms the evidence of personal interviews that candidates need to devote themselves wholeheartedly to the task for a long time before the start of the official campaign. But, once more, the greatest contrasts were between the elite and members, since half the Labour members were entirely passive.

Financial resources

In Britain financial resources are less significant today than in the pre-war period, where contemporary accounts suggest personal expenditure was sometimes decisive in gaining good seats. Reform of the campaign finance laws in the 1880s, combined with the 1949 Maxwell-Fyfe rules in the Conservative Party and the 1957 Wilson reforms in the Labour Party, strictly limited the nature and amount of money individual candidates can contribute to their election expenses and the constituency association. Financial barriers for British candidates do not provide the formidable barrier faced by candidates for the United States Congress (see chapter 10) or the Japanese Diet (see chapter 6). Nevertheless personal

Table 9.5. *Time resources*

| | Conservative | | | Labour | | | |
	MPs %	PPCs %	List %	MPs %	PPCs %	List %	Members %
0 hours	0	0	0	0	0	0	50
0–5 hours	7	1	18	0	0	12	30
5–10 hours	10	5	18	9	2	15	9
10–15 hours	10	3	18	17	7	12	4
15–20 hours	10	5	12	14	9	10	2
<20 hours	64	87	35	60	83	53	4
	100	100	100	100	100	100	100

Note:

Q. 'How much time do you usually devote to party activities in the average month?'

Source: BCS 1992, Labour Party Membership Survey, 1989.

expenses, met by the candidate, may be a problem. As one Conservative women candidate remarked:

The financial side of it is, I think, prohibitive, because it's almost selective in itself, as I said, if I had had children, and been in a different situation financially, then there's no way I could've contemplated it.

There are the expenses associated with being selected: travel, clothes, local research, accommodation, training sessions and party conferences. Applicants travelling around the country for interviews pay their own expenses. Recent Labour Party reforms have lengthened the process, and increased the number of ward and constituency meetings candidates must attend. If adopted, candidates must meet their personal expenses in nursing the constituency, often for one or two years before the campaign. This includes direct expenses like communications and transportation, plus the hidden costs of time away from work, possibly child care or home help. How much does it all cost? Estimates varied. Local candidates already resident in the constituency, or those sponsored by their trade union, thought it only cost a few hundred pounds. Those with more distant seats thought it cost them anywhere from £3,000 to £10,000. For some this proved prohibitive.

To assess the effect of financial resources, party strata were compared by the household's total income, divided into seven bands (see Table 9.6). Candidates were found to have very similar incomes to applicants. Indeed in the Conservative Party applicants were slightly more affluent, although

Table 9.6. *Financial resources*

£	Conservative				Labour				
	MPs %	PPCs %	List %	Voters %	MPs %	PPCs %	List %	Members %	Voters %
>5,000	0	1	1	18	0	0	5	16	36
5,000–10,000	0	1	1	24	0	7	11	21	31
10,000–20,000	0	15	9	39	2	26	24	32	27
20,000–30,000	5	22	19	13	31	28	30	17	5
30,000–40,000	12	16	17	6	37	21	15	8	1
40,000–50,000	22	14	11	–	20	11	11	4	–
<50,000	61	31	43	–	10	7	4	–	–
100	100	100	100	100	100	100	100	100	100

Note:
The scale for voters only extends to £30,000+ and for Labour party members to £40,000+
Source: BCS 1992; BES 1987; Labour Party Membership Survey, 1989.

in the Labour Party slightly more applicants were in the lower bands. But the most striking contrast was between the political elite and voters: two thirds of Labour voters were in households with incomes of less than £10,000 compared with one third of members and only 8 per cent of the Labour elite. As we might expect there were also noticeable differences between parties, with Conservative MPs by far the most affluent group. The results confirm the thesis that financial resources affect supply rather than demand: those without a comfortable income may feel they just cannot afford the financial investment required to nurse a seat, particularly given the risk of electoral failure.

Political experience

Political experience may provide political capital. Members who have already held public office can be expected to have developed political expertise, speaking skills, practical knowledge of government and social contacts, which will be useful in gaining a seat. A Parliamentary career in Britain is usually the apex of years involved in ward, constituency and executive party meetings, the local or county council, the trade union movement, community work or public service. As one Conservative MP described the process it was a gradual escalator:

After I'd been a councillor for a while – a borough councillor – I started to see some of the decisions taken a bit further away at County Council. I became a County Councillor immediately after that and then, of course, one sees all the big decisions taken in Parliament, and I became more and more interested in that.

Most noted how many overlapping political commitments they had, which gradually took over their lives. Ranney (1965) suggests long-standing party or union service was particularly important in the Labour Party. Candidates often assume that they have to be 'bloodied' by fighting a hopeless seat before they will be considered for a good one, although too many consecutive failures may count against applicants.

We compare the political experience of party strata by measuring a range of different types of activism: including whether party members had ever held local, regional or national party office; considered standing, been a candidate or been elected to the local council; and been a candidate at a previous general election. These items were added for a summary scale, weighted according to the level of office (see Table 9.7). Nearly all the elite had been active in their local party, while the majority had been local councillors and had served on local public bodies as the first steps up the ladder. The most striking finding is that candidates were no more experienced than applicants, indeed in the Conservative Party

Table 9.7. *Political experience*

Have you ever . . .	Conservative				Labour				Scale Weight %
	MPs %	PPCs %	List %	Members %	MPs %	PPCs %	List %	Members %	
Stood for Parliament before	100	31	49		100	32	32		[12]
PPC how many times?	4.5	1.5	1.4		3.3	1.3	1.3		
Held local party office	87	90	90	32	96	95	96	50	[3]
Held regional party office	38	35	36	8	47	19	24	4	[6]
Held national party office	31	19	21	2	19	4	8	1	[9]
Been candidate for local government	61	75	70	14	79	85	81	20	[6]
Been elected to local government	50	44	57	15	65	66	61	19	[9]
Been candidate Euro. Parliament	4	5	6		9	6	4		[6]
Been elected Euro. Parliament	3	1	1		6	1	0		[9]
Served on local public body	47	57	62		67	68	76		[3]
Served on national public body	28	8	12		34	9	13		[9]
Held office in local pressure group	39	35	36		56	58	61		[3]
Held office in national pressure group	39	18	21		36	20	24		[9]
Held office in other community group	30	36	42		43	49	55		[3]
Held office in professional association	22	22	26		25	24	24		[3]
Held office in student organisation	28	41	39		22	32	31		[3]
Held office in trade union	8	9	11		63	63	61		[3]
Held office in women's organisation	3	4	6		5	11	20		[3]
Summary weighted scale	39	27	21		45	31	31		[100]

Note:
Q. "Have you ever held office/served on . . ."
Source: BCS 1992.

the reverse held true; applicants had slightly more experience through standing for Parliament and holding local office. Once more the main contrast, where comparisons could be drawn, was between members and the party elite; for example, less than one-fifth of members had run for local government compared with 80 per cent of the elite. We can conclude that candidates need to demonstrate some political experience, to have 'done their bit', but given the amateur tradition no more is required. As one Conservative MP noted, applicants have a good chance:

So long as you fulfil the criteria of having done something to help the party – been a local councillor, done a bit of work in a constituency, and you've got the backing of one or two people who are prepared to say you are a fairly sane and rational human being.

Support networks

Support networks may be an important resource of information, advice and direct endorsements. We would expect that those who received wide-spread encouragement from close friends, party members, party agents, community groups, business associates, trade unionists and employers, as well as their immediate family, would be more likely to consider a Parliamentary career, and would be better placed to get a good seat. In the Labour Party many stressed the importance of local contacts, especially with trade union branches.

Through having worked in the area I did develop a lot of contacts and a lot of friends, and especially the person who encouraged me to go for seats in the first place, and so he was there, and actually on the ground, and knew what was happening, and there was therefore very much of a support network available.

In the Conservative Party social networks, developed through national fundraisers, constituency work, or Central Office, were seen as invaluable in identifying good opportunities and getting advice about procedures, or simply as a source of encouragement, a steer in the right direction:

When you get to a certain level these contacts really can be very, very useful to you. Very useful. One word from the right person in the right place can actually open a door. Can't get you a seat, but it can open a door. Just draw your attention to opportunities.

The survey used a fifty-point scale measured according to the level of support which applicants reported from ten different groups, ranging from family to employers. The results in Table 9.8 again indicate minimal differences between candidates and applicants; all reported fairly positive support from most groups.

Table 9.8. *Support networks*

	Conservative			Labour		
	MPs	PPCs	List	MPs	PPCs	List
Spouse or partner	4.2	4.2	3.9	4.1	4.1	3.9
Other family members	4.0	4.0	3.8	4.0	3.8	3.7
Personal friends	4.1	4.2	4.0	4.3	4.2	4.2
Women's groups	3.3	3.5	3.5	3.5	3.8	3.5
Community groups	3.4	3.5	3.5	3.9	3.7	3.6
Business associates	3.5	3.7	3.5	3.4	3.4	3.1
Trade unionists	2.9	3.2	3.1	4.5	4.1	3.8
Party members	4.5	4.6	4.4	4.6	4.4	4.2
Party agents	4.4	4.4	4.2	4.3	4.0	3.4
Employers	3.3	3.4	3.2	2.9	3.0	2.7
Summary index	26.0	28.0	28.0	30.0	32.0	30.0

Note:
Q. 'Some people receive encouragement from those around them when they decide to stand for public office, while others experience indifference or disapproval. How positive or negative were the following people in encouraging you to become a candidate in the next election?' Scaled from 5 (very positive) to 1 (very negative). The summary index is scored from 0 (very negative) to 50 (very positive). Figures represent the mean response.
Source: BCS 1992.

Motivation: political ambition

Lastly, although many people have resources, only a few choose a political career. The combination of resources plus motivation produces the necessary and sufficient conditions for candidacies. Motivational factors are defined as psychological predispositions to become involved in politics. Previous research has commonly explained activism by higher levels of political ambition, interest and confidence (Fowler and McClure 1989). Although intuitively plausible, motivational factors are some of the most difficult variables to measure. Motivation is hidden; older MPs may have forgotten their initial impetus; candidates may disguise naked ambition under the cloak of public service; bitter failure may produce plausible rationalisations.

The ambition of applicants was explored using an open-ended question: 'What was the single most important reason why you first wanted to stand for Parliament?' This is a limited measure but it provides an indication of the initial motivation. Reasons for standing were explored in greater depth in the personal interviews with some respondents. Based on this, survey responses were coded into six major categories according

Table 9.9. *Motivation*

	Conservative			Labour		
	MPs %	PPCs %	List %	MPs %	PPCs %	List %
Personal ambition	46	42	51	45	40	37
Ideology	20	20	21	25	18	21
Public service	20	22	16	14	9	11
Party standard-bearer	6	12	5	4	12	7
Single issue	6	2	4	1	4	4
Group representation	0	1	3	1	12	19
Invited	2	2	1	9	4	1
	100	100	100	100	100	100

Note:
Q. 'What was the most important reason why you first wanted to stand for Parliament?'
Source: BCS 1992.

to whether applicants were motivated primarily by personal career, ideology, public service, party standard-bearers, single issues and group representatives. Our hypothesis assumed that candidates with personal career motives would be more ambitious than those standing for other reasons. Accordingly in the final model ambition was coded as a dichotomous variable. The results of this classification, given in Table 9.9, suggest a party difference: perhaps due to ideological reasons the Conservatives tended to stress the public service role while Labour favoured that of 'group representative'. Nevertheless by this measure there was no major difference in the motivation of candidates and applicants.

Drive

Plausibly we would expect drive to be important, since candidates who were more persistent would be expected to be more successful. One Labour MP suggested that one of the main difficulties in the initial stages was maintaining motivation:

Keeping going. There were lots of reasons why I shouldn't go on, like...thinking life's passing you by and you should be getting on with your career. It's ups and downs. The hardest part was keeping determined during the troughs.

Drive is another difficult psychological concept to assess. In this model it is gauged by a proxy behavioural measure, namely the number of seats applied for in the 1992 election. Logically the more tenacious the appli-

Table 9.10. *Demand-side model predicting whether respondents were candidates or applicants*

	Conservative	Labour	Coding
Social background:			
Social class	0.09	0.07	Manual/Non-manual
Education (years)	−0.01	0.08	Years
Public + Oxbridge	0.01	−0.02	Public + Oxbridge/Other
Trade union	−0.06	0.04	Member/Non-member
Age	−0.14**	0.01	Years
Children	−0.12**	0.04	Any children under 16/None
Marital status	0.11**	−0.07	Married/Not married
Gender	0.00	0.09*	Man/Woman
Resources:			
Time	0.49**	0.42**	Hours of party work
Financial resources	−0.07	0.03	Household income
Political experience	−0.11**	−0.09	100-point scale
Support networks	−0.04	0.08	50-point scale
Motivation:			
Ambition	−0.06	−0.05	Personal career/other
Drive/seats applied for	−0.19**	0.03	Number of seats applied for
	0.35	0.18	Candidate/Applicant

Notes:
The figures represent standardised Beta coefficients using a least-squared multiple regression analysis. Ethnic identity was dropped from the model, due to the small number of cases. The graduate/non-graduate variable was excluded due to multi-collinearity with years of education.
**=p.>.01 *=p.>.05.
Source: BCS 1992.

cant, this hypothesis assumes, the better their chances of being interviewed and adopted for a good seat.

Contrary to expectations, Conservative candidates applied for fewer seats (12) than applicants (17). In the Labour Party there was little difference between applicants and candidates, although due to the greater emphasis on localism both applied for fewer seats than Conservatives. This throws doubt on the idea that people on the party list are not actively pursuing vacancies. Particularly in the Conservative Party they are trying but failing. What still requires explanation, therefore, is why applicants are less successful despite their tenacity. On the basis of more detailed analysis of these applicants it seems plausible to suggest that these are usually experienced members who have given years of faithful party service, and have stood before, but who are no longer seen as attractive or electable candidates due to their age. They find themselves, often bitterly, left on the party shelf.

Conclusions

Taken together, what is the relative importance of social background, resources and motivation? How do these effects interact? Since there are separate surveys of members and applicants, based on different samples, unfortunately it is not possible to use the standard multivariate tests to evaluate the relative impact of these variables on the supply of applicants. It is possible, however, to test whether these variables influence demand. Based on the discussion so far, the null hypothesis would suggest that these factors would have little ability to predict whether respondents were candidates or applicants. Accordingly after testing for multi-collinearity, the variables measuring resources, motivation and social background were entered into a least-squared regression model, in this order, to see whether these factors distinguished between candidates and applicants. Since we would anticipate that the effects might be different in the Conservative and the Labour Party, the model was run separately for each party.

Three major points emerge from this analysis (see Table 9.10). First, most importantly, in most respects the results confirm the null hypothesis. According to this evidence party selectors did not choose candidates on the basis of education, social class, trade union membership, financial resources, ambition or support networks. The evidence suggests that these factors influence supply rather than demand. Second, time proved significant in both parties, as we have noted candidates devote far more hours to party work than applicants. Yet this finding is open to interpretation. Whether selectors look for candidates who have time to devote to their constituency, or candidates spend more time on party work by virtue of their official position, remains an open question.

Lastly, in the Conservative Party, contrary to expectations, successful candidates applied for fewer seats, had less political experience, and were less likely to be married or to have children than applicants. This poses a puzzle. Based on everything else we know, it seems counter-intuitive to propose that party selectors are looking for less-experienced applicants. The most convincing explanation points to the critical importance of the age of those short-listed; many on the Conservative approved list are older members who, despite extensive local government experience and party service, may be seen by selectors as less attractive than younger and potentially more dynamic contenders.

In conclusion, as J.F.S. Ross (1944) observed in analysing the composition of Parliament in the inter-war years:

In no single respect – age, education, occupation, sex, social standing, party – does the composition of the House of Commons reflect that of the community. The differences, moreover, are not the minor deviations inseparable from any system of representation: they are radical divergences.

Forty years later we are little closer to demographic representation in Parliament. The most plausible explanation of the social bias, on the basis of this analysis, is that supply-side factors play a major role in recruitment. The most important of these factors – determining who came forward to pursue a Parliamentary career – were age, class and education. The well-established socioeconomic bias seems attributable to the resources and motivation associated with higher education and brokerage occupations. Those aspiring to Parliament need professions which allow them, at an early age, flexibility over time-management, financial security, transferable skills, horizontal mobility, and interrupted career paths. These occupations minimise the costs, and maximise the opportunities, associated with the risks of a political life.

On the demand side this analysis provides no evidence that party selectors choose applicants on the grounds of education or class. Women candidates seem to experience some discrimination against them by Labour, but not Conservative, party selectors. As in other careers, the age of applicants seems important, with selectors favouring younger contenders. Lastly the analysis of race is hampered by the number of cases available, but the provisional results indicate that in the Conservative Party this is a problem of supply, while in the Labour Party supply and demand factors play a role.

Does the social bias in Parliament matter anyway? Does it make any difference to the behaviour of members, the debates about major national issues, or the legislation which is passed? Some are sceptical, on the grounds that the British political system is based on the model of responsible party government. As such, what matters for defending the interests of the poorer, less-educated sectors of society, women and ethnic minorities is getting policies accepted by parties which defend their interests. But for defenders of the demographic theory of representation what matters is not just the policy outcome but who takes the decisions. By this standard a Parliament which does not 'look like Britain', no matter how much it claims to speak on behalf of its constituents, remains fundamentally unrepresentative.

10   United States

Paul S. Herrnson

Can I win? Is this the right time for me to run? Who is my competition likely to be? These are the kinds of questions that go through the minds of prospective candidates. This chapter examines who decides to run for the US Congress, how potential candidates reach their decisions, and the influence that different individuals and groups have on these decisions. It also examines the impact of political experience on a candidate's prospects of winning the nomination and the influence of the nomination process on the representativeness of the national legislature.[1]

Strategic ambition

The Constitution, state laws and the political parties pose few formal barriers to running for Congress, enabling virtually anyone to declare him- or herself a candidate. Members of the House are required to be at least twenty-five years of age, to have been US citizens for at least seven years, and to reside in the state they represent. The requirements for the Senate are only slightly more stringent. In addition to residing in the state they represent, senators must be at least thirty years old and must have been US citizens for at least nine years. Some states bar prison inmates or individuals who have been declared insane from running for Congress or voting in an election, and most states require candidates to pay a small filing fee or to collect anywhere from a few hundred to several thousand signatures prior to having their names placed on the ballot. As is typical for election to public offices in many democracies, a dearth of formal requirements allows almost anyone to run for Congress. And more than a thousand people run in an average two-year election cycle.

Although the formal requirements are minimal, other factors, related to the candidate-centred nature of the electoral system, favour individuals with certain personal characteristics. Strategic ambition, which is the combination of a desire to get elected, a realistic understanding of what it

---

[1]   This chapter is drawn from Paul Herrnson, *Congressional Elections* (Washington, DC: CQ Press, 1995).

takes to win, and an ability to assess the opportunities presented by a given political context, is one such characteristic that distinguishes most successful candidates for Congress from the general public. Most successful candidates must also be self-starters, since the electoral system lacks a tightly controlled party-recruitment process or a well-defined career path to the national legislature. And, because the electoral system is candidate-centred, the desire, skills and attitudes that candidates bring to the electoral arena are the most important criteria separating serious candidates from those who have little chance of getting elected. Ambitious candidates, sometimes referred to as *strategic*, *rational* or *quality* candidates, are political entrepreneurs who make rational calculations about when to run. Rather than plunge right in, they assess the political context in which they would have to wage their campaigns, consider the effects that a bid for office could have on their professional careers and families, and carefully weigh their prospects for success (Kazee 1994).

Strategic politicians examine a number of institutional, structural and subjective factors when considering a bid for Congress. The institutional factors include filing deadlines, campaign finance laws, prohibitions for or against preprimary endorsements, and other election statutes or party rules. The structural factors include the social, economic, and partisan composition of the district, its geographic compactness, the media markets that serve it, the degree of overlap between the district and lower-level electoral constituencies, and the possibilities that exist for election to some alternative office. One structural factor that greatly affects the strategic calculations of nonincumbents and is prone to fluctuate more often than others is whether an incumbent plans to run for re-election.

Potential candidates also assess the political climate in deciding whether to run. Strategic politicians focus mainly on local circumstances, particularly whether a seat will be vacant or an incumbent appears to be vulnerable. National forces, such as a public mood that favours Democrats or Republicans or challengers or incumbents, are usually of secondary importance. The convergence of local and national forces can have a strong impact on the decisions of potential candidates. The bounced cheques and other ethical transgressions that cast a shadow over many House incumbents and the widespread hostility that was directed against Congress as an institution played a major role in shaping the pool of candidates that competed in the 1992 primaries and general election. These forces motivated many House incumbents to retire. They also encouraged many would-be House members to believe that a seat in Congress was not beyond their reach. Favourable circumstances and the candidates' positive assessment of their own abilities encouraged the candidates to think they could win the support of local, state and national political elites, raise the money, build the name recognition, and generate the momentum needed to propel them into office.

Incumbents

For House incumbents the decision to run for re-election is usually an easy one. Congress offers its members many reasons to want to stay, including the ability to affect issues they care about, a challenging environment in which to work, political power and public recognition. Moreover, incumbents are usually confident of their ability to get re-elected. Name recognition and the advantages inherent in incumbency – such as paid staff and the franking privilege (which have an estimated worth of more than $1.5 million over a two-year House term) – are two factors that discourage strong opposition from arising. Furthermore, most House members recognise that the 'home styles' they use to present themselves to constituents create bonds of trust that have important electoral implications.

Incumbents undertake a number of additional pre-election activities to build support and ward off opposition. Many raise large war chests early in the election cycle in order to intimidate potential opponents. Many also keep a skeletal campaign organisation intact between elections and send to their supporters campaign newsletters and other political communications. Some even shower their constituents with greeting cards, flowers and other gifts. Their congressional activities, pre-election efforts, and the fact that they have been elected to Congress at least once before make most incumbents fairly secure in the knowledge that they will be re-elected.

Under certain situations, however, incumbents recognise that it may be more difficult than usual for them to hold on to their seats. Redistricting, for example, can change the partisan composition of a House member's district or it can force two incumbents to compete for one seat. Ethical transgressions, such as involvement in a highly publicised scandal, can also weaken an incumbent's re-election prospects. A poor economy, an unpopular president or presidential candidate, or a wave of antigovernment hostility also has the potential to bring down legislators who represent marginal districts. These factors can influence incumbents' expectations about the quality of the opposition they are likely to face, the kinds of re-election campaigns they will need to wage, the toll those campaigns could take on themselves and their families, and their desire to stay in Congress.

When the demands of campaigning outweigh the benefits of getting re-elected, strategic incumbents retire. Elections that immediately follow redistricting are often preceded by a jump in the number of incumbents who retire, as was the case in 1952, 1972, 1982 and 1992. Elections held during periods of voter frustration or congressional scandal are also preceded by high numbers of retirements. A combination of redistricting and anti-incumbent sentiments led 15 per cent of all House members to retire in 1992 – a post-World War II record.

Elections that occur following upheaval within Congress itself are also marked by large numbers of congressional retirements. The political reforms passed during the mid-1970s, which redistributed power from conservative senior House members to more liberal junior ones, encouraged many senior members to retire from the House between 1974 and 1978.

Among the individuals who are most likely to retire from Congress are senior members who decide they would rather enjoy the fruits of old age than face a tough opponent, members who find their districts largely obliterated, and those who are implicated in some kind of scandal. The pre-1992 election period was marked by several retirements that were motivated by these reasons.

Nonincumbents

The conditions that affect the strategic calculations of incumbents also influence the decision-making of nonincumbents who plan their political careers strategically. Redistricting has a tremendous impact on these individuals. More state and local officeholders run for the House in election cycles that follow redistricting than in other years. Many of these candidates anticipate the opportunities that arise from the creation of new seats, the redrawing of old ones, or the retirements that often accompany post-redistricting elections. The effects of redistricting and the anti-incumbent mood that gripped the nation encouraged roughly 350 candidates who had officeholding experience to run in 1992.

Candidates who have significant campaign and political experience but who have never held elective office also respond to the opportunities that emerge in specific election years. These 'unelected politicians' include legislative and executive branch aides, political appointees, state and local party officials, political consultants, and individuals who have previously lost a bid for Congress. Most of these politicians think strategically. Prior to deciding to run, they monitor voter sentiment, assess the willingness of political activists and contributors to support their campaigns, and keep close tabs on who is likely to oppose them for the nomination or in the general election.

Unelected politicians differ from elected officials in their perceptions of what constitutes a good time to run. Elected officials are more likely than unelected politicians to view post-redistricting elections favourably.

The major reason for this difference is that the candidacies of elected officials weigh heavily in the strategic calculations of unelected politicians. Unelected politicians are well aware that most elected officials possess name recognition and fund-raising advantages over them. Unelected politicians typically balk at the opportunity to contest a primary against an elected official, even when other circumstances appear favourable. Indeed, the two most recent post-redistricting elections witnessed large numbers of candidates who had previously held elective office and correspondingly few unelected politicians.

Political amateurs are an extremely diverse group, and it is difficult to generalise about their political decision-making. Only a small subgroup of amateurs, referred to as *ambitious amateurs*, behave strategically, responding to the same opportunities and incentives that influence the decisions of more experienced politicians. The majority of amateurs do not spend much time assessing these factors. *Policy amateurs*, comprising another subgroup, are driven by issues, while *experience-seeking* or *hopeless amateurs* run out of a sense of civic duty or for the thrill of running itself.

Record numbers of amateurs ran in the 1982 and 1992 elections. A few of these amateurs were ambitious challengers, who after weighing the costs of campaigning and the probability of winning declared their candidacies. Many policy and experience-seeking amateurs also felt compelled to run in 1992. They found in the political landscape an ideal backdrop for running advocacy-oriented or anti-incumbency campaigns. Calls for change, pervasive incumbent-bashing in the press, and the predictions of tremendous turnover attracted all types of amateurs.

Because it is so difficult to defeat an incumbent, most of the best-qualified office-seekers usually wait until a seat opens, through either retirement or death of the incumbent, before throwing their hats into the ring. Once a seat becomes vacant, it acts like a magnet, drawing the attention and candidacies of many individuals. Several strategic politicians will usually express their interest in an open seat. Sixty-three per cent of the Democratic state and local officials who ran for the House in 1992 ran in the 18 per cent of the races in which there was no incumbent at the beginning of the 1992 election. Open seats also drew the greatest number of Republicans with officeholding experience and disproportionate numbers of unelected politicians from both parties.

Others involved in the decision to run

The drive to hold elective office may be rooted in an individual's personality and tempered by the larger political environment, but potential candidates rarely reach a decision about running for Congress without touching base with a variety of people. Nearly all candidates single out their family and friends as having a decisive impact on their decision to enter or to forgo the race. In Virginia's 8th district, for example, Kerry Donley, a young, ambitious and highly regarded Democrat from a politically active family, remarked that his family 'would probably shoot him' if he decided to run in 1992. Donley's sentiments echo those of multitudes of politicians who decide not to set their sights on a seat in Congress because of family pressures or for career reasons.

Political parties, labour unions and other organised groups, and political consultants can also affect a prospective candidate's decision, but they have far less impact than the people who are directly involved in an individual's daily life. Potential candidates usually discuss their plans with these groups only after mulling over for a long time the idea of running. Sometimes, would-be candidates approach local party leaders, fellow party members in the House or the Senate, or officials from their party's state, national, congressional or senatorial campaign committee to learn about the kinds of assistance that would be available should they decide to run. On other occasions the party initiates the contact, seeking to nurture the interest of good prospects.

Barred from simply handing out the nomination, party leaders can influence a prospective candidate's decision to run in a variety of ways. State and local party leaders can help size up the potential competition and try to discourage others from contesting the nomination. In some states party leaders can help a candidate secure a pre-primary endorsement, but this does not guarantee nomination.

Members of Congress and the staffs of the Democratic and Republican congressional and senatorial campaign committees often encourage prospective candidates to run. Armed with favourable polling figures and the promise of party assistance in the general election, they search out local talent. Promising individuals are invited to meet with members of Congress and party leaders in Washington and to attend campaign seminars. They are also given lists of political action committees (PACs) and political consultants who possess some of the resources and skills needed to conduct a congressional campaign.

During the early and mid-1980s, national party committees also attempted to winnow the field of primary contestants by discouraging some individuals from filing candidacies. The goal of this activity, dubbed 'negative recruitment', was to prevent candidates from damaging one another in a decisive primary and to enable party members to unify quickly behind a nominee. National party activity in candidate recruitment can be risky, however. If the national party backs a candidate who is not the favourite of state or local party activists, it can demoralise local party members and damage the chances of the eventual nominee. As a result of the conflicts that occasionally emerged and a belief that negative recruitment caused more harm than good, party organisations in Washington reduced their intervention in congressional primaries in the late 1980s. Since that time, when more than one candidate has signed up to run for a nomination the national parties usually have remained neutral, waiting until the primary was over before becoming involved. The major exception to this rule has been when a primary challenger seriously threatens an incumbent.

Party recruitment is especially important and difficult when local or national forces favour the opposing party. Just as a strong economy or popular president can encourage members of the president's party to run, it can discourage members of the opposition party from declaring their candidacies, especially when an incumbent of the opposing party is seeking to remain in the seat. Sometimes the promise of party support can encourage a wavering politician to run under what at the outset appear to be less than optimal conditions.

Recruiting candidates to run for traditionally uncompetitive seats is not a major priority, but party committees work to prevent those seats from going uncontested. According to staffers from both parties' congressional and senatorial campaign committees, getting candidates to run for these seats is an important part of building for the future. These candidates can strengthen state and especially local party committees by giving them a campaign on which to focus and deepening the farm team from which candidates emerge. These candidacies help prepare a party for opportunities that might arise when an incumbent retires, House districts are redrawn, or a scandal or some other event changes the partisan dynamics in the district.

Labour unions, PACs and other organised groups typically play more limited roles in candidate recruitment than do parties. A few labour PACs and some trade association committees, such as the American Federation of Labor-Congress of Industrial Organisations (AFL-C10)'s Committee on Political Education (COPE) and the American Medical Association's AMPAC, take polls to encourage experienced politicians to run. Others, such as the Women's Campaign Fund, EMILY's List, and WISH List, which are pro-women PACs, search out members of specific demographic groups and offer them financial support. Labour unions focus most of their candidate-recruitment efforts, and campaign activities in general, on Democrats. Ideological PACs are among the most aggressive in searching out candidates, and many offer primary assistance to those who share their views. Few corporate PACs become involved in recruiting candidates because they fear offending incumbents.

Finally, political consultants can become involved in a potential candidate's decision-making. In addition to taking polls and participating in candidate-training seminars, consultants can use their knowledge of a state or district to assist a would-be candidate in assessing political conditions and sizing up the potential competition.

Passing the primary test

There are two ways to win a major-party nomination for Congress: in an uncontested nominating race or by defeating an opponent. Victory in an uncontested primary or caucus is common in situations where a congressional seat is held by an incumbent. Even in the 1992 elections, which were marked by a record number of nonimcumbent candidacies, 52 per cent of all representatives and 42 per cent of all senators who sought re-election were awarded their party's nomination without having to defeat an opponent.

Incumbent victories in uncontested primaries

Victories by default occur mainly when an incumbent is perceived to be invulnerable. The same advantages of incumbency and pre-election activities that make incumbents confident of re-election make them seem invincible to those contemplating a primary challenge. Good constituent relations, policy representation and other job-related activities are sources of incumbent strength. A hefty campaign account is another.

The loyalties of political activists and organised groups also discourage party members from challenging their representatives for the nomination. While in office, members of Congress work to advance the interests of those who supported their previous election, and in return they routinely receive the support of these individuals and groups. With this support comes the promise of endorsements, campaign contributions, volunteer campaign workers, and votes. Would-be primary challengers often recognise that the groups whose support they would need to win the nomination are often among the incumbent's staunchest supporters. Senior incumbents also benefit from the clout – real and perceived – that comes with moving up the ranks of the congressional leadership.

Junior incumbents rarely have the same kind of clout in Washington or as broad a base of support as senior legislators, but because they tend to devote a great deal of time to expanding their bases of support they too typically discourage inside challenges. Junior members also may receive special attention from national, state and local party organisations. Both the Democratic Congressional Campaign Committee and the National

Republican Congressional Committee hold seminars immediately after the election to instruct junior members on how to use franked mail, town meetings and local press to build voter support. Prior to the start of the campaign season these party committees advise junior members on how to defend their congressional roll-call votes, raise money and discourage opposition.

Local party activists, who form the pool of potential candidates from which inside opposition usually emerges, are generally more inclined to help junior legislators than to challenge them because these activists often worked to elect that individual in the first place. Their loyalties tend to be especially strong when the seat is competitive or was held by the opposition party for a long period of time.

This rarely protects House members who are vulnerable because of scandal. Incumbents who are implicated in some highly publicised ethical transgression face more challenges from within their own party than others. The 1992 elections were unique for the number of House members who were under the cloud of scandal. Yet some of these legislators, including several who were implicated in the House banking scandal, faced no primary opposition. Most often, opposition failed to materialise because the member's ethical difficulties did not become public until after the state's primary filing deadline had already passed or it was too late for a challenger to mount a campaign.

Contested primaries with an incumbent

When incumbents do face challenges for their party's nomination, they almost always win. Of the 174 House members who had to compete for their party's nomination in 1992, only 19 were defeated, including 4 who were defeated in incumbent-versus-incumbent primaries that were brought about by redistricting. Only those members of Congress who have been accused of an ethical transgression, lost touch with their district, or suffer from failing health run a significant risk of falling to a primary challenger.

What kinds of challengers succeed in knocking off an incumbent for the nomination? The answer is candidates who have either held lower-level office or had some other significant political experience. Only 14 per cent of the 1992 challengers who sought to defeat an incumbent in the primary had been elected to lower office, and fewer than 3 per cent had significant nonelective political experience. Yet these candidates accounted for 60 per cent of the Democrats and 40 per cent of the Republicans who defeated an incumbent in the primary.

Individuals who have held elective office or have some significant unelective political experience are generally more successful than political amateurs. Experienced candidates are able to take advantage of previous contacts to gain the support of the political and financial elites who contribute to or volunteer in political campaigns. Candidates who have officeholding experience are usually in a very strong position in this regard because they often enjoyed these elites' backing in previous campaigns and can make the case that they know what it takes to get elected. Some of these candidates have consciously used a lower-level office as a stepping-stone to Congress. The success rates that these candidates enjoy demonstrate that political experience can improve one's odds of wresting a party nomination from an incumbent.

Open primaries

Opposing-incumbent primaries are those primaries in which an incumbent of the opposing party has decided to seek re-election. A second type of open nomination, called open-seat primaries, occurs in districts in which there is no incumbent seeking re-election. Both types of primary attract more candidates than contests in which a nonincumbent must defeat an incumbent in the primary in order to win the nomination, but opposing-incumbent primaries are usually the less hotly contested of the two.

Political experience was a determining factor in many opposing-incumbent primaries in 1992. Elected officials comprised about 14 per cent of the candidates but 22 per cent of the winners in these contests. They enjoyed a success rate of about 65 per cent. Unelected politicians accounted for a smaller portion of the candidates and winners, but they had very high success rates. Political amateurs overwhelmed the other two groups both in numbers of candidates and in numbers of victorious candidates. Nevertheless, their success rates were far lower than those of more experienced primary contestants.

Nominations, elections and representation

The electoral process – which transforms private citizen to candidate to major-party nominee to House member – greatly influences the makeup of the first branch of the national government. Those parts of the process leading up to the general election, especially the decision to run, play a major role in producing a Congress that is not demographically representative of the US population. The willingness of women and minorities to run for Congress during the past few decades and of voters to support them have helped make the national legislature somewhat more representative in terms of gender and race. Still, in many respects Congress does not mirror American society.

Occupation

Occupation has a tremendous impact on the pool of House candidates and on the candidates' prospects for success. Individuals who claim law, politics or public service (many of whom have legal training) as their profession are a minuscule portion of the general population but comprise 35 per cent of all nomination candidates, 46 per cent of all successful primary candidates, and 57 per cent of all House members (see Table 10.1). The analytical, verbal and organisational skills that it takes to succeed in the legal profession or in public service help these individuals undertake a successful bid for Congress. The high salaries that members of these professions earn give them the wherewithal to take a leave of absence from work so they can campaign full time. These highly paid professionals can also afford to make the initial investment that is needed to get a campaign off the ground. Moreover, their professions place many attorneys and public servants in a position to rub elbows with political activists and contributors whose support can be crucial to winning a House primary or general election.

Business professionals and bankers are not as over-represented among nomination candidates, major-party nominees or House members as are public servants and lawyers, but persons in business tend to be very successful in congressional elections. Many possess money, skills and contacts that are useful in politics. Educators (particularly college professors), entertainers and other white-collar professionals also enjoy a modicum of success in congressional elections. Of these, educators comprise the largest group of candidates. They rarely possess the wealth of lawyers and business professionals, but educators frequently have the verbal, analytical and organisational skills that are needed to get elected.

Just as some professions are over-represented in Congress, others are under-represented. Disproportionately few persons employed in agriculture or blue-collar professions either run for Congress or are elected. Even fewer students, homemakers, and others who are considered outside the workforce attempt to win a congressional seat.

Closely related to the issue of occupation is wealth. There were seventy-two millionaires in the House – 17 per cent of its members – following the 1992 election, far outstripping the less than one-half of one per cent of the population who enjoy similar wealth.

Table 10.1. *Occupational representativeness of House candidates and members, 1992*

Occupation	General population	Nomination candidates	General election candidates	House members
Agricultural or blue-collar workers	26%	7%	6%	4%
Business or banking	12	18	18	17
Clergy or social work	0.4	1	1	1
Education	2	7	9	10
Entertainer, actor, writer or artist	1	1	2	3
Law	0.3	16	23	34
Medicine	1	3	2	1
Military or veteran	1	0.5	1	0.2
Politics or public service	–	19	23	23
Other white-collar professionals	17	6	5	6
Outside workforce	35	2	1	1
Unemployed	4	–	–	–
Unidentified, nonpolitical occupation	–	20	8	0
(N)	(248,718,000)	(2,015)	(843)	(435)

Notes:
Figures include all 1992 major-party House candidates and all members of the 103rd Congress, including Rep. Bernard Sanders (I-Vt.). The figures for the general population are from 1990. Some columns do not add to 100 per cent because of rounding.
Sources: General population figures are from U.S. Department of Commerce, Bureau of the Census, *Statistical Abstract of the United States* (Washington, DC: US Government Printing Office, 1992), xii, 18, 392–4; candidate occupation data are from various issues of *Congressional Quarterly Weekly Report*.

Gender

Far fewer women than men run for Congress (see Figure 10.1). Even in 1992, which was widely proclaimed the "Year of the Woman', only 13 per cent of all contestants for major-party nominations were female. Women are under-represented among congressional candidates for a number of reasons. Active campaigning demands greater time and flexibility than most people – but in particular, women – can afford. Women continue to assume primary parenting responsibilities in most families, a role that is difficult to combine with long hours of campaigning. It is only since the 1980s that significant numbers of women have entered the legal and busi-

Percent

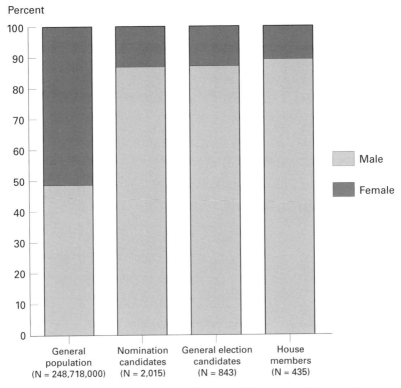

Figure 10.1 Gender representativeness of House candidates and
members.
Sources: General population figures are from U.S. Department of
Commerce, Bureau of the Census, *Statistical Abstract of the United
States* (Washington, DC: U.S. Government Printing Office, 1992), xii,
18, 392–4; candidate gender data are from various issues of
Congressional Quarterly Weekly Report.
Notes: Figures include all 1992 major-party House candidates and all
members of the 103rd Congress, including Rep. Bernard Sanders
(I–Vt.). The figures for the general population are from 1990.

ness professions, which often serve as training grounds for elected
officials and political activists. Women also continue to be under-
represented in state legislatures and other elective offices, which commonly serve as stepping-stones to Congress.

Once women decide to run, gender does not affect their election
prospects. Women are just as likely to advance from primary candidate to
nominee to House member as are men. As more women come to occupy

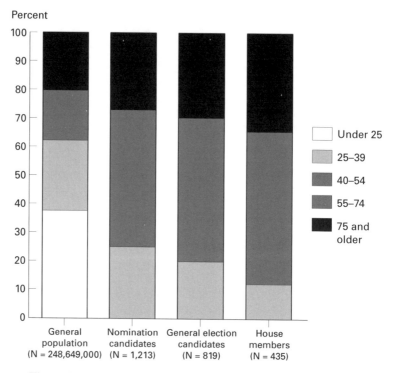

Figure 10.2 Age representativeness of House candidates and members, 1992.
Sources: General population figures are from U.S. Department of Commerce, Bureau of the Census, *Statistical Abstract of the United States* (Washington, DC: U.S. Government Printing Office, 1992), xii, 18, 392–4; candidate age data are from various issues of *Congressional Quarterly Weekly Report.*
Notes: Figures include 1992 major-party House candidates and all members of the 103rd Congress, including Rep. Bernard Sanders I–Vt.). The figures for the general population are from 1990. The Ns differ from those in Figures 10.1 and 10.3 because of missing data.

lower-level offices or to hold positions in the professions from which congressional candidates usually emerge, the proportion of women candidates and members of Congress can be expected to increase.

Age

Congressional candidates are also somewhat older than the general population, and this is only partly due to the age requirements imposed by the

Constitution. The average candidate for the nomination is almost twice as likely to be between forty and fifty-four years of age as to be between twenty-five and thirty-nine years of age (see Figure 10.2). Moreover, successful nomination candidates tend to be older than those whom they defeat. The selection bias in favour of forty to seventy-four year olds continues into the general election; as a result, Congress is made up largely of persons who are middle-aged or older.

The under-representation of young people is due to an electoral process that allows older individuals to benefit from their greater life experiences. People who have reached middle age typically have greater financial resources, more political experience, and a wider network of political and professional associates to help them with their campaigns. Moreover, a formidable group of forty to seventy-four year olds – current representatives – also benefit from considerable incumbency advantages.

Race and ethnicity

Race and ethnicity, like gender, have a greater impact on candidate emergence than on electoral success. Whites are heavily over-represented in the pool of nomination candidates, while persons of other races are underrepresented (see Figure 10.3). This reflects the disproportionately small numbers of minorities who have entered the legal or business professions or who occupy state or local offices.

Once minority persons declare their candidacies, they have fairly good odds of winning. The recent successes of minority House candidates are largely due to redistricting processes that were intended to promote minority representation. A few House members, such as Gary Franks, an African American Republican who represents the 5th district of Connecticut, Jay Kim, an Asian American Republican Party (GOP) member who was recently elected in California's 41st district, and Ron Dellums, a twelve-term African American Democrat from California's 9th district, were elected in districts that were not specifically carved to promote minority representation in Congress. However, most minority candidates are elected in districts that have large numbers of votes belonging to their racial or ethnic group.

Party differences

Public servants and members of the legal profession comprise a large portion of each party's candidate pool, but many Republican candidates come from the business world, and many Democratic candidates are educators (see Table 10.2). These differences reflect patterns of support that

Percent

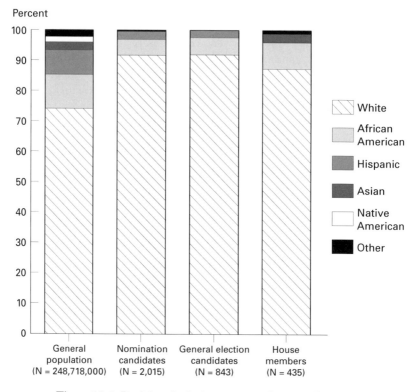

Figure 10.3 Racial and ethnic representativeness of House candidates and members, 1992.
Sources: General population figures are from U.S. Department of Commerce, Bureau of the Census, *Statistical Abstract of the United States* (Washington, DC: U.S. Government Printing Office, 1992), xii, 18, 392–4; candidates race data are from various issues of *Congressional Quarterly Weekly Report*.
Notes: Figures include all 1992 major-party House candidates and all members of the 103rd Congress, including Rep. Bernard Sanders (I–Vt.). The figures for the general population are from 1990.

exist for the parties among voters. The GOP's over-representation of business professionals continues through each stage of the election, but the differences for teachers disappear after the nomination stage. Educators comprised 10 per cent of both the House Democratic Caucus and the House Republican Conference after the 1992 election.

Candidates from the legal and entertainment professions are the sources of the largest occupational differences between the parties. Attorneys from both parties do well in House elections, but lawyers are

Table 10.2. *Major-party nomination candidates, general election candidates, and House members, 1992*

	Nomination candidates		General election candidates		House members	
	Democrats	Republicans	Democrats	Republicans	Democrats	Republicans
Occupation						
Agricultural or blue-collar workers	6%	7%	5%	8%	3%	6%
Business or banking	13	23	13	23	12	25
Clergy or social work	1	1	2	1	2	1
Education	8	5	11	7	10	10
Entertainer, actor, writer or artist	1	2	1	3	1	5
Law	16	14	27	19	37	27
Medicine	3	3	2	2	1	1
Military or veteran	0.3	1	0.2	2	0.4	1
Politics or public service	20	18	24	23	24	23
Other white-collar professionals	7	6	6	4	8	3
Outside workforce	2	2	1	1	1	1
Unidentified, not politics	22	18	8	9	0	0
(N)	(1,039)	(976)	(424)	(419)	(258)	(176)
Gender						
Male	85%	91%	83%	91%	86%	94%
Female	15	9	17	9	14	6
(N)	(1,039)	(976)	(424)	(419)	(258)	(176)
40–54	53	43	57	44	59	47

Table 10.2. (cont.)

	Nomination candidates		General election candidates		House members	
	Democrats	Republicans	Democrats	Republicans	Democrats	Republicans
Age						
Under 25	0%	0.2%	0%	0%	0%	0%
25–39	21	28	15	26	10	16
55–74	24	28	27	30	30	38
75 and older	1	1	2	0.3	2	1
(N)	(878)	(835)	(413)	(406)	(258)	(176)
Race and Ethnicity						
White	87%	98%	84%	96%	79%	97%
African American	9	0.4	9	3	14	0.6
Other	4	2	6	2	6	3
(N)	(1,039)	(976)	(424)	(419)	(258)	(176)

Notes:

Figures are full or major-party nomination candidates, all major-party general election candidates, and all major-party members of the 103rd Congress (which excludes Rep. Bernard Sanders (I-Vt.). Some data are missing for the age representation of nomination and general election candidates. Some columns do not add to 100 per cent because of rounding.

Sources: Compiled by the author from various issues of *Congressional Quarterly Weekly Report.*

more heavily over-represented in the Democratic than the Republican Party. Entertainers, on the other hand, have a bigger presence in the ranks of Republican legislators. Even though Republicans have historically been viewed as the defenders of the rich, slightly more House Democrats than Republicans are among Congress's wealthiest members.

More women run for Democratic than Republican nominations for Congress. This gender gap reflects the greater number of women who identify with the Democratic party and that party's greater acceptance of female candidates. Democratic and Republican women enjoy similar success rates in congressional primaries, but Democratic women have greater success in the general election than their GOP counterparts.

More Democratic than Republican primary candidates are between forty and fifty-four years of age, reflecting the different orientation of the two parties' activists toward politics. Democratic activists are more likely to consider politics a profession and to view a congressional election as an opportunity for midcareer advancement. Their Republican counterparts are more apt to pursue careers in the private sector. Many Republican activists run for Congress before they have taken major strides in their profession or after they have reached fifty-five, an age at which many individuals' careers have peaked. The initial age difference between Democrat and Republican candidates lays the foundation for an uneven trend toward a middle-aged Congress that continues through the primary and the general election.

The parties also draw candidates from different racial and ethnic groups. Republican primary contestants are overwhelmingly white, as are the GOP's nominees and House members. The Democratic Party attracts candidates from a wider array of groups. African Americans comprise 9 per cent of all Democratic primary winners and 14 per cent of all Democratic members of the House. Candidates of other races and Hispanics also do well, comprising 6 per cent of all victorious Democratic primary contestants and House members.

The Senate

The Senate historically has been less demographically representative than the House, but it, too, has been moving toward more accurately mirroring the US population in some important ways. Prior to the 1992 elections, the Senate had only two women. It also had two Asian American members (both from Hawaii), but no Native Americans or African Americans. Over 60 per cent of its members were at least fifty-five years of age. Senate members came from a variety of occupations, but most – roughly 47 per cent – were lawyers. Another 25 per cent were drawn from the business and banking communities, and 8 per cent were journalists. An additional 8 per cent were educators, and 6 per cent were from the agricultural sector. The remainder held a variety of positions, with 4 per cent claiming politics or public service as their profession. In short, descriptions of the Senate as a bastion of white, middle-aged, professional men were very close to the mark.

Part of the reason that the Senate has been slower to change than the House is that Senate terms are six years, and only one-third of the upper chamber is up for election at a time. Other reasons have to do with the heightened demands of Senate campaigns. As statewide races, Senate primary and general election campaigns require larger amounts of money, more extensive organisations and more complex strategies than do House campaigns. Successful Senate candidates generally possess more skill, political connections and campaign experience than do their House counterparts. The fact that so many members of the Senate had extensive political experience prior to their election suggests that the dearth of minorities in lower-level offices may help to explain why the upper chamber is changing more slowly than the lower. In order to gain seats in the Senate, members of traditionally under-represented groups have had first to place citizens in the offices that serve as stepping-stones to that body. As more women, African Americans and members of other under-represented groups are elected or appointed to local, state and federal offices, their numbers in the Senate will probably increase.

Nevertheless, a single election can have a tremendous impact on the Senate's makeup. After the polls closed in 1992, twelve new members had been elected to the upper chamber. Among these were five women, including the Senate's first African American woman, Carol Moseley-Braun (D-Ill.), as well as its first Native American, Ben Nighthorse Campbell (D-Colo.). The election also lowered the age distribution of senators but not enough to bring the members' average age below fifty-eight years. Some noteworthy changes took place in the professional backgrounds of members: the numbers of business executives and bankers fell from thirty-two to twenty-four, the number of lawyers fell by three, and the number of members claiming politics or public service as a career rose by five. The number of millionaires in the Senate remained unchanged at twenty-eight.

The addition of many new senators who claim public service as a profession is particularly telling, as it alludes to the fact that few of the individuals who are nominated to run for the Senate or eventually win a seat in the upper chamber lack political experience. Even 1992, which was considered one of the most promising years for outsider candidates in decades, resulted in the election of only one individual who had not previously worked in politics or run for office – Robert Bennett (R-Utah). Even Bennett was no newcomer to politics, having grown up the son of a senator. Despite the rhetoric of some of the candidates or the insurgent nature of their campaigns, all of those who were elected had some form of political experience. Senator Moseley-Braun had been Cook County recorder of deeds from 1988 through 1992 and assistant majority leader in the Illinois state house prior to that. Patty Murray (D-Wash.), the self-styled 'mom in tennis shoes', had served four years in the state senate. And Russ Feingold (D-Wis.), a 'liberal-populist' who went so far as to paint a contract with the voters on the garage doors of his middle-class home, had been a state senator for ten years.

A total of thirty-two of the senators in the 103rd Congress had previously served in the US House of Representatives, sixteen had been governors of their states, thirteen previously held some other statewide office, twelve had been state legislators, and fifteen had served in a local office. Another eight had served as party officials, political aides or presidential appointees, or had previously run for the Senate. Besides Bennett, only three senators – Bill Bradley (D-N.J.), Frank Lautenberg (D-N.J.) and Orrin Hatch (R-Utah) – were elected to the Senate without having previously held public office or some other important political position.

Although senators are more likely than representatives to have to defend their nominations, Senate primaries tend to be less competitive than those for the House. Not a single senator who sought to be renominated was defeated between 1982 and 1990. This helps to explain why Moseley-Braun's 1992 defeat of Sen. Alan Dixon in the Illinois primary sent such shock waves through Congress. The relative ease with which members of the Senate secure renomination can be attributed to a number of factors besides the tremendous demands that Senate primary contests make on challengers and their supporters. Like their counterparts in the House, members of the Senate use their office to help their state receive its share of federal projects, to garner positive coverage in the press, and to build support among voters. Senators, like representatives, also build huge campaign treasuries to discourage potential opponents. Finally, members of the Senate are shrewd enough to recognise when it is time to retire. The impact that scandal has on Senate turnover tends to be felt more through strategic retirements than primary defeats.

On the other side of the ledger, the most qualified opponent that a senator is likely to face in a primary is a current House member or some other elected official. Because these individuals are also highly strategic, only a few are willing to risk their current positions by picking a primary fight. Most prefer to wait until a seat becomes open.

When an incumbent does announce his or her retirement, or a member of the opposite party appears vulnerable, political parties, interest groups and even some campaign consultants help to shape the field of Senate candidates by encouraging potential candidates to declare their candidacies. These organisations promise the same types of support and under the same kinds of circumstances to potential Senate candidates as they offer to House candidates.

Party organisations rarely become involved in contested Senate primaries even though they may promise a candidate hundreds of thousands of dollars in campaign support upon winning the nomination. The parties' senatorial campaign committees are singled out by candidates as the most influential organisations in the candidate-recruitment process. Nevertheless, the decision to run for the Senate, like the decision to run for the House, is a highly personal one. Political organisations are not nearly as important as are the candidate's family and friends, nor are they as important as issues or ideology, a desire to improve governments, or the goal of becoming a national leader. In other words, the decisions made by potential Senate candidates may be influenced by a variety of political organisations, but these candidates, like most potential officeholders, tend to be self-starters.

11   Conclusions: comparing passages to power

Pippa Norris

Chapters in this book have looked at the process of recruitment in a range of advanced industrialised countries, focussing on common concerns in different systems. In order to explore this further on a more systematic basis we can turn to comparing simultaneous elections to the European Parliament in twelve member states. As discussed in the Introduction, one of the primary concerns driving interest in political recruitment lies in issues of 'social representation', meaning how far legislatures reflect the society from which they are drawn in terms of salient political cleavages like gender, class and region. The European Parliament would be ideally constituted, in this sense, if it were a microcosm of European society. Yet far from reflecting the electorate, the European parliament, in common with most legislatures, draws disproportionately from certain sections of society: the better educated, more affluent, middle aged and male (see Norris 1996a; Putnam 1976; Loewenberg and Patterson 1979; Lovenduski and Norris 1993). Moreover the proportion of working-class MPs in many parliaments has declined over time, with the professionalisation of political careers. Since the mid-1960s women have gradually edged towards increased representation in many European countries, although they remain far from parity (Lovenduski 1986; Lovenduski and Norris 1993).

To compare social representation across Europe we can first establish the background of candidates and incumbents in the 1994 European elections. We can go on to analyse how far this pattern of legislative recruitment can be explained by the supply and demand for candidates in the political market-place. In seeking to explain cross-national variations we will use the analytical framework outlined in the Introduction, which identifies four components of the recruitment process. In this framework the *supply* of candidates is understood to be determined by the motivation and political capital of candidates. By 'political capital' we mean all the assets which facilitate a political career, which vary by party, such as a record of party service, financial resources, or political networks. The *demand* for candidates is produced by the attitudes of gatekeepers. The structure of opportunities in the political market-place is influenced by the *recruitment process*, including party rules and procedures, and the *political system* including the legal regulations, electoral system, party system and political culture.

Supply-side explanations stress that the outcome reflects the aspirants who choose to pursue a political career. If few women, younger people or working-class aspirants want to become MEPs, perhaps because they lack ambition or political experience, then we would expect these groups to be scarce in the European assembly. On the other hand if these groups are seeking elected office, but core gatekeepers are not supporting them, then the explanation rests on the demand side of the equation. Supply and demand interact, as in the economic market-place. The introduction of gender quotas, for example, may change the behaviour of key gatekeepers, and may encourage more women to come forward. Candidates and selectors can also be expected to be influenced by the systemic structure of opportunities. Unfortunately most studies are limited to examining only one component of the process, usually cross-national variations in the political system or the party rules. In this analysis we can start to examine the interaction of all components simultaneously, thereby understanding supply and demand in the context of the political market-place.

This analysis uses data derived from the *European Candidate Study*, based on a mail questionnaire with responses from 1,233 EP candidates in nine member countries. Certain features of elections to the European parliament make them particularly suitable for this analysis. One long-standing problem with comparative studies of the proportion of social groups in the British House of Commons, the Japanese Diet and the German Bundestag is that it is not clear that we are comparing like with like, given the different powers, functions and rewards of elected office in these bodies. We know that the costs and benefits of running for office at different levels within one country – for example for the US Senate or the House of Representatives – produce candidates with widely different backgrounds. Even greater contrasts may be expected to be evident between parliaments cross-nationally. The advantage of focussing on European election in this Conclusion is that they occur simultaneously in members states, with candidates running for the *same* office in the context of different institutional and party settings. This provides a unique opportunity to test a variety of propositions about recruitment.

Nevertheless we should note certain serious limitations with this data set for our purposes. First, the evidence does not allow us to look directly at the attitudes of gatekeepers, although we can examine candidates' perceptions of selectors' powers and priorities. Even more importantly, there is no available evidence about the pool of eligibles who never succeeded in becoming European candidates. This means we cannot compare the supply of those pursuing a political career with those actually selected. Despite this serious limitation, we can draw an important distinction between candidates and elected members. Some face hopeless prospects, at the bottom of party lists or in unwinnable single-member districts. Others fight winnable contests where selection is tantamount to election. By comparing winners and losers we can analyse the characteristics which most enable candidates to succeed in selection and election.

First we can establish the basic pattern in social representation which we are seeking to explain in the context of the 1994 elections to the European parliament. While ideally it would be useful to compare the full range of social cleavages, in practice the limited number of working-class candidates for the European parliament (4.3 per cent of the sample in the survey) restricts the reliability of any analysis by socioeconomic group. This reflects the overwhelmingly middle-class and professional nature of legislative careers. Yet we can compare candidates and incumbent Members of the European Parliament in terms of their gender, generation, educational qualifications and employment sector, and focus on analysing the factors which promote or deter the election of women, where there have been strong demands for equal representation in recent years (Lovenduski and Norris 1993).

The social background of members

Gender

The representation of women in the European Parliament has gradually grown during the past four decades. The Common Assembly (1952–8) included one woman out of seventy-eight representatives, or 1.3 per cent of the total. This increased marginally to 3 per cent of members in the Parliament of the Six (1958–72), then 5.5 per cent in 1978 (European Commission 1979). Originally MEPs were nominated by national legislatures, and responsibility for the low representation of women rested squarely with the parliamentary parties. The major breakthrough came in the first direct elections in 1979, resulting in 69 women out of 410 representatives, or 16.8 per cent. The proportion increased, with some fluctuations, during the next decade until by 1994 one quarter of all MEPs were female. Based on trends since the first direct elections, we can estimate that women will achieve parity in the European Parliament in the year 2044.

Although members are being elected to a common body, female repre-

Table 11.1. *Women elected in European elections, 1979–94 (%)*

	1979	1984	1989	1994
Belgium	8	21	17	32
Denmark	31	38	38	44
Germany	15	20	31	35
France	22	21	23	31
Ireland	13	13	7	26
Italy	14	10	10	10
Luxembourg	33	17	33	33
Netherlands	24	28	28	32
UK	14	15	13	18
All nine	19	20	22	29
Greece		8	4	16
Portugal		4	13	8
Spain		10	15	33
All Twelve	19	16	19	25

Source: The Times Guide to the European Parliament successive volumes (Times Publications).

sentation varies substantially across member states (see Table 11.1). In 1994, women were 8 per cent of representatives in Portugal compared with 44 per cent in Denmark. Women are over a third of the members in six other countries. Women's representation in the European Parliament lags behind other member states most clearly in the UK, Greece, Italy and Portugal, respectively, often by a large margin. The comparison reveals a strong link between the proportion of women elected in each country to the European and national parliaments ($r=.63$, $p>.05$), as well as a strong correlation between the proportion of women MEPs and women members of national cabinets ($r=.73$, $p>.05$). This pattern strongly suggests that systematic patterns affect women's recruitment across these levels. Nevertheless countries such as France and Belgium have a far higher proportion of women in the European than national parliaments, while the reverse is true in the Netherlands and Denmark.

Generation

There are certain significant variations in the age of candidates (see Table 11.2), who were classified into the younger generation (under 35), the

Table 11.2. *Age of candidates*

	Younger	Middle	Older
All	24	59	17
Candidates	26	58	16
MEPs	6	70	24
Belgium	23	58	19
Britain	19	67	14
Denmark	28	55	17
France	18	62	20
Germany	31	53	16
Ireland	9	64	27
Italy	15	69	17
Luxembourg	13	65	23
Netherlands	19	66	16
Spain	24	54	21
PES – Socialists	18	68	15
ERP – Christian Democrats	30	56	15
LDR – Liberals	19	60	21
Greens	22	66	12
ERA	22	68	11
EDN	27	59	15
Independent	25	47	38
Men	23	59	18
Women	25	62	14

Note:
Younger (18–35 years), Middle (36–55), Older (56 plus).
Source: ECS-94.

middle-aged (36–55), and the older members (56 or older). The results of the survey show that across the whole pool about a quarter of all candidates came from the younger generation. The proportion was highest in Germany and Denmark and lowest in Ireland and Luxembourg. Not surprisingly, the majority of candidates were middle-aged (59 per cent), while less than a fifth (17 per cent) were in the oldest category. In terms of party group, there was little variation by age, except that, perhaps surprisingly, there were slightly more younger candidates in the Christian Democrats (EPP) than in any other party group, including the Greens. The age profile of candidates could be significant if, as Inglehart suggests, the younger generation bring a distinctive set of values and priorities to public life (Inglehart 1977, 1991; Abramson and Inglehart 1995).

Education

One of the most striking long-term trends in many parliaments is the gradual rise in university-educated members, documented in earlier chapters. As shown in Table 11.3, the majority of the candidates were university graduates, as were three-quarters of the MEPs. Educational qualification showed some variations by party and country, with candidates most highly educated from Spain, Britain and France, with fewer university graduates in Ireland, Germany and Belgium. Women were also less likely to be graduates than men.

Employment Sector

Lastly the majority of respondents worked in the public sector (see Table 11.3), although this was more common for MEPs than for candidates. As one might expect the sectoral cleavage did divide the parties of left and right in the expected direction, with more Christian Democrats, Liberals and Independents drawn from private sector employment. Public sector workers were also more common in the Netherlands than elsewhere, and such employment was also slightly more typical for women. Given this pattern, how do we start to explain the social biases?

The structure of opportunities

The structure of opportunities is determined first by the *legal* requirements which make citizens eligible to stand for election. The laws controlling candidacies vary in the nationality requirements, the use of dual mandates, public funding of campaigns, and the method of filling vacancies between elections (see Jacobs and Corbett 1990: 13–24; Nugent 1994: 186–9). In most European countries, except for Germany and Finland, the law does not influence the procedures parties use to select their candidates. The legal requirements cannot explain the under-representation of most social groups in the European Parliament: women and working-class citizens have equal rights to stand as candidates in every European country. There are some age barriers since normally citizens have to be at least eighteen years old but other legal restrictions on candidacies are minimal.

The *electoral system* may prove a more significant barrier. One of the best-established generalisations about female representation suggests that the electoral system plays a decisive role (Darcy et al.1994; Rule and Zimmerman 1992; Rule 1987; Norris 1985; Norris 1996a). Three pos-

Table 11.3. *Background of candidates*

	Women %	Graduate %	Public sector %
All	28	59	59
Candidates	31	57	47
MEPs	28	76	59
Belgium	45	53	48
Britain	27	72	41
Denmark	34	38	47
France	30	72	53
Germany	24	51	44
Ireland	8	50	50
Italy	21	67	50
Luxembourg	38	58	38
Netherlands	26	66	71
Spain	32	78	49
PES – Socialists	39	68	62
ERP – Christian Democrats	25	56	44
LDR – Liberals	27	60	41
Greens	39	66	56
ERA	33	68	50
EDN	30	59	67
Independent	18	47	46
Men		63	47
Women		50	54

Source: ECS-94.

sible factors may affect women's representation: the ballot structure (whether party list, semi-proportional or single candidate); district magnitude (the number of seats per district); and the degree of proportionality (the allocation of votes to seats). The literature remains divided about which of these factors is most important. Darcy et al. (1994) suggest that in the United States ballot structure (whether single or multimember) is significant, whereas district magnitude (how large a multimember district is) does not seem to affect women's representation. Similar findings have been reported for Britain (Studlar and Welch 1991; Welch and Studlar 1990). In contrast previous work by Norris (1996a), comparing female representation in forty-seven democracies, suggests that, all other things being equal, district magnitude seems the most significant component of electoral systems.

Table 11.4. *Electoral system in European elections*

Country	No. of MEPs	Eligibility for candidacy	Electoral system	Open or closed lists	No. of seats	District Magnitude
Belgium	25	21	PR	Open	4	6.3
Denmark	16	18	PR	Open	1	16.0
Germany	99	18	PR	Closed	1	99.0
Greece	25	21	PR	Closed	1	25.0
Spain	64	18	PR	Closed	1	64.0
France	87	23	PR	Closed	1	87.0
Ireland	15	21	STV		4	3.8
Italy	87	21	PR	Open	5	17.4
Luxembourg	6	21	PR	Open	1	6.0
Netherlands	31	25	PR	Open	1	31.0
Portugal	25	18	PR	Closed	1	25.0
UK	84	21	Plurality		84	1.0
N. Ireland	1	21	STV		3	0.3

Source: Neil Nugent *The Government and Politics of the European Union* Durham NC: Duke University Press, 1994.

There are limited but important cross-national variations in the electoral systems used for the European Parliament, which allow these factors to be tested systematically (see Table 11.4). In European elections Britain is the only country using single member districts with simple plurality voting (first-past-the-post). Northern Ireland and Eire use a single transferable vote system in multi-member districts. The remaining countries use party list proportional representation, with d'Hondt quotas, based on either regional lists (Belgium, Italy), or the whole country as one constituency (Denmark, Greece, Germany, Spain, Portugal, France, Luxembourg, Netherlands). There are other variations, including the use of closed party lists (Germany, Greece, France, Spain and Portugal), or those which allow preferential voting in the order of candidates within the party list, or even vote splitting for candidates from different lists (Luxembourg).

The party system – the relatively enduring features of party competition within a country – may also influence candidate recruitment. Since Duverger, studies have suggested that a major factor facilitating women's entry into elected office is the strength of parties on the centre-left, including Labour, Social Democrat and Communist parties, with the more recent addition of the Greens (Duverger 1955: 82; European Commission 1979: 3; Lovenduski and Norris 1993; Norris 1985). We can compare the percentage of seats won by parties on the left, classified

Table 11.5. *Impact of the political system on women's representation*

	Stand. Betas	Sig. T	Coding
Electoral system			
Ballot structure	0.70	0.01	FPTP (0), STV (0.5), Party List (1)
District magnitude	0.08	0.45	Seats per district
Proportionality	0.22	0.07	Votes/seat
Party system			
Strength of left parties	0.41	0.01	% party seats in EP
Political culture			
Catholicism	0.77	0.01	% Catholic pop.
R^2	0.67		

Note:
Standardised beta coefficients in regression analysis with the percentage of women MEPs per country per election (N.46) as the dependent variable.

by their affiliation with European Parliamentary groups. Left-wing parties are defined as those affiliated with the Group of the Party of European Socialists (PES), Group of the Greens in the European Parliament, the Rainbow Alliance (RBW), and the Left Unity (LU).

The *political culture* – the dominant norms and values in any country – may also influence recruitment. Evidence from the series of EuroBarometers in the 1980s has demonstrated how attitudes towards female equality vary substantially among member states (deVaus and McAllister 1989; European Commission 1979, 1983, 1987; Wilcox 1991). The strength of Catholicism provides a cultural indicator of traditional attitudes which has been used to investigate this relationship (Mayer and Smith 1985; Rule 1987), and which provides a consistent measure over time.

To analyse the effects of these variables an OLS multiple regression model can be used. The dependent variable is the proportion of women elected in each country in the four successive contests from 1979 to 1994, producing forty-six separate units of analysis. Looking first at the effects of the electoral system, the results in Table 11.5 show that the type of ballot structure was significantly related to the election of women MEPs, although not the proportionality or district magnitude of electoral systems used for European Parliamentary elections. The critical difference seems to be whether or not electoral systems use party lists.

The strength of left-wing parties also proved highly significant. This may reflect a more egalitarian ideology in these parties, which stresses access for all political minorities, gender equality in other spheres of public policy, and favours the use of gender quotas. In contrast European parties of the right, such as the Christian Democrats, Conservative and Liberal parties, seem less favourably inclined towards selecting women candidates. Of course, in countries where parties of the left adopt many women candidates this in turn may stimulate parties of the right to follow suit. Yet the results confirm as we would expect that the stronger the left-wing share of EP seats, the higher the proportion of women MEPs.

The cultural measure of Catholicism was also linked to the representation of women. Cultural attitudes towards traditional sex roles may influence the willingness of women to come forward as candidates, and the support they receive from party members, community groups, local factions and voters. In total, the model explained a high proportion (67 per cent) of variance in the country/election results for women MEPs. This confirms the significance of the political system in setting the context for legislative recruitment. Even if every EP candidate was selected using identical recruitment procedures within parties, we would still expect to find significant cross-national variations in social representation.

The effects of the recruitment process

The political system sets the general structure of opportunities within any country. But entry into elected office can be expected to be influenced by the recruitment process. Political parties remain the main gatekeepers to elected office throughout Europe, although interest groups, the media and financial supporters may play a crucial role. The key selectors within parties may be grassroots members, delegates at local conventions, regional officers, factions, affiliated interest groups or national leaders, depending on the centralisation of the system. Decisions by gatekeepers take place within the context of formal rules, and informal practices, which constrain choice (for comparative studies see Lovenduski and Norris 1993; Gallagher and Marsh 1988; Gallagher, Laver and Mair 1995; Epstein 1980; Ranney 1981; Katz and Mair 1992; Norris 1997). Previous studies emphasise that the use of affirmative action strategies, and the centralisation of the selection process, may be expected to have a significant impact on the outcome.

In terms of affirmative action programmes, many parties in Europe have adopted gender quotas in an attempt to boost women's representation (Lovenduski and Norris 1993; Norris 1994). There is considerable

Table 11.6. *Perceived support by gatekeepers*

	Men	Women	Difference
Women's organisations	4.15	5.62	1.47**
Party officials	5..49	5.77	0.28*
Other groups	4.53	4.80	0.27
Local party members	6.06	6.23	0.17
National party factions	5.07	5.24	0.17
National party leaders	5.70	5.81	0.11
Community groups	4.76	4.82	0.06
Local party leaders	6.01	6.04	0.03
Regional party leaders	5.93	5.86	−0.07
Youth organisations	4.99	4.91	−0.08
Trade unions	4.14	4.04	−0.1
Business groups	4.02	3.82	−0.2

Notes:
Q. 'In becoming a candidate for the EP, did you get opposition or
support from the following . . .?', with a list of groups involved in
recruitment, using a seven-point scale ranging from high opposition
(1) to high support (7).
* $p<.05$ ** $p<.001$.
Source: ECS-94.

variation in the measures adopted worldwide. Quotas are enacted by
legislation in a few countries, for example where religious groups, ethnic
minorities and/or women are entitled to a certain proportion of places on
party lists of candidates, or reserved seats in parliaments. More commonly, quotas are implemented by internal party rules, constitutions and
procedures. The worldwide review by the *Inter-Parliamentary Union*
(1992) found that twenty-two parties employed gender quotas for legislative elections, while fifty-one parties used them for elections to internal
party posts. These measures were commonly introduced in Western
Europe during the 1980s by parties of the left (Social Democratic,
Labour, Communist, Socialist and Greens) (see Table 11.6) although in
some countries they have been adopted across all parties.

The centralisation of decision-making

Another factor which may affect demand for women candidates is *who*
selects. The primary gatekeepers to elected office may be highly centralised, if national leaders and party officials are empowered to handpick

candidates through a process of personal patronage, as in the Greek PASOK party. Alternatively the decision-making process may be devolved downwards if key gatekeepers are local organisations, constituency officials, grassroots members and voters, as in the German SDP. One hypothesis which has been suggested (Randall 1987), but never examined systematically, is that more centralised recruitment is beneficial to women, on the grounds that the party leadership is more likely to be well educated and relatively liberal in their attitudes towards gender equality. Yet alternatively, equally plausibly, a selection process with decision-making devolved downwards towards ordinary party members may prove more permeable for entry by minority challengers.

In previous studies it has proved difficult to identify the key players in the selection process at anything more than an anecdotal level due to the complexities of the decision-making process within each party. Reviews have attempted to summarise the primary 'selecting agency' in each country, such as the national executive or constituency committee (Ranney 1981; Gallagher, Laver and Mair 1995: 254), but these summaries represent a considerable oversimplification: in practice many groups influence different stages of the recruitment process; a series of decisions, not one, produces the eventual outcome; practices vary substantially between different parties in a country; and formal constitutional powers may disguise de facto control. The formal rules (see Katz and Mair 1994) provide only an approximate guide to procedures.

Nevertheless we have candidate perceptions of the relative influence of different bodies on the selection process within their own party (see Table 11.7). Candidates were asked: 'In your party, how much power do the following groups have to select candidates for the European parliament?', using a seven-point scale ranging from 'little power' to 'much power'. Based on this data, we can develop a cumulative weighted scale, ranging from highly centralised recruitment processes, where national leaders and bodies are perceived to have the greatest influence, down to highly localised systems, where grassroots party members and local groups are believed to have the greatest influence. The results of the comparison show considerable cross-national variations, with Ireland and Britain having the most localised decision-making process in this comparison, while central party leaders played the greatest role in Luxembourg, Spain and the Netherlands. Nevertheless a simple correlation between the centralisation of the selection process and the gender of candidacies proved to be insignificant. While *who* selects may therefore prove critical for issues of internal party democracy, this seems to have no direct impact on the relative success of women candidates.

Table 11.7. *Parties using gender quotas in EU countries (1992)*

		Party quotas	Candidate quotas	%
Belgium	CVP	Y	Y	–
	PS	Y	N	20
	PVV	Y	Y	20
Denmark	SDP	Y	Y	40
	SPP	Y	Y	40
France	PS	Y	N	–
Germany	SDP	Y	Y	40
	Greens	Y	Y	50
Greece	NDP	Y	N	–
	CPL	Y	N	40
Ireland	Labour	Y	N	20
Italy	DC–	–	Y	
	CP	Y	Y	30
	Greens	–	Y	50
Luxembourg	GAP	Y	N	40
	Socialist	Y	N	–
Netherlands	PvdA	–	Y	33
	Groes Lin	–	Y	40
	CDA	–	Y	26
Portugal	Socialist	Y	N	25
Spain	PSOE	Y	N	25
	CP	Y	N	25
UK	Lab	Y	Y	
	Lib Dem	Y	N	33
	PC	Y	N	
		20	13	

Source: Women and Political Power (Inter-Parliamentary Union, Geneva, 1992).

The demands of selectors

One pervasive theme in the scholarly literature, and in popular wisdom, is that women and working-class candidates face a major barrier in the attitudes of selectors. Many believe that party members and voters hold sex-role stereotypes which reinforce images of women in traditional roles, and thereby undermine the qualities and experience which women bring to public life. These attitudes may be particularly influential in preventing women from being selected to fight winnable contests (Vallance 1979;

Table 11.8. *Powers of selectorate*

	Central summary scale	National party leaders	National party factions	Regional party leaders	Local party leaders	Local party members	Party officials
Luxembourg	3.8	6.4	5.6	4.3	2.8	2.6	3.1
Spain	3.4	6.1	4.5	5.4	3.6	3.1	5.2
Netherlands	3.0	5.5	3.7	4.1	3.1	2.9	4.5
Belgium	3.0	5.6	3.9	3.9	2.6	2.6	3.3
Italy	2.8	5.8	4.0	5.3	4.4	3.9	3.2
France	2.8	6.3	3.6	4.0	3.2	3.1	3.0
Denmark	2.6	3.8	4.4	4.5	4.0	4.4	2.7
Germany	2.5	4.7	3.5	5.2	4.6	3.9	4.2
Britain	1.5	1.7	1.7	2.5	3.9	6.8	2.5
Ireland	1.2	1.4	1.4	1.4	1.4	1.4	3.1

Notes:
'In your party, how much power do the following groups have to select candidates for the European parliament?' Measured from 1 'Not very important' to 7 "Very important'. The Central summary scale added the party items weighted by national (*3), regional (×2) and local (×1).
Source: ERS-94.

Rasmussen 1983). Plausible evidence for direct or indirect discrimination is notoriously difficult to establish. One effective strategy is to examine the perceptions of candidates, to see whether they believed that they received support or opposition from key groups of selectors. To examine this the ECS-94 survey asked: 'In becoming a candidate for the EP, did you get opposition or support from the following...?', with a list of groups involved in recruitment, using a seven-point scale ranging from strong opposition (1) to strong support (7).

The results proved contrary to our initial hypotheses. In response to this item, as shown in Table 11.8, women candidates reported that they received more support than men from party officials, national party leaders and local party members, as well as from women's groups, although the gender difference did not prove statistically significant. Moreover, women candidates were also more likely than men to have been asked to stand. There are a number of ways to interpret the available evidence. It is possible that female candidates may have been being discriminated against, and they may not have been aware of it. Women aspirants who never became nominated as candidates may have received less support from selectors at an earlier stage of the process prior to formal nomination. Equally, it may be that women may not have come forward because they anticipated being discriminated against. These propositions are worth exploring further in subsequent research, but the available evidence strongly suggests that women who succeed in becoming candidates did not believe they were discriminated against by party selectors.

Voters' preferences

Another alternative is that, because of traditional attitudes, voters may discriminate against women candidates at the ballot boxes. Here we have a range of questions used in the *1994 European Election Study*, which provide indirect evidence about voter's attitudes towards women in power. The overall results proved broadly positive. In the study European voters were asked:

Several bodies, institutions or organizations in your country are supposed to deal with questions relating to the European Union. Do you think that these questions would be better dealt with or not if there were more women in decision-making positions in these bodies, institutions or organizations?

Only a third of European voters (32 per cent) gave a negative response to this while almost half (47 per cent) responded that there should be more women in power. Voters who expressed support for the inclusion of more women in decision-making positions were asked to which institutions this applied. People were particularly likely to cite the need to have more women in government (69 per cent), political parties (68 per cent), education (66 per cent), local authorities (64 per cent) and EU institutions (54 per cent).

The European Election Study also asked about the expected policy impact of women: 'In your opinion, would a greater number of women within decision-making bodies have a positive influence or not on decisions taken in the areas...?' The impact was thought to be most positive on family policy (81 per cent), equal opportunities policy (79 per cent), and education (69 per cent), perhaps reflecting traditional sex-role stereotypes, while there was far less support for the impact of women in the fields of industrial or foreign policy. Lastly, voters were asked whether they 'would have liked there to have been more female candidates put forward for the European elections in your country', where far more proved positive (48 per cent) than negative (32 per cent). Public support for the inclusion of more women in power, as measured by the series of EuroBarometers, has also steadily become more positive over the years (European Commission 1976, 1979, 1983, 1987).

Yet these changing attitudes cannot have a major effect on the outcome, since voters have little influence over which individual candidates win European elections, except in Eire and Northern Ireland. In countries using closed party list elections, if there is a swing towards their party, then candidates on the list will be elected in rank order. Countries like the Netherlands and Italy allow voters to express preferences for candidates within party lists, but in practice this rarely changes the rank order determined by parties. British voters can cast their ballot for individual candidates in single-member districts, but there is no evidence from aggregate data that electors discriminate for or against women candidates (Crewe, Norris and Waller 1992). Within the European Union only the Single Transferable Vote electoral system, used in Eire and Northern Ireland, routinely allows voters to prioritise candidates from the party slate within limited multi-member districts. In most countries, therefore, individual candidates for the European Parliament are dragged in and out of office, like flotsam and jetsam, on electoral tides beyond their making. Plausible explanations for female under-representation therefore do not seem to rest with the electorate.

The effect of supply

On the supply-side there are a range of complex factors which may influence whether candidates come forward to pursue a European parliamentary career. Turning first to the motivation of candidates, the literature which has developed in the United States places greatest emphasis on the *political ambition* of candidates (see Herrnson chapter 10; Kazee 1994; Ehrenhalt 1992; Fowler and McClure 1989). With the rise of political entrepreneurs, personal ambition has been found the best predictor of who runs for Congress from among the large pool of eligibles. American studies have also found a gender gap in political ambition, which may be attributable to early patterns of sex-role socialisation (Carroll 1994: 121–37). Along similar lines, at mass level European studies have noted a persistent gender difference in political interest, political discussion, party membership and participation in activities other than voting, which has diminished but not disappeared over time (Inglehart 1981; European Commission 1983; Klingemann and Fuchs 1995).

We can compare the ambition expressed by women and men candidates running for the European Parliament. In the survey, candidates were asked 'Where you most like to be ten years from now?', where they could give multiple answers to a series of alternatives such as a career in the European parliament, the national parliament, European leadership or wholly retired from public life. Yet again contrary to expectations, as shown in Table 11.9, women emerged as slightly more ambitious than men across each category, with the exception of being a member of the

Table 11.9. *Political ambition*

	Men	Women	Difference
European parliamentary career			
Member EP	43.1	48.3	5.2
Chair EP committee	12.5	17.7	5.2★
Rapporteur EP committee	7.1	10.1	3.0
National parliamentary career			
Member national parliament	24.7	28.4	3.7
Member national government	19.9	17.0	−2.9
European leadership			
European Commission	11.9	12.0	0.1
Head European agency	6.4	6.9	0.5
Chair parliamentary group	5.1	7.9	2.8
Retired from public life	22.9	25.2	2.3

Note:
Q: 'Where would you most like to be 10 years from now?' ★ p<.05.
Source: ECS 94.

national government, although the differences were usually not statistically significant. There is no evidence from this measure that women who run as European candidates are less serious in their political ambitions, or more willing to take a back-seat role in public life. Of course this measure is limited to information about candidates, and it cannot tell us whether there are gender differences in political ambition among activists at lower levels of party or elected office.

Motivational factors could be explored further since candidates were asked to rank the importance (1st, 2nd and 3rd) of different reasons for becoming a candidate. The list of reasons included standing because they wanted to support their party, they were asked to stand, they wanted to further their political career, they wanted to become an MEP, and because they were restanding as incumbent MEPs. There are plausible grounds to expect that candidates who saw themselves as party standard-bearers would be less likely to be in winnable seats than those who were more actively pursuing a European political career. The comparison in Table 11.10 suggest that there were few significant gender differences in results except that, interestingly, more women were candidates as a result of being asked to stand, while more men expressed overtly careerist sentiments. This supports anecdotal evidence that women candidates need greater encouragement to run than men, and this finding may have

Table 11.10. *Reasons for standing*

	Men	Women	Difference
I was asked to support my party	74.1	77.0	2.9
I was asked to stand	57.3	65.0	7.7**
I wanted to become an MEP	46.6	47.6	1.0
I thought it would help my political career	29.0	22.1	−6.9**
I am an MEP standing for re-election	6.6	7.3	0.7

Note:
Q: 'Why did you become a candidate for the European Parliament? Please rank the
following reasons in order of importance . . . 1st, . . . 2nd, . . . 3rd.' ** p<.01.
Source: ECS-94.

important implications for party strategies to boost female representation.

As discussed in this book's Introduction, an alternative supply-side
explanation is that the women and men have different amounts of *political
capital* which can be used to pursue office. People may be equally ambitious, but they may differ in the time they have available for campaigning,
in their political experience, and in their occupations, all of which can be
vital assets for legislative careers. 'Political capital' which may help candidates get selected for winnable contests can include the advantages of
incumbency, prior political experience, available time, occupational
background, age and educational qualifications.

Political careers in countries with strong mass-branch party systems,
like Australia, Germany and Britain, usually involve a long series of steps
which require work within parties and lower levels of office before applicants are considered credible candidates for Europe (see Wessels chapter
5; McAllister chapter 2). Yet, as we have seen in earlier chapters, in
countries like Canada and Finland the process is far more open to inexperienced political amateurs. New parties, like Berlusconi's Forza Italia,
often allow rapid promotion for many with little conventional political
experience. To examine the routes into European politics the survey
asked candidates whether they had ever held office in their party, in local,
regional and national government, in public bodies, and in group
organisations, as well as prior experience as EP candidates and MEPs.
The results, in Table 11.11, suggest that women and men differ somewhat in their political backgrounds. Men are more likely to have come
through the local government route, while women have slightly more
experience in local interest groups, and, more importantly, national
government. The findings reinforce the way women's organisations are an

Table 11.11. *Political experience*

	Men	Women	Difference
European parliament			
Been candidate	23.8	25.6	1.8
How often?	0.4	0.4	0.0
Been elected	8.0	9.5	1.5
How often?	0.2	0.1	0.0
Party office			
Local/regional party	33.3	32.5	−0.8
National party office	30.9	30.6	−0.3
Local government			
Candidate	59.7	55.2	−4.5
Elected	38.9	33.1	−5.8
National parliament			
Candidate	38.9	34.1	−4.8
Elected	7.7	12.3	4.6*
Member of government	4.9	7.6	2.7
Public body			
Local	26.2	27.1	0.9
National	20.2	18.0	−2.3
Group organisations			
Professional	22.5	21.8	0.7
Student	26.8	19.6	−7.2***
Trade union	19.1	18.9	−0.2
Women's organisations	3.6	30.0	26.4***
Local interest groups	28.6	34.1	5.5**
National interest groups	20.4	24.3	3.9
Summary experience scale	41.5	43.4	1.9

Notes:
Q: 'Have you ever . . . held office . . .?'
* $<.05$ ** $p<.01$ *** $p<.001$
Source: ECS-94.

important route for female candidates. But the overall summary scale suggests that, contrary to expectations, there were no significant differences in the political experience of women and men candidates.

Turning to *occupational experience*, brokerage careers such as those in the law or journalism may provide the flexibility, security and skills which serve as a launchpad for political office. The prior occupational experience for candidates shows predictable gender differences, which reflect the familiar horizontal and vertical patterns of occupational segregation

Table 11.12. *Influence of supply and demand*

	All	Women	Men	Coding
Political capital				
Incumbent MEP	0.50**	0.49**	0.49**	Incumbent MEP (1)
Others (0)				
Time	0.14**	0.23**	0.10**	Scale (v7) 1–35
Political experience	0.01	0.01	0.01	Scale from 0 to 15
Motivation				
MEP ambition	0.08**	0.11*	0.07**	v1 'I wanted to become an MEP'
Party standard-bearer	−0.05*	−0.09*	−0.03	v1 'I was asked to stand'
Gatekeeper demand				
Party support	0.04	0.03	0.06	Scale (v9) Support from group
Centralised selection	0.01	−0.04	0.03	Scale (v10) Power of selectors
Left–Right Party	0.05*	0.07	0.06*	L–R Scale EP Group
Personal background				
Age	0.05*	0.02	0.07*	Age categories (6)
Education	0.08*	0.03	0.09**	Graduate degree
Class	0.01	0.01	0.01	Middle/working
Sector	0.03	0.01	0.04	Public/private
Gender	0.01			Male/Female
R^2	0.35	0.36	0.36	

Notes:
The OLS regression analysis uses whether candidates won or lost as the dependent variable. The figures represent standardised (beta) coefficients.
See text for coding. * $p<.05$ ** $p<.01$.
Source: ECS-94.

in the workforce. More women candidates were drawn from the educational professions, secretarial work and political research, while more men were in commerce, business and management. Nevertheless it was not apparent that these gender differences among candidates were large enough to have a major impact on women's representation.

Political capital also includes the *time resources* which candidates can invest in pursuing winnable seats and campaigning. This emerged as one of the factors prioritised by selectors in Britain (Norris and Lovenduski 1995), and one of the factors which best predicted which such applicants became candidates. Time resources have also been found to play a major role in determining political participation at mass levels (Verba, Schlozman and Brady 1995). To assess these resources, candidates were asked how much time they planned to invest in a variety of political activities, such as public and party meetings, canvassing voters and contacting the media, during the May 1994 European campaign.

To consider whether supply or demand factors best predict who gets into the European Parliament, OLS regression analysis was used. The dependent variable was whether candidates won or lost. The results in Table 11.12 suggest the greater importance of supply over demand for winning candidacies. The analysis confirms the overwhelming advantages of incumbency status, and the importance of time resources, both of which proved highly significant in gaining winnable seats. Those who already held office in the European Parliament, and who could invest many hours in the forthcoming campaign, were at a clear advantage. The motivational factors also proved important in the expected direction, that is, those who were more ambitious to become an MEP won their contests, while party loyalists who stood as standard-bearers were less successful. In contrast in terms of gatekeeper demand, it did not seem to matter whether candidates received a great deal of support from different groups of selectors, nor whether the process of selection was localised or centralised. Lastly, turning to the personal background of candidates, age and education were significantly related to gaining winnable contests. In contrast gender, class and sector of employment dropped out of the equation. Overall the general model explained 35 per cent of variance in distinguishing winners and losers.

The model was run for all candidates, then separately for women and men to see if they came to parliament through different routes. The results indicate that the supply-side factors of incumbency status, time and motivation proved important for the success of men and women candidates in entering parliament, while in contrast gatekeeper demand did not prove significant for either. There were some other minor variations, in particular age and education served to distinguish the more successful men, but not women. Nevertheless in general it is the similarities in the factors leading to the election of women and men which are most striking.

Conclusions

The most important conclusion from this comparison is that *supply-side* factors proved more strongly related to candidates gaining winnable contests – and thus election to the European parliament – than demand-side factors. This confirms studies in earlier chapters which also found that the resources and motivation which candidates bring to the recruitment process are the primary factors explaining why some aspirants succeed while others fail. This suggests that one important reason why few women come forward to enter politics may be that they lack the time to pursue office. Politics is usually a highly demanding, taxing and risky career, made even more arduous by the additional travel requirements of the European parliament. With the familiar and well-established patterns of women's 'dual careers', at home and at work, the additional burden of politics could produce 'triple careers' which may prove too much.

Even more importantly, at the national level the results confirm once more the influence of the institutional structure of opportunities on women's representation, particularly the electoral system, party system and political culture. More women are elected in countries with egalitarian attitudes, with strong left-wing parties, and with proportional party-list electoral systems, than elsewhere.

Does this matter? Concern about social representation rests on a variety of claims. It can be argued that all major groups of citizens should be included in any elected body on the simple grounds of equity and fairness (Phillips 1994). Moreover, the under-representation of certain social groups may undermine the democratic legitimacy of parliaments. In elections for the German Bundestag Wessels notes that more than a fifth of all voters believe it is important that candidates come from the same region, class and generation as themselves, while 40 per cent of workers regard having a working-class background as an essential prerequisite for candidates to receive their support (Wessels chapter 5; Rebenstorf and Wessels 1989).

These arguments become more compelling if, in addition, members drawn from different social groups bring distinctive perspectives and priorities to the policymaking process. The assumption behind this meaning is that the personal characteristics of an elected official may influence their behaviour, attitudes and interests. This claim, associated with post-modern identity politics, reflects a long tradition. At the turn of this century Social Democratic, Labour and Communist parties were founded as the political voice of the working class and organised trade union movement. Regional parties are based on the same rationale: that only Catalonians, Quebecois or Scots can articulate the concerns of citizens living in these areas.

In the older literature it was commonly argued that the social origins of political elites did not have a significant impact on their attitudes or behaviour (Edinger and Searing 1967; Schleth 1971; Matthews 1985). Yet there is a growing consensus in more recent research that the background of members (their education, class, age and gender) may influence the attitudes, priorities and behaviour of representatives *within* parties. Studies have found that education, class and age of members are significantly related to attitudes in the German Bundestag, the Swedish parliament (Esaiason and Holmburg 1996), while gender, age and religion (although not class) proved significant predictors of members' values in the British House of Commons (Norris and Lovenduski 1995). It has been found that when sex equality issues were discussed in the European Parliament, this was invariably due to initiatives by women members (Vallance 1988; Vallance and Davies 1986). Since the European Union has been at the forefront of equal opportunity policies, forcing the pace of change in member states which have dragged their heels in this area (Meehan 1993), women MEPs can have a significant impact on public policy with ramifications throughout European society. Evidence from the United States and Scandinavia suggests that women's election to office has the potential to make a substantive, as well as symbolic, difference to public life (Thomas 1994; Dahlerup 1988; Karvonen and Selle 1995; Norris 1996b). During the 1980s increased demands for greater political inclusion have produced some progress towards greater social diversity in many parliaments, but the global pace of change remains painfully slow. There are many issues facing parliaments trying to respond to pressures for greater diversity in elected bodies, and concerns about social representation add to the overall problems of democratic legitimacy, and thus the difficulties of institutional reform facing modern legislatures.

Bibliography

Aaronovitch, S. 1961. *The Ruling Class*. London: Lawrence and Wishart.

Aberbach, J.D., R.D. Putnam and B.A. Rockman. 1981. *Bureaucrats and Politicians in Western Democracies*. Cambridge, MA: Harvard University Press.

Abramson, Paul and Ronald Inglehart. 1995. *Value Change in Global Perspective*. Ann Arbor: University of Michigan Press.

Aitkin, Don. 1982. *Stability and Change in Australian Politics*. Canberra: Australian National University Press (2nd edn).

Allardt, Erik. 1968. 'Past and Emerging Cleavages'. In *Party Systems, Party Organizations and the Politics of the New Masses*, ed. Otto Stammer. Conference of the Committee on Political Sociology of the International Sociological Association, Berlin. Printed manuscript: 66–76.

ALLBUS. 1990. *Allgemeine Bevölkerungsumfrage der Sozialwissenschaften, Codebook No. 1800*. Köln: Central Archive for Empirical Social Research.

Almond, Gabriel and J.S. Coleman. 1960. *The Politics of Developing Areas*. Princeton: Princeton University Press.

Asahi nenkan [Asahi yearbook]. 1995. Tokyo: Asahi shinbunsha.

Asahi senkyo taikan [Asahi compendium on elections]. Tokyo: Asahi shinbunsha.

Asahi shinbun senkyo honbu [Asahi newspaper election headquarters]. 1990.

Asahi shinbun. 1989. (22 July).

Asahi shinbun. 1990a.(4 February).

Asahi shinbun. 1990b.(17 February).

Asahi shinbun. 1990c. (20 February).

Asahi shinbun. 1992 (9 July).

Atkinson, Michael M. and David C. Docherty. 1992. 'Moving Right Along: The Roots of Amateurism in the Canadian House of Commons'. *Canadian Journal of Political Science* 25: 295–318.

Bagehot, Walter. 1872. *The English Constitution*. London: Thomas Nelson and Sons.

Barber, James. 1965. *The Lawmakers*. New Haven, CT: Yale University Press.

Barber, James. 1972. *The Presidential Character: Predicting Performance in the White House*. Englewood Cliffs, NJ: Prentice Hall.

Barnes, Samuel H. 1977. *Representation in Italy*. Chicago: University of Chicago Press.

Bean, Clive. 1993. 'Conservative Cynicism: Political Culture in Australia'. *International Journal of Public Opinion Research* 5: 58–77.

Beer, S.H. 1982. *Modern British Politics: Parties and Pressure Groups in the Collectivist Age*. London: Faber and Faber (3rd edn).

Bentley, Michael. 1987. *The Climax of Liberal Politics: British Liberalism in Theory and Practice, 1868–1918*. Winchester, MA: Edward Arnold.

Berg, J.Th.J. van den. 1981. 'Herkomst, ervaring en toekomstperspectief van Kamerleden'. *In Leden van de Staten-Generaal*, ed. M. van Schendelen, J.J.A. Thomassen and H. Daudt. Den Haag: Vuga.

Berg, J.Th.J. van den. 1983. *Der toegand tot het Binnenhof*. Weesp: Van Holkema en Warendorf.

Berg, J.Th.J. van den. 1989. Het pre-fab Kamerlid. In *Tussen Nieuwspoort & Binnenhof. De jaren 60 als breuklijn in de naamloze ontwikkelingen in politiek en journalistiek*, ed. J.Th.J. van den Berg. Den Haag: SDU.

Birch, A.H. 1964. *Representative and Responsible Government*. London: Allen and Unwin.

Birch, A.H. 1971. *Representation*. Macmillan: London.

Birch, A.H. 1993. *The Concepts and Theories of Modern Democracy*. London: Routledge.

Blake, Donald E. 1991. 'Party Competition and Electoral Volatility: Canada in Comparative Perspective'. In *Representation, Integration and Political Parties in Canada*, ed. Herman Bakvis. Toronto: Dundurn Press and the Royal Commission on Electoral Reform and Party Financing.

Bloc Québécois. 1993. *Réglements et procédures concernant la tenue et le déroulement d'une assemblée d'investitue du Bloc Québécois*. Montréal.

Blondel, Jean. 1963. *Votes, Parties and Leaders*. London: Penguin.

Blondel, Jean. 1973. *Comparative Legislatures*. Englewood Cliffs, NJ: Prentice Hall.

Blondel, Jean. 1987. *Political Leadership*. London: Sage Publications.

Blondel, Jean. 1995. *Comparative Government*. Hemel Hempstead: Prentice Hall.

Bochel, John and David Denver. 1983. 'Candidate Selection in the Labour Party: What the Selectors Seek'. *British Journal of Political Science* 13: 45–69.

Bogdanor, Vernon, ed. 1985. *Representatives of the People? Parliamentarians and Constituents in Western Democracies*. Hants: Gower.

Bogdanor, Vernon and David Butler. 1983. *Democracy and Elections*. Cambridge: Cambridge University Press.

Borchert, Jens and Lutz Golsch. 1995. 'Die politische Klasse in westlichen Demokratien'. *Politische Vierteljahresschrift* 36: 609–29.

Bottomore, Tom. 1964. *Elites and Society*. London: Watts.

Brand, Jack. 1989. 'Faction as its Own Reward: Groups in the British Parliament 1945 to 1986'. *Public Administration* 42, (2): 148–64.

Brodie, Janine (with the assistance of Celia Chandler). 1991. 'Women and the Electoral Process in Canada'. In *Women in Canadian Politics: Toward Equity in Representation*, ed. Kathy Megyery. Vol. 6 of the research studies of the Royal Commission on Electoral Reform and Party Financing. Ottawa and Toronto: RCERPF/Dundern.

Brooks, Rachel, Angela Eagle and Clare Short. 1990. *Quotas Now: Women in the Labour Party*. London: Fabian Society Tract 541.

Buck, J. Vincent and Bruce E. Cain. 1990. 'British MPs in Their Constituencies'. *Legislative Studies Quarterly* 15 (1) (February): 127–43.

Buck, P.W. 1963. *Amateurs and Professionals in British Politics 1918–59*. Chicago: University of Chicago Press.

Burch, M. and M. Moran. 1985. 'The Changing Political Elite'. *Parliamentary Affairs* 38: 1–15.

Butler, David. 1978. 'The Renomination of MPs'. *Parliamentary Affairs* Spring.

Butler, David. 1988. 'Electors and Elected'. In *British Social Trends Since 1900*, ed. A.H. Halsey. London: Macmillan.

Butler, David and Gareth Butler. 1986. *British Political Facts, 1900–1985*. London: Macmillan.

Butler, David and Gareth Butler. 1986. *British Political Facts, 1900–1985*. London: Macmillan.

Butler, David and Dennis Kavanagh. 1992. *The British General Election of 1992*. London: Macmillan.

Butler, David and Michael Pinto-Duschinsky. 1980. 'The Conservative Elite 1918–78: Does Unrepresentativeness Matter?' In *Conservative Party Politics*, ed. Zig Layton Henry. London: Macmillan.

Byrne, Tony. 1986. 'The Councillors'. *Local Government in Britain*. Middlesex: Penguin (Ch. 8).

Cain, Bruce, John Ferejohn and Morris Fiorina. 1987. *The Personal Vote: Constituency Service and Electoral Independence*. Cambridge, MA: Harvard University Press.

Callaghan, John. 1989. 'Fabian Socialism, Democracy and the State'. In *Democracy and the Capitalist State*, ed. G. Duncan. Cambridge: Cambridge University Press.

Carroll, Susan. 1994. *Women as Candidates in American Politics*. Indiana: University of Indiana Press.

Carty, R.K. 1991. *Canadian Political Parties in the Constituencies*. Toronto and Oxford: Dundurn Press.

Carty, R.K. and Lynda Erickson. 1991. 'Candidate Nomination in Canada's National Political Parties'. In *Canadian Political Parties: Leaders, Candidates and Organization*, ed. Herman Bakvis. Vol. 13 of the research studies of the Royal Commission on Electoral Reform and Party Financing. Ottawa and Toronto: RCERPF/Dundern.

Chambers, William Nesbit and Walter Dean Burnham, eds. 1967. *The American Party Systems: Stages of Political Development*. London, Toronto: Oxford University Press.

Chandler, J.A. and D. Morris. 1983. 'The Selection of Local Candidates'. In *The Redundant Counties?*, ed. S. Bristow, D. Kermode and M. Manning. Ormskirk: Hesketh Press.

Chapman, Jenny. 1993. *Politics, Feminism and the Reformation of Gender*. London: Routledge.

Charnock, David. 1992. 'Party Identification in Australia, 1967–90: Implications for Methods Effects from Different Survey Procedures'. *Australian Journal of Political Science* 27: 510–16.

Child, V.G. 1923. *How Labour Governs*. London: The Labour Publishing Co.

Clarke, Peter B. and James Q. Wilson. 1961. 'Incentive Systems: A Theory of Organizations'. *Administrative Science Quarterly* 4: 129–66.

Collins, Hugh. 1985. 'Political Ideology in Australia: the Distinctiveness of a Benthamite Society'. *Daedalus* 114: 147–69.

Conservative Party. 1980. *Rules and Standing Orders of the National Union of Conservative and Unionist Associations*. London: Conservative Central Office.

Converse, Philip E. and Roy Pierce. 1986. *Political Representation in France*. Cambridge, MA: Harvard University Press.

Cook, Chris and Ian Taylor. 1980. *The Labour Party*. London: Longman.

Craig, F.W.S. 1989. *British Electoral Facts, 1832–1987*. Dartmouth: Parliamentary Research Services.

Crewe, Ivor. 1983. 'Representation and the Ethnic Minorities in Britain'. In *Ethnic Pluralism and Public Policy*, ed. Nathan Glazer and Ken Young. London: Heinemann Educational Books.

Crewe, Ivor. 1985. 'MPs and Their Constituents in Britain: How Strong are the Links?' In *Representatives of the People?*, ed. Vernon Bogdanor. Hants: Gower.

Crewe, Ivor, Pippa Norris and Robert Waller. 1992. 'The 1992 general election'. In Pippa Norris et al., *British Elections and Parties Yearbook, 1992*. Herts: Harvester Wheatsheaf.

Criddle, Byron. 1992. 'MPs and Candidates'. In *The British General Election of 1992*, ed. David Butler and Dennis Kavanagh. London: Macmillan.

Crisp, L.F. 1985. *Australian National Government*. Melbourne: Longman Cheshire.

Curtis, Gerald. 1988. *The Japanese Way of Politics*. New York; Columbia University Press.

Czudnowski, Moshe M. 1975. 'Political Recruitment'. In *Handbook of Political Science*, Vol. II: *Micro-Political Theory* Reading, MA: Addison-Wesley.

Daalder, Hans. 1992. In *Geachte Afgevaardigde*, ed. J.J.A. Thomassen, M.P.C.M. van Schendelen and M.L. Zielinka-Geoi. Muiderberg: Couthino.

Dahl, Robert. 1981. *Who Governs?* New Haven: Yale University Press.

Dahl, Robert. 1984. *Modern Political Analysis*. New York: Prentice-Hall International (4th edn).

Dahlerup, Drude. 1985. *Unfinished Democracy*. Oxford: Pergamon Press.

Dahlerup, Drude. 1988. 'From a Small to a Large Minority: Women in Scandinavian Politics'. *Scandinavian Political Studies* 11(4): 275–98.

Dalton, Russell J. 1988. *Citizen Politics in Western Democracies*. Chatham, NJ: Chatham House.

Darcy, R., Susan Welch and Janet Clark. 1994. *Women, Elections and Representation*. Lincoln: Nebraska University Press (2nd edn).

Dawson, Richard E. 1967. 'Social, Development, Party Competition and Policy'. In Chambers and Burnham 1967, 203–37.

Delacourt, Susan and Craig McInnes. 1993. '"Bad apples" Can't Run Chrétien Says'. *The Globe and Mail*. 29 July.

Denters, S.A.H., H.M. de Jong and J.J.A. Thomassen. 1990. *Kwaliteit van Gemeenten*. Den Haag: Vuga.

Denters, S.A.H. and H.v.d. Kolk (ed.). 1993. *Leden van de Raad . . .* Delft: Eburon.

DeVaus, David and Ian McAllister. 1989. 'The Changing Politics of Women: Gender and Political Alignment in Western Democracies'. *European Journal of Political Research*. 17: 241–62.

Diamond, Irene. 1977. *Sex Roles in the State House*. New Haven, CT: Yale University Press.

Dittrich, K. and R.B. Andewag. 1982. 'De mythologie van het meerderheidsdenken'. *Socialisme en Demokratie*. Oct.: 324–32.

Dowse, Robert E. 1963. 'The M.P. and His Surgery'. *Political Studies*. October: 333–41.

Dunleavy, Patrick and Brendan O'Leary. 1984. *Theories of the State: The Politics of Liberal Democracy*. Basingstoke: Macmillan.

Duverger, Maurice. 1951. *Political Parties: Their Organisation and Activity in the Modern State*. London: Methuen and Co.

Duverger, Maurice. 1955. *The Political Role of Women*. Paris: UNESCO.

Edinger, Lewis J. and Donald D. Searing. 1967. 'Social Background in Elite Analysis: A Methodological Inquiry'. *American Political Science Review* 61: 428–45.

Edney, Ray. 1991. 'Affirmative Action Given Green Light'. *The Democrat* June–July: 14.

Ehrenhalt, Alan. 1992. *The United States of Ambition*. New York: Times Books.

Eldersveld, Samuel J. 1964. *Political Parties: An Organizational Analysis*. Chicago: Rand McNally.

Emy, Hugh V. 1974. *The Politics of Australian Democracy*. Melbourne: Macmillan.

Epstein, L.D. 1980. *Political Parties in Western Democracies*. New York: Praeger Publishers.

Epstein, L.D. 1986. *Political Parties in the American Mold*. Madison: The University of Wisconsin Press.

Erickson, Lynda. 1991. 'Women and Candidacies for the House of Commons'. In *Women in Federal Politics: Towards Equity in Representation*, ed. K. Megyery. Vol. 6 of the research studies of the Royal Commission on Electoral Reform and Party Financing. Ottawa and Toronto: RCERPF/Dundern

Erickson, Lynda. 1993. 'Making Her Way In: Women, Parties and Candidacies in Canada'. In *Gender and Party Politics*, ed. Joni Lovenduski and Pippa Norris. London: Sage Publications.

Erickson, Lynda. 1995a. 'The 1993 October Election and the Canadian Party System'. *Party Politics* 1: 133–43.

Erickson, Lynda. 1995b. *Entry to the Commons: Parties, Recruitment and the Election of Women in 1993*. Burnaby, BC: Simon Fraser University.

Erickson, Lynda and R.K. Carty. 1991. 'Parties and Candidate Selection in the 1988 Canadian General Election'. *Canadian Journal of Political Science* 24: 331–49.

Esaiasson, Peter and Sören Holmberg. 1996. *Representation from Above: Members of Parliament and Representative Democracy in Sweden*. Aldershot: Dartmouth.

Eulau, Heinz and Jon C. Wahlke. 1978. *The Politics of Representation*. London: Sage Publications.

European Commission. 1976. *Women of Europe*, No. 3. Brussels: European Commission.

European Commission. 1979. *European Men and Women in 1978*. Brussels: European Commission.

European Commission, 1980. 'Women in the European Parliament'. Supplement No 4, *Women of Europe*. Brussels.

European Commission. 1983. *Women and Men of Europe in 1983* Brussels: European Commission.

European Commission. 1987. 'Men and Women of Europe in 1987'. In *Women of Europe* No. 26, Brussels.

Farrell, David and Ian McAllister. 1995. 'Legislative Recruitment to Upper Houses: The Australian Senate and the House of Representatives Compared'. *Journal of Legislative Studies*.

Ferejohn, John and Brian Gaines. 1991. 'The Personal Vote in Canada'. In *Representation, Integration and Political Parties in Canada*, ed. Herman Bakvis. Toronto: Dundurn Press and the Royal Commission on Electoral Reform and Party Financing.

Finer, S., H.B. Berrington and D.J. Bartholemew. 1961. *Backbench Opinion in the House of Commons, 1955–59*. Oxford: Pergammon Press.

Finer, S.E. 1980. *The Changing British Party System, 1945–79*. Washington, DC: American Enterprise Institute.

Fowler, Linda. 1993.*Candidates, Congress and the American Democracy*. Ann Arbor: University of Michigan Press.

Fowler, Linda and Robert D. McClure. 1989. *Political Ambition: Who Decides to Run for Congress*. Yale: Yale University Press.

Fukui, Haruhiro, and Shigeko N. Fukai. 1991. 'Nihon ni okeru infomaru poritikkusu to itto yui taisei: kesu sutadei to shoho riron [Informal Politics in Japan and the One-party Dominant System: A Case Study and Rudimentary Theory]'. *Leviathan* 9: 55–79.

Fukui, Haruhiro and Shigeko N. Fukai. 1994. 'The Political Economy of Electoral *Keiretsu*: Cases and Interpretations'. Paper presented at the annual meeting of the *Association for Asian Studies*, Boston, 23-7 March.

Fukui, Haruhiro, and Shigeko N. Fukai. 1996a. 'Pork Barrel Politics Networks and Local Economic Development in Contemporary Japan'. *Asian Survey* 36: 3.

Fukui, Haruhiro, and Shigeko N. Fukai. 1996b. 'Japan'. In *Comparative Politics at the Crossroads*, ed. Joel Krieger, Mark Kesselman and William Joseph. Lexington, MA: D.C. Heath.

Fukui, Haruhiro, and Shigeko N. Fukai. Forthcoming. 'Campaigning for the Japanese Diet'. In *Elections and Campaigning in Japan, Korea, and Taiwan: Toward a Theory of Embedded Institutions*, ed. Bernard Grofman et al. Ann Arbor: University of Michigan Press.

Gallagher, Michael. 1988. 'Conclusion'. In Gallagher and Marsh 1988.

Gallagher, M., M. Laver and P. Mair. 1995. *Representative Government in Modern Europe*. New York: McGraw Hill.

Gallagher, Michael and Michael Marsh, eds. 1988. *The Secret Garden: Candidate Selection in Comparative Perspective*. London: Sage.

Garner, Robert and Richard Kelly. 1993. *British Political Parties Today*. Manchester: Manchester University Press.

Geddes, Andrew, Joni Lovenduski, and Pippa Norris. 1991. 'Candidate Selection: Reform in Britain'. *Contemporary Record* 4 April: 19–22.

German Bundestag Candidate Data. 1994. 'Dataset on the basis of information from the Federal Statistical Office on 3931 candidates'. Compiled by Achim Kielhorn and Bernhard Wessels, both Wissenschaftszentrum Berlin.

German Representation Study. 1988/89. 'Three hundred twenty-nine face-to-face interviews with MPs (response rate 62 percent)'. Principal investigators:

Dietrich Herzog, Free University of Berlin, and Bernhard Wessels, Wissenschaftszentrum Berlin.

'Germany'. In *Panorama Strategies: Expert Network Women in Decision Making*. Brussels: Equal Opportunities Unit.

Gow, Neil. 1971. 'The Introduction of Compulsory Voting in the Australian Commonwealth'. *Politics* 6: 201–10.

Graham, B.D. 1993. *Representation and Party Politics: A Comparative Perspective*. Oxford: Blackwell.

Greenwood, John. 1988. 'Promoting Working-Class Candidatures in the Conservative Party: The Limits of Central Office Power'. *Parliamentary Affairs* 41(4) October: 456–68.

Griffith, J.A.G. and M. Ryle. 1989. *Parliament: Functions, Practice and Procedures*. London: Sweet & Maxwell.

Guadagnini, M. 1993. 'A 'Partitocrazia Without Women: The Case of the Italian Party System'. In *Gender and Party Politics*, ed. J. Lovenduski and P. Norris. London: Sage Publications.

Guttsman, W.L. 1968. *The British Political Elite*. London: MacGibbon and Kee.

Haavio-Mannila, Elina et al. 1985. *Unfinished Democracy: Women in Nordic Politics*. NY: Pergamon.

Hanham, H.J. 1978. *Elections and Party Management: Politics in the Time of Disraeli and Gladstone*. London: Harvester Press.

Harmel, Robert and Kenneth Janda. 1992. *Parties and Their Environments*. New York: Longmans.

Held, David and C. Pollitt, eds. 1986. *New Forms of Democracy*. London: Sage Publications.

Herzog, Dietrich. 1975. *Politische Karrieren*. Opladen: Westdeutscher Verlag.

Herzog, Dietrich. 1991. 'Brauchen wir eine Politische Klasse?' *Aus Politik und Zeitgeschichte*. Beilage zur Wochenzeitung Das Parlament B50/91: 3–13.

Herzog, Dietrich, Hilke Rebenstorf and Bernhard Wessels, eds. 1993. *Parlament und Gesellschaft. Eine Funktionsanalyse der repräsentativen Demokratie*. Opladen: Westdeutscher Verlag.

Hess, Adalbert. 1995. 'Sozialstruktur des 13. Deutschen Bundestages'. *Zeitschrift für Parlamentsfragen* 26: 567–85.

Hillebrand, Ron. 1992. *De antichambre van het Parlement*. Leiden: DSWO press.

Hills, Jill. 1981. 'Candidates, the Impact of Gender'. *Parliamentary Affairs* 34: 221–8.

Hindess, Barry. 1971. *The Decline of Working Class Politics*. London: McGibbon and Kee.

Holland, Martin. 1986. *Candidates for Europe*. Farnborough, Hants: Gower.

Holland, Martin. 1987. 'The Selection of Parliamentary Candidates: Contemporary Developments and the Impact of the European Elections'. *Parliamentary Affairs* 34(2): 28–46.

Holzapfel, Andreas. 1995. *Deutschland/Bundestag*. Rhinbreitbach: NDV.

Holzapfel, Klaus-J. 1995. *Kürschners Volkshandbuch Deutscher Bundestag: 13. Wahlperiode 1994*. Rheinbreitbach: Neue Darmstädter Verlagsanstalt.

Horie, Fukashi. 1993. *Seiji kaikaku to senkyo seido* [Political reform and election systems]. Tokyo: Ashi shobo.

Hrebenar, Ronald J., ed. 1986. *The Japanese Party System: From One Party Rule to Coalition Government*. Boulder, CO: Westview.

Hughes, Colin A. 1968. 'Compulsory Voting'. In *Readings in Australian Government*, ed. Colin A. Hughes. St. Lucia: University of Queensland Press.

Ike, Nobutaka. 1980. *A Theory of Japanese Democracy*. Boulder, CO: Westview.

Imidas. 1995. Tokyo: Shueisha.

Inglehart, Margaret. 1981. 'Political interest in West European women'. *Comparative Political Studies*, 14: 299–326.

Inglehart, Ronald. 1977. *Silent Revolution*. Princeton: University of Princeton Press.

Inglehart, Ronald. 1991. *Culture Shift*. Princeton: University of Princeton Press.

Inoguchi, Takashi, and Tomoaki Iwai. 1988. *Zoku giin no kenkyu* [A study of tribe members in the Diet]. Tokyo: Nihon keizai shinbunsha.

Inter-Parliamentary Union. 1986. *Parliaments of the World: A Comparative Reference Compendium*. Hants: Gower (2nd edn).

Inter-Parliamentary Union. 1992a. *Chronicle of Elections*. Geneva: Interparliamentary Union (Quarterly Series to 1992).

Inter-Parliamentary Union. 1992b. *Women and Political Power*. Reports and Documents No. 19, Geneva: Interparliamentary Union.

Inter-Parliamentary Union. 1993. *Electoral Systems*. Geneva: Inter-Parliamentary Union.

Iremonger, Lucille. 1970. *The Fiery Chariot: A Study of British Prime Ministers and the Search for Love*. London: Secker and Warburg.

Jacobs, Francis and Richard Corbett. 1990. *The European Parliament*. Essex: Longman.

Jaensch, Dean. 1983. *The Australian Party System*. Sydney: Allen and Unwin.

Jaensch, Dean. 1994. *Power Politics: Australia's Party System*. Sydney: Allen and Unwin.

Janosik, Edwards G. 1968. *Constituency Labour Parties in Britain*. London: Pall Mall Press.

Jennings, Sir Ivor. 1958. *The British Constitution*. Cambridge: The University Press (3rd edn).

Jewell, Malcolm E. 1985. 'Legislators and Constituents in the Representative Process'. In *Handbook of Legislative Research*, ed. Gerhard Loewenberg, Samuel C. Patterson and Malcolm E. Jewell. Cambridge, MA: Harvard University Press.

Jiyuminshuto [LDP]. 1994a. *Senkyo taisaku yoko* [Guidelines for election policy]. 24 November. Mimeo. Tokyo: Jiyuminshuto.

Jiyuminshuto. 1994b. *Kohosha sentei kijun* [Criteria for candidate selection]. 24 November. Mimeo. Tokyo: Jiyuminshuto.

Jiyuminshuto. 1994c. *Dai 17–kai sangiin giin tsujo senkyo hirei daihyo senshutsu giin kohosha meibo sakusei kijun* [Criteria for the compilation of the candidate list for the proportional representation contests in the 17th house of councillors regular election] (28 June). Mimeo. Tokyo: Jiyuminshuto.

Judge, David, ed. 1983. *The Politics of Parliamentary Reform*. London: Heinemann.

Judge, David. 1993. *The Parliamentary State*. London: Sage.

Karvonen, Lauri and Per Selle. 1995. *Women in Nordic Politics*. Aldershot: Dartmouth Press.

Katz, Richard S., ed. 1987. *Party Governments: European and American Experiences*. Berlin: Walter de Gruyter.

Katz, Richard and Peter Mair. 1992. *Party Organisations: A Data Handbook on Party Organisations in Western Democracies, 1960–90*. London: Sage.

Katz, Richard S. and Peter Mair, eds. 1994. *How Parties Organize*. London: Sage.

Kavanagh, Dennis. 1992. 'The Political Class and its Culture'. *Parliamentary Affairs* 45: 18–32.

Kazee, Thomas A. 1994. 'The Emergence of Congressional Candidates', in *Who Runs for Congress? Ambition, Context, and Candidate Emergence*, ed. Kazee. Washington DC: Congressional Quarterly.

Key, V.O. 1950. *Southern Politics in State and Nation*. New York: Knopf Books.

Key. V.O. 1964. *Politics, Parties and Pressure Groups*. New York: Crowell-Collier.

Kilroy-Silk, Robert. 1986. *Hard Labour*. London: Chatto and Windus.

King, Anthony. 1974. *British Members of Parliament: A Self-Portrait*. London: Macmillan.

King, A. 1981. 'The Rise of the Career Politician in Britain and its Consequences'. *British Journal of Political Science* 11: 249–63.

King, Anthony and Anne Sloman. 1974. *Westminster and Beyond*. London: Macmillan.

Kirchheimer, Otto. 1966. 'The Transformation of the Western European Party Systems'. In La Palombara and Weiner 1996a: 177–200.

Kirchheimer, Otto. 1990. 'The Catch-all Party'. In *The West European Party System*, ed Peter Moir. Oxford: Oxford University Press.

Klingemann, Hans-Dieter and Dieter Fuchs, eds. 1995. *Citizens and the State*. Oxford: Oxford University Press.

Klingemann, Hans-Dieter, Richard I. Hofferbert and Ian Budge. 1994. *Parties, Policies and Democracy*. Boulder, CO: Westview.

Klingemann, Hans-Dieter, Richard Stöss and Bernhard Wessels. 1991. 'Politische Klasse und politische Institutionen'. In *Politische Klasse und politische Institutionen. Probleme und Perspektiven der Elitenforschung*, ed. Hans-Dieter Klingemann, Richard Stöss and Bernhard Wessels. Opladen: Westdeutscher Verlag.

Kogan, D. and M. Kogan. 1982. *The Battle for the Labour Party*. London: Fontana.

Kohn, Walter S.G. 1981. 'Women in the European Parliament'. *Parliamentary Affairs* 34(1).

Kokkai benran [Diet handbook], 91st edn. 1994. Tokyo: Nihon seikei shinbunsha.

Koole, Ruud. 1992. *De opkomst van de moderne kaderpartij*. Zwolle: Spectrum B.V.

Koole, Ruud and Monique Leijenaar. 1988. 'The Netherlands: the predominance of regionalism'. In *Candidate Selection in Comparative Perspective*, ed. Michael Gallagher and Michael Marsh. London: Sage Publications.

Kuusela, Kimmo. 1995. 'The Finnish Electoral System: Basic Features and Developmental Tendencies'. In *The Finnish Voter*, ed. Sami Borg and Risto Sänkiaho. Tampere: The Finnish Political Science Association.

La Palombara, J. and Myron Weiner, eds. 1966a. *Political Parties and Political Development*. Princeton: Princeton University Press.

La Palombara, J. and Myron Weiner, eds. 1966b. 'The Original Development of Political Parties'. In *Political Parties and Political Development*: 3–42.

Labour Party. 1990a. *NEC Report*. London: The Labour Party.

Labour Party. 1990b. *Representation of Women in the Labour Party: Statement by the National Executive Committee*. London: The Labour Party.

Labour Party. 1990c. *Selection of Parliamentary Candidates: Report of the NEC Consultation.* London: The Labour Party.

Labour Party. 1991. *Selection and Reselection of Parliamentary Candidates.* London: The Labour Party.

Labour Party. 1992. *Rule Book, 1991–2.* London: The Labour Party.

Lasswell, Harold. 1960. *Psychopathology and Politics.* NY: Viking.

Lasswell, Harold, David Lerner, and C. Easton Rothwell. 1952. *The Comparative Study of Political Elites.* Stanford, CA: Stanford University Press.

Lawson, K. 1988. 'When Linkage Fails.' In *When Parties Fail.* ed. K. Lawson and P. Merkl. Princeton: Princeton University Press.

Layton-Henry, Zig. 1984. *The Politics of Race in Britain.* London: Allen and Unwin.

Layton-Henry, Zig and Donley Studlar. 1985. 'The Electoral Participation of Black and Asian Britains: Integration or Alienation?' *Parliamentary Affairs* 38(3) Summer: 307–18.

Lees, J.D. and R. Kimber. 1972. *Political Parties in Modern Britain.* London: Routledge.

Leif, Thomas, Hans-Josef Legrand and Ansgar Klein, eds. 1992. 'Die Politische Klasse'. In *Deutschland. Eliten auf dem Prüfstand.* Bonn/Berlin: Bouvier.

Leijenaar, Monique. 1989. *De geschade heerlijkheid.* Den Haag: Staatsuitgeverij.

Leijenaar, Monique. 1993. 'A Battle for Power: Selecting Candidates in the Netherlands'. In *Gender and Party Politics*, ed. Joni Lovenduski and Pippa Norris. London: Sage Publications.

Leiserson, Avery. 1967. 'The Place of Parties in the Study of Politics'. In *Political Parties*, ed. R.C. Macridis. New York: Harper and Row.

Lijphart, Arendt. 1984. *Democracies: Patterns of Majoritarian and Consensus Government in 21 Countries.* New Haven: Yale University Press.

Lijphart, Arend. 1989. 'From the politics of accommodation to adversial politics in the Netherlands: A reassessment'. In *Politics in the Netherlands: How much change?*, ed. Hans Daalder and Galen Irwin. London: Cass.

Lindsay, T.F. and M. Harrington. 1979. *The Conservative Party, 1918–1979.* London: Macmillan (2nd edn).

Lipset, S.M. and Rokkan, Stein. 1967. 'Cleavage Structures, Party Systems and Voter Alignments: An Introduction'. In *Party Systems and Voter Alignments*, ed. S.M. Lipset and Stein Rokkan. New York: The Free Press.

Locke, John. 1948. *The Second Treatise of Civil Government.* Oxford: Basil Blackwell.

Loewenberg, Gerhard and Samuel C. Patterson. 1979. *Comparing Legislatures.* Boston: Little, Brown and Company.

Loewenberg, Gerhard, Samuel C. Patterson and Malcolm Jewell, eds. 1985. *Handbook of Legislative Research.* Cambridge, MA: Harvard University Press.

Loveday, Peter and A.W. Martin. 1965. *Parliament, Factions and Parties : The First Thirty Years of Responsible Government in New South Wales, 1856–1889.* Melbourne: Melbourne University Press.

Loveday, Peter et al. 1977. *The Emergence of the Australian Party System.* Sydney: Hale and Iremonger.

Lovenduski, Joni. 1986. *Women and European Politics.* Sussex: Wheatsheaf Books.

Lovenduski, Joni and Pippa Norris. 1989. 'Selecting Women Candidates: Obstacles to the Feminisation of the House of Commons'. *European Journal of Political Research* 17, Autumn: 533–62.

Lovenduski, Joni and Pippa Norris. 1991. 'Party Rules and Women's Representation: Reforming the British Labour Party'. In *British Elections and Parties Yearbook, 1991*, ed. Ivor Crewe et al., 189–206. Herts: Harvester Wheatsheaf Press.

Lovenduski, Joni and Pippa Norris, eds. 1993. *Gender and Party Politics*. London: Sage.

Lovenduski, Joni and Pippa Norris. 1994a. 'Labour and the Unions: Contentious Issues?' *Government and Opposition*, 1994.

Lovenduski, Joni and Pippa Norris. 1994b. 'Political Recruitment: Gender, Class and Ethnicity'. In *British Parties in Transition*, ed. Lynton Robbins, Hilary Blackmore and Robert Pyper. London: Leicester University Press.

Lovenduski, Joni, Pippa Norris, and Catriona Burgess. 1995. 'The Party and Women'. In *Conservative Century*, ed. Anthony Seldon and Stuart Ball. Oxford: Oxford University Press.

Lovenduski, Joni and Vicky Randall. 1993. *Contemporary Feminist Politics*. Oxford: Oxford University Press.

Lowi, Theodore. 1967. 'Party, Policy and Constitution'. In *The American Party System: Stages of Political Development*. London, Toronto: Oxford University Press.

Luhmann, Niklas. 1984. *Soziale Systeme: Grundriss einer allgemeinen Theorie*. Frankfurt A.M.: Suhrkamp.

MacGregor, Burns. 1963. *The Deadlock of Democracy: Four-Party Politics in America*. New Jersey: Prentice-Hall.

Macridis, R.C., ed. 1967. *Political Parties: Contemporary Thoughts and Ideas*. New York: Harper Textbooks.

Mainichi shinbun. 1993a: 2 July.

Mainichi shinbun. 1993b: 5 July.

Mainichi shinbun. 1993c: 19 July.

Maisel, L. and P.M. Sacks. 1975. *The Future of Political Parties*. Beverly Hills: Sage.

Manning, D.J. 1976. *Liberalism*. London: J.M. Dent and Sons.

March, James and Johan Olsen. 1989. *Rediscovering Institutions*. New York: Free Press.

Matthews, Donald. 1984. 'Legislative recruitment and legislative careers'. *Legislative Studies Quarterly*. November: 547–85.

Matland, Richard E. and Donley T. Studlar. 1995. 'Turnover Patterns and Explanations of Variations in Turnover in Parliamentary Democracies'. Paper presented at the Working Group on Legislative Recruitment and the Structure of Opportunities, *European Consortium for Political Research*, Bordeaux, France.

Matthews, Donald R. 1985. 'Legislative Recruitment and Legislative Careers'. In *Handbook of Legislative Research*, ed. Gerhard Loewenberg, Samuel C. Patterson and Malcolm E. Jewell, 17–55. Cambridge, MA: Harvard University Press.

Maud Committee Report. 1967. *Report of the Committee on the Management of Local Government, Vol. 2: The Local Government Councillor*. London: HMSO.

Mayer, L. and R. Smith. 1985. 'Feminism and religiosity: female electoral behaviour in Western Europe'. *West European Politics* 8: 38–49.

McAllister, Ian. 1985. 'Party Membership, Party Service and Legislative Recruitment in Australia'. Paper presented at the Working Group on Legislative Recruitment and the Structure of Opportunities, European Consortium for Political Research, Bordeaux, France.

McAllister, Ian. 1991. 'Party Adaptation and Factionalism within the Australian Party System'. *Australian Journal of Political Science* 35: 206–27.

McAllister, Ian. 1992. *Political Behaviour: Citizens, Parties and Elites in Australia.* Melbourne: Longman Cheshire.

McConnell, Grant. 1966. *Private Power and American Democracy.* New York: Vintage Books.

McCubbins, Mathew D. and Gregory W. Noble. 1995. 'The Appearance of Power: Legislators, Bureaucrats, and the Budget Process in the United States and Japan'. In *Structure and Policy in Japan and the United States*, ed. Peter F. Cowhey and Mathew D. McCubbbins. Cambridge, UK: Cambridge University Press.

McCubbins, Mathew D. and Frances M. Rosenbluth. 1995. 'Party provision for Personal Politics: Dividing the Vote in Japan'. In *Structure and Policy in Japan and the United States*, ed. Peter F. Cowhey and Mathew D. McCubbins. Cambridge, UK: Cambridge University Press.

McKenzie, R.T. 1955. *British Political Parties.* London: Heinemann.

MccLean, Iain. 1991. 'Forms of Representation and Systems of Voting'. In *Political Theory Today*, ed. David Held. Palo Alto, CA: Stanford University Press.

McLellan, David. 1980. *The Thought of Karl Marx: An Introduction.* Basingstoke: Macmillan (2nd edn).

Meehan, Elizabeth. 1993. *Citizenship and the European Community.* London: Sage Publications.

Mellors, Colin. 1978. *The British MP: A Socio-Economic Study of the House of Commons.* Farnborough, Hants: Saxon House.

Messina, Anthony. 1989. *Race and Party Competition in Britain.* Oxford: Clarendon Press.

Mezey, Michael L. 1979. *Comparative Legislatures.* Durham, NC: Duke University Press.

Mezey, Michael L. 1993. 'Legislatures: Individual Purpose and Institutional Performance'. In *Political Science: The State of the Discipline*, II, ed. Ada Finifter. Washington, DC: American Political Science Association.

Michels, Robert. 1949. *Political Parties.* Glencoe: The Free Press.

Miliband, Ralph. 1969. *The State in Capitalist Society.* London: Weidenfeld and Nicholson.

Miliband, Ralph. 1982. *Capitalist Democracy in Britain.* Oxford: Oxford University Press.

Mill, John Stuart. 1974. *On Liberty, Representative Government, The Subjection of Women, Three Essays.* London: Oxford University Press.

Miller, Raymond. 1992. 'The Minor Parties'. In *New Zealand Politics in Perspective*, ed. Hyam Gold. Auckland: Longman Paul.

Miller, Warren E. and M. Kent Jennings. 1986. *Parties in Transition: A Longitudinal Study of Party Elites and Party Supporters.* New York: Russell Sage.

Mills, C. Wright. 1956. *The Power Elite*. Oxford: Oxford University Press.

Minkin, Louis. 1992. *The Contentious Alliance*. Edinburgh: Edinburgh University Press.

Mitchell, Austin. 1982. *Westminster Man*. London: Methuen.

Mulgan, Richard. 1994. *Politics in New Zealand*. Auckland: Auckland University Press.

Myrskylä, Pekka. 1995. 'The Background of the Candidates by Party'. *Parliamentary Elections 1995*. Helsinki: Statistics Finland.

Needham, Richard. 1983. *Honourable Member: An Inside Look at the House of Commons*. London: Patrick Stephens.

Nettl, J.P. 1965. 'The German Social Democratic Party 1890–1914 as a Political Model'. *Past and Present* No. 30: 65–95.

Nettl, J.P. 1966. 'Are Two-Party Systems symmetrical?' *Parliamentary Affairs* 19, (2): 218–23.

Niemöller, Kees. 1991. *Partijleden: achtergronden en houdingen*. Amsterdam: University of Amsterdam.

Nihon shakaito [SDPJ]. 1995. *Senkyo toso hoshin an* [Draft plan for election struggle]. Mimeo. Tokyo: Nihon shakaito chuo honbu.

Nihon shakaito chuo honbu. 1991. *Nihon shakaito kiyaku (1991–nen 2–gatsu dai 56–kai taikai kaisei), soshiki kaikaku no gutaiteki koso, un'ei yoko* [The rules of the social democratic party of Japan, as revised at the 56th national meeting, February 1991; a concrete plan for organizational reform; guidelines for action]. Tokyo: Nihon shakaito chuo honbu soshikikyoku.

Nihon shakaito senkyo taisaku iinkai [SDPJ election policy committee]. 1995. *Sanko shiryo 4: Shugiin sosenkyo taisaku hoshin* [Reference material 4: Policy plan for the house of representatives general election]. (9 February). Tokyo: Nihon shakaito chuo honbu.

Noponen, Martti. 1989. 'Eduskunan jäsenistön vaihturuus ja lainsäätäjän ura'. In *Suomen kansanedustusjärjestelmä* (ed. Naponen). Juva: WSDY.

Norris, Pippa. 1985. 'Women's Legislative Participation in Western Europe'. *West European Politics*, 8 (4): 90–101.

Norris, Pippa. 1991. *British By-elections: The Volatile Electorate*. Oxford: Clarendon Press.

Norris, Pippa. 1993. 'The Gender Generation Gap in British Elections'. In *British Parties and Elections Yearbook, 1993*, ed. David Denver et al. Herts: Harvester Wheatsheaf.

Norris, Pippa. 1994. 'Labour Party Factionalism and Extremism: Changing the Party and Hanging the Image'. In *Can Labour Win?*, ed. Anthony Heath et al. Dartmouth Press.

Norris, Pippa. 1996a. 'Legislative Recruitment'. In *Comparing Democracies: Elections and Voting in Global Perspective*, ed. Lawrence LeDuc, Richard Niemi and Pippa Norris, Newbury Park, CA: Sage.

Norris, Pippa. 1996b. 'Women Politicians: Transforming Westminster?' *Parliamentary Affairs*, 49(1): 89–102.

Norris, Pippa, R.K. Carty, Lynda Erickson, Joni Lovenduski and Marian Simms. 1990. 'Party Selectorates in Australia, Britain and Canada: Prolegomena for Research in the 1990s'. *The Journal of Commonwealth and Comparative Politics* 28:2 July, 219–45.

Norris, Pippa and Ivor Crewe. 1994. 'Did the British Marginals Vanish?

Proportionality and Exaggeration in the British Electoral System Revisited'. *Electoral Studies*, June.

Norris, Pippa, Andrew Geddes and Joni Lovenduski. 1992. 'Race and Parliamentary Representation'. In *British Parties and Elections Yearbook 1992*, ed. Pippa Norris et al. Herts: Harvester Wheatsheaf.

Norris, Pippa and Joni Lovenduski. 1989a. 'Pathways to Parliament'. *Talking Politics* 1(3), Summer: 90–4.

Norris, Pippa and Joni Lovenduski. 1989b. 'Women Candidates for Parliament: Transforming the Agenda?' *British Journal of Political Science* 19 (1), January: 106–15.

Norris, Pippa and Joni Lovenduski. 1993a. '"If Only More Candidates Came Forward": Supply-side Explanations of Candidate Selection in Britain'. *British Journal of Political Science* 23, June: 373–408.

Norris, Pippa and Joni Lovenduski. 1993b. 'Gender and Party Politics in Britain'. In *Gender and Party Politics*, ed. Joni Lovenduski and Pippa Norris. London: Sage.

Norris, Pippa and Joni Lovenduski. 1995. *Political Recruitment: Gender, Race and Class in British Parliament*. Cambridge: Cambridge University Press.

Norris, Pippa, Elizabeth Vallance and Joni Lovenduski. 1992. 'Do Candidates Make a Difference?: Gender, Race, Ideology and Incumbency'. *Parliamentary Affairs* 45(4) October: 496–517.

Norton, Philip. 1978. *Conservative Dissidents*. London: Temple Smith.

Norton, Philip. 1980. *Dissension in the House of Commons, 1945–1979*. Oxford: Clarendon Press.

Norton, Philip. 1981. *The Commons in Perspective*. Oxford: Martin Robertson.

Norton, Philip. 1985. 'The House of Commons: Behavioural Changes'. In *Parliament in the 1980s*, ed. Philip Norton. Oxford: Basil Blackwell.

Norton, Philip. 1989. 'The Glorious Revolution of 1688/89: Its Continuing Relevance'. *Parliamentary Affairs* 42, (2): 135–147.

Norton, Philip and Arthur Aughey. 1981. *Conservatives and Conservatism*. London: Temple Smith.

Norton, Philip and David Wood. 1990. 'Constituency Service by Members of Parliament: Does it Contribute to a Personal Vote?' *Parliamentary Affairs* 43(2) April: 196–208.

Nugent, Neil. 1994. *The Government and Politics of the European Union*. Durham, NC: Duke University Press.

Nurmi, Hannu and Erik Lagerspetz. 1984. 'Observations on the Finnish Electoral System'. In *Essays on Democratic Theory*, ed. Dag Anckar and Erkki Berndtson. Yampere: Finnpublishers.

Ostrogorski, M. 1902. *Democracy and the Organisation of Political Parties*. London.

Painebanco, Angelo. 1988. *Political Parties: Organisation and Power*. Cambridge: Cambridge University Press.

Parkin, Frank. 1968. *Middle Class Radicals*. Manchester: Manchester University Press.

Parkinson, M. 'Central-Local Relations in British Parties: A Local View'. *Political Studies* 19 (4): 440–6.

Parliamentary Candidates in England, Wales and Northern Ireland. London: Conservative and Unionist Central Office.

Parry, Geraint. 1969. *Political Elites*. London: Allen and Unwin.

Parry, Geraint, George Moyser and Neil Day. 1992. *Political Participation and Democracy in Britain*. Cambridge: Cambridge University Press.

Pateman, Carole. 1972. *Participation and Democratic Theory*. Cambridge: Cambridge University Press.

Patterson, Peter. 1966. *The Selectorate*. London: Macmillan.

Pennock, J.R. and J.W. Chapman, eds. 1968. *Nomos X, Representation*. New York: Atherton Press.

Perlin, George. 1980. *The Tory Syndrome*. Montréal: McGill-Queen's University Press.

Pesonen, Pertti. 1972. 'Political Parties in the Finnish Eduskunta'. In *Comparative Legislative Behaviour: Frontiers of Research*, ed. Samuel Patterson and John C. Wahlke. New York: John Wiley & Sons, Inc.

Pesonen, Pertti. 1995. 'The Evolution of Finland's Party Divisions and Social Structure'. In *The Finnish Voter*, ed. Sami Borg and Risto Sänkiaho, Tampere: The Finnish Political Science Association.

Phillips, Anne. 1994. *Democracy and Difference*. Pennsylvania: University of Pennsylvania Press.

Pimlott, Ben and Chris Cook. 1991. *Trade Unions in British Politics: The First 250 Years*. London: Longman.

Pinto-Duschinsky, Michael. 'Central Office and "Power" in the Conservative Party'. *Political Studies* 20(1): 1–16.

Pitkin, Hanna. 1967. *The Concept of Representation*. Berkeley: University of California Press.

Plaid Cymru. 1991. *Procedure for Selection of Parliamentary Candidates*. Cardiff: Plaid Cymru.

Polsby, Nelson W. 1963. *Community Power and Political Theory*. New Haven and London: Yale University Press.

Porter, Stephen R. 1995. 'Political Representation in Germany: The Effects of the Candidate Selection Committees'. PhD. Thesis, University of Rochester.

Powell, G. Bingham. 1982. *Contemporary Democracies: Participation, Stability and Violence*. Cambridge, MA: Harvard University Press.

Powell, Walter and Paul J. Dimaggio. 1991. *The New Institutionalism in Organizational Analysis*. Chicago: University of Chicago Press.

Putnam, R.D. 1976. *The Comparative Study of Political Elites*. Englewood Cliffs, NJ: Prentice Hall.

Radice, Lisanne, Elizabeth Vallance and Virginia Willis. 1987. *Members of Parliament*. New York: St. Martin's Press.

Ragsdale, Lyn. 1985. 'Legislative Elections'. In *Handbook of Legislative Research*, ed. Gerhard Loewenberg, Samuel C. Patterson and Malcolm E. Jewell, 57–96. Cambridge, MA: Harvard University Press.

Randall, Vicky. 1987. *Women and Politics*. London: Macmillan (2nd edn).

Ranney, Austin. 1965a. 'Inter-Constituency Movement of British Parliamentary Candidates, 1951–1959'. *American Political Science Review*, 59.

Ranney, Austin. 1965b. *Pathways to Parliament: Candidate Selection in Britain*. London: Macmillan.

Ranney, Austin. 1968. 'Candidate Selection and Party Cohesion in Britain and the United States'. In *Approaches to the Study of Party Organisation*, ed. William J. Crotty. Boston, MA: Allyn and Bacon.

Ranney, Austin. 1981. 'Candidate Selection'. In *Democracy at the Polls*, ed. D. Butler, H. Penniman, and A. Ranney, 75-106. Washington, DC: AEI.

Rasmussen, Jorgen. 1983. 'The Electoral Costs of Being a Woman in the 1979 British General Election'. *Comparative Politics* July: 460–75.

Rebenstorf, Hilke. 1993. 'Gesellschaftliche Interessenrepräsentation und politische Integration'. In *Parlament und Gesellschaft. Eine Funktionsanalyse der repräsentativen Demokratie*, ed. Dietrich Herzog, Hilke Rebenstorf and Bernhard Wessels. Opladen: Westdeutscher Verlag.

Rebenstorf, Hilke and Bernhard Wessels. 1989. 'Wie wünschen die Wähler ihre Abgeordneten?' *Zeitschrift für Parlamentsfragen* 20: 408–24.

Reif, Karlheinz, ed. 1985. *Ten European Elections*. Hants: Gower.

Reimer, Neal. 1967. *The Democratic Experiment*. Princeton, NJ: D. Van Nostra and Company Inc.

Richards, Peter. 1964. *Honourable Members*. London: Faber and Faber.

Richards, Peter. 1972. *The Backbenchers*. London: Faber and Faber.

Richardson, Bradley M. and Scott C. Flanagan. 1984. *Politics in Japan*. Boston: Little, Brown.

Riddell, Peter. 1993. *Honest Opportunism: The Rise of the Career Politician*. London: Hamish Hamilton.

Riker, William H. 1986. 'Duverger's Law Revisited'. In *Electoral Laws and Their Political Consequences*, ed. Bernard Grofman and Arend Lijphart. New York: Agathon Press.

Roberts, Geoffrey. 1988. 'The German Federal Republic: The Two-Lane Route to Bonn'. In *Candidate Selection in Comparative Perspective*, ed. Michael Gallagher and Michael Marsh. London: Sage Publications.

Rose, Paul. 1981. *Backbench Dilemma*. London: Frederick Muller Ltd.

Rose, Richard. 1962. 'The Policy Ideas of English Party Activists'. *American Political Science Review* 56(2): 360–71.

Rose, Richard. 1969. *Studies in British Politics*. London: Macmillan.

Rose, Richard. 1974. *The Problem of Party Government*. New York: The Free Press.

Rose, Richard. 1986. *Party Politics*. Harmondsworth: Penguin.

Ross, J.F.S. 1944. *Parliamentary Representation*. New Haven, CT: Yale University Press.

Ross, J.F.S. 1955. *Elections and Electors*. London: Eyre and Spottiswoode.

Royal Commission on Electoral Reform and Party Financing. 1991. *Reforming Electoral Democracy, Vol. 1*. Ottawa: Minister of Supply and Services.

Rudig, Wolfgang, Bennie Lynn and Mark N. Franklin. 1991. *Green Party Members: A Profile*. Glasgow: Delta Publications. Rule, Wilma. 'Why Women Don't Run: The Critical Contextual Factors in Women's Legislative Recruitment'. *Western Political Quarterly*, 34: 60–77.

Rule, Wilma. 1981. 'Why Woman Don't Run: The Critical Contextual Factors in Women's Legislation Recruitment'. *Western Political Quarterly* 34: 60–77.

Rule, Wilma. 1987. 'Electoral Systems, Contextual Factors and Women's Opportunity for Election to Parliament in Twenty-Three Democracies'. *Western Political Quarterly* 50(3): 477–98.

Rule, Wilma and Joseph F. Zimmerman, eds. 1992. *U.S. Electoral Systems: Their Impact on Minorities and Women*. Westport, CT: Greenwood Press.

Rush, Michael. 1969. *The Selection of Parliamentary Candidates*. London: Nelson.

Rush, Michael. 1986. 'The Selectorate Revisited'. *Teaching Politics* 15:1

Rydon, Joan. 1968. 'Electoral Methods and the Australian Party System, 1910–1952'. In *Readings in Australian Government*, ed. Colin A. Hughes. St. Lucia: University of Queensland Press.

Rydon, Joan. 1986. *A Federal Legislature: The Australian Commonwealth Parliament, 1901–80*. Melbourne: Oxford University Press.

Sampson, Anthony. 1982. *The Changing Anatomy of Britain*. London: Hodder and Stoughton.

Sartori, Giovanni. 1966. 'European Political Parties: The Case of Polarized Pluralism'. In La Palombara and Weiner 1966a: 137–77.

Sartori, Giovanni. 1976. *Parties and Party Systems: A Framework for Analysis*. Cambridge: Cambridge University Press.

Sartori, Giovanni. 1987. *The Theory of Democracy Revisited*. New Jersey: Chatham House (2 vols.).

Schattschneider, E.E. 1942. *Party Government*. New York: Rinehart and Company.

Schattschneider, E.E. 1960. *The Semi-Sovereign People*. New York: Holt, Rinehart and Winston.

Schindler, Peter. 1983. *Deutscher Bundestag: Datenhandbuch zur Geschichte des Deutschen Bundestages 1949 bis 1982*. Bonn: Presse- und Informationszentrum des Deutschen Bundestages.

Schindler, Peter. 1986. *Datenhandbuch zur Geschichte des Deutschen Bundestages 1980–1984*, ed. Verwaltung des Deutschen Bundestages, Dept Wissenschaftliche Dokumentation. Baden- Baden: Nomos.

Schindler, Peter. 1994. *Datenhandbuch zur Geschichte des Deutschen Bundestages 1983–1991*. Baden-Baden: Nomos.

Schindler, Peter. 1995. 'Deutscher Bundestag 1976–1994: Parlaments-und Wahlstatistik'. *Zeitschrift für Parlamentsfragen* 26: 551–66.

Schlesinger, Joseph. 1966. *Ambition and Politics: Political Careers in the United States*. Chicago: Rand McNally and Co.

Schlesinger, Joseph. 1991. *Political Parties and the Winning of Office*. Ann Arbor, MI: University of Michigan Press.

Schleth, Uwe. 1971. 'Once Again: Does it Pay to Study Social Background in Elite Analysis?' In *Sozialwissenschaftliches Jahrbuch für Politik*, ed. Rudolf Wildenmann. München: Olzog.

Schnatterschneider. 1942. *Party Government*. New York: Holt, Rinehart and Winston.

Schoonmaker, D. 1988. 'The Challenge of the Greens to the West German Party System'. In *When Parties Fail*, ed. L. Lawson and P. Merkl. Princeton: Princeton University Press.

Schumpeter, Joseph A. 1962. *Socialism, Capitalism and Democracy*. New York: Harper (orig. 1942).

Scott, John. 1982. *The Upper Classes*. London: Macmillan.

Scott, John. 1985. *Corporations, Classes and Capitalism*. London: Hutchinson (2nd edn).

Scott, John. 1991. *Who Rules Britain?* Cambridge: Polity.

Scottish National Party. 1991. *Constituency Association Selection Meetings – Notes for Guidance*. Edinburgh: Scottish National Party.

Searing, Donald. 1978. 'Measuring Politicians' Values: Administration and Assessment of a Ranking Technique in the British House of Commons'. *American Political Science Review* March, 72: 65–79.

Searing, Donald D. 1985. 'The Role of the Good Constituency Member and the Practice of Representation in Great Britain'. *Journal of Politics* 47, May: 348–81.

Searing, Donald. 1987. 'New Roles for Postwar British Politicians: Ideologues, Generalists, Specialists and the Progressive Professionalisation of Parliament'. *Comparative Politics* July, 19(4): 431–53.

Searing, Donald D. 1991. 'Role, Rules, and Rationality in the New Institutionalism'. *American Political Science Review* 85: 1239–60.

Searing, Donald D. 1994. *Westminster's World*. Cambridge: Harvard University Press.

Seldon, Anthony and Stuart Ball, eds. 1995. *Conservative Century*. Oxford: Clarendon Press.

Seyd, Patrick. 1987. *The Rise and Fall of the Labour Left*. Hamps.: Macmillan Educational.

Seyd, Patrick and Paul Whiteley. 1992. *Labour's Grassroots: The Politics of Party Membership*. Oxford: Oxford University Press.

Shaw, Eric. 1988. *Discipline and Discord in the Labour Party*. Manchester: Manchester University Press.

Smith, Martin J. and Joanna Spear, eds. 1992. *The Changing Labour Party*. London: Routledge.

Smith, Susan J. 1989. *The Politics of 'Race' and Residence*. Cambridge: Polity Press.

Solomos, John. 1980. *Race and Racism in Contemporary Britain*. London: Macmillan.

Somit, Albert, Rudolf Wildemann, Bernhard Boll and Andrea Römmele. 1994. *The Victorious Incumbent*. Aldershot: Dartmouth.

Sorauf, Frank. 1984. *Party Politics in America*. Boston: Little, Brown.

Sorauf, Frank. 1992. *Inside Campaign Finance*. New Haven, CT: Yale University Press.

Sorifu [Office of the Prime Minister]. 1994. *Josei no genjo to shisaku: Sekai no naka no nihon no josei* [The present state of women and policy: Japanese women in global perspective]. Tokyo: Okurasho insatsukyoku.

Sorifu tokeikyoku [Bureau of Statistics, Office of the Prime Minister], ed. 1995. *Nihon no tokei* [Statistics on Japan]. Tokyo: Okurasho insatsukyoku.

Stanley, Harold and Richard Niemi. 1995. *Vital Statistics on American Politics*. Washington, DC: CQ Press.

Stanyer, Jeff. 1976. *Understanding Local Government*. London: Martin Robertson/Fontana.

Statistisches Bundesamt. 1995. *Statistisches Jahrbuch der Bundesrepublik Deutschland 1994*. Wiesbaden.

Stevenson, John. 1993. *Third Party Politics Since 1945*. Oxford: Blackwell Publishers.

Stewart, G.T. 1986. *The Origins of Canadian Politics: A Comparative Approach*. Vancouver: University of British Columbia Press.

Stewart, Robert. 1978. *The Foundation of the Conservative Party*. London: Longman.

Studlar, Donley T. and Ian McAllister. 1991. 'The Recruitment of Women to the Australian Legislature: Toward an Explanation of Women's Electoral Disadvantages'. *Western Political Quarterly* 44 (3): 67–85.

Studlar, Donley T. and Ian McAllister. 1996. 'Constituency Activity and Representational Roles Among Australian Legislators'. *Journal of Politics*.

Studlar, Donley, Ian McAllister and Alvaro Ascui. 1988. 'Electing Women to the British Commons: Breakout from the Beleaguered Beachhead'. *Legislative Studies Quarterly* 13(4), November: 515–28.

Studlar, Donley and Susan Welch. 1987. 'Understanding the Iron Law of Andrarchy: the Effect of Candidate Gender on Voting in Scotland'. *Comparative Political Studies* 20(2) July: 174–91.

Studlar, Donley T. and Susan Welch. 1991. 'Does District Magnitude Matter? Women Candidates in Local London Elections'. *Western Political Quarterly*. March.

Sundberg, Jan. 1989. *Lokala partioganisationer i kommunala och nationella val. Bidrig till kännedom av Finlands natur och Folk*. Helingfors: Finiska Vetenskaps–Societen No. 140.

Sundberg, Jan. 1990. 'The Role of Party Organization in the Electoral Process: Membership Activity in National and Local Elections in Finland'. In *Finnish Democracy*, ed. Jan Sundberg and Sten Berglund. Jyvöskylä: The Finnish Political Science Association.

Sundberg, Jan. 1995. 'Organisational Structures of Parties, Candidate Selection and Campaigning'. In *Finnish Democracy*, ed. Jan Sundberg and Sten Berglund. Tampere: The Finnish Political Science Association.

Sundberg, Jan and Christel Gylling. 1992. 'Finland'. In *Party Organisations*, ed. Richard S. Katz and Peter Mair. London: Sage.

Swain, Carol. 1993. *Black Faces, Black Interests*. Cambridge, MA: Harvard University Press.

Tether, Philip. 1991. 'Recruiting Conservative Party Members: A Changing Role for Central Office'. *Parliamentary Affairs* 44(1) January: 20–9.

The Times Guide to the House of Commons. London: Times Books, 1945–1992.

Thijn, Ed van. 1967. 'Van partijen naar stembusaccoorden'. In *Partijvernieuwing*, ed. E. Jurgens et al. Amsterdam: Arbeiderspers.

Thomas, J.A. 1939. *The House of Commons, 1832–1901: A Study of its Economic and Functional Character*. Cardiff: University of Wales Press.

Thomas, Sue. 1994. *How Women Legislate*. Oxford: Oxford Universty Press.

Thomassen, J.J.A. 1993. Democratie en representatie. In *Handboek Politicologie*, ed. Jan van Deth. Assen: Van Gorkum.

Thomassen, J.J.A., M.P.C.M. van Schendelen and M.L. Zielonka-Goei. 1992 *Geachte Afgevaardigde*. Muiderberg: Couthino.

Thomassen, Jacques. 1994. 'Empirical Research into Political Representation'. In *Elections at Home and Abroad*, ed. M. Kent Jennings and Thomas E. Mann. Ann Arbor: University of Michigan Press.

Timonen, Pertti. 1972. 'Edustajaehdokkaiden valikoituminen puoluejärjestön jäsenääneskyksessä'. In *Protestivaalit – nuorisovaalit*, ed. Pertti Pesonen. Helsinki: Gaudeamus.

Timonen, Pertti. 1981. *Puolueiden ehdokkaiden asettaminen*. University of Tampere: Institute of Political Science. Research Report No. 58.

Tops, Pieter, S.A.H. Denters, P. Depla, J.W. van Deth, M.H. Leijenaar and B. Niemöller. 1991. *Lokale Democratie en Bestuurlijke Vernieuwing*. Delft: Eburon.

United Nations. 1995. *The World's Women 1995: Trends and Statistics*. New York: United Nations Publications.

Urry, John and John Wakeford. 1973. *Power in Britain*. London: Heinemann Educational Books.

Uyl, Joop den. 1967. 'Een stem die telt'. In *Partijvernieuwing*, ed. E. Jurgens et al. Amsterdam: Arbeiderspers.

Valen, Henry. 1988. 'Norway: Decentralization and Group Representation'. In Gallagher and Marsh 1988.

Valen, Henry. 1994. 'List Alliances: An Experiment in Political Representation'. In *Elections at Home and Abroad*, ed. M. Kent Jennings and Thomas E. Mann. Ann Arbor: The University of Michigan Press.

Vallance, Elizabeth. 1979. *Women in the House: A Study of Women Members of Parliament*. London: Althone Press.

Vallance, Elizabeth. 1984. 'Women Candidates in the 1983 General Election'. *Parliamentary Affairs* 37: 301–9.

Vallance, Elizabeth. 1988. 'Do Women Make a Difference? The Impact of Women MEPs on Community Equality Policy'. In *Women, Equality and Europe*, ed. Mary Buckley and Malcolm Anderson. London: Macmillan.

Vallance, Elizabeth and Elizabeth Davies. 1986. *Women of Europe: Women MEPs and Equality Policy*. Cambridge: Cambridge University Press.

Verba, S., N. Nie and J. Kim. 1978. *Participation and Political Equality: A Seven Nation Comparison*. Cambridge: Cambridge University Press.

Verba, Sidney, Kay Schlozman and Henry Brady. 1995. *Voice and Equality*. Cambridge, MA: Harvard University Press.

Velde, Hella van de. 1994. *Vrouwen van de Partij*. Leiden: DSWO Press.

Vogel-Polsky, E. 1993. 'Belgium'. In *Panorama Strategies: Expert Network Women in Decision Making*. Brussel: Equal Opportunities Unit.

Vowles, Jack. 1985. 'Delegates Compared: A Sociology of the National, Labour and Social Credit Party Conferences, 1983'. *Political Science* 37: 1–17.

Vowles, Jack, Peter Aimer, Helena Catt, Raymond Miller and Jim Lamare. 1995. *Towards Consensus?: The 1993 Election in New Zealand and the Transition to Proportional Representation*. Auckland: Auckland University Press.

Ward, Doug. 1993. 'Pending Lawsuit Cited as Liberals Reject Would-be Candidate in Vancouver South'. *Vancouver Sun* 19 June A3.

Ware, Alan. 1979. *The Logic of Party Democracy*. New York: St. Martin's Press.

Ware, Alan. 1986. 'Political Parties'. In Held and Pollitt: 110–34.

Ware, Alan. 1995. *Political Parties and Party Systems*. Oxford: Oxford University Press.

Ware, Alan. 1996. *Political Parties and Party Systems*. Oxford: Oxford University Press.

Warner, Gerald. 1988. *The Scottish Tory Party: A History*. London: Weidenfeld and Nicholson.

Weber, Max. 1958. 'Politik als Beruf'. In *Gesammelte politische Schriften*. Tübingen: Mohr.

Weber, Max. 1976. *Wirtschaft und Gesellschaft*. Tübingen: Mohr.

Welch, Susan and Donley T. Studlar. 1990. 'Multi-Member Districts and the Representation of Women: Evidence from Britain and the United States'. *Journal of Politics*.

Welch, Susan. 1985. 'Are Women More Liberal than Men in the U.S. Congress?' *Legislative Studies Quarterly* 10(1) February: 125–34.

Welch, Susan and Donley Studlar. 1988. 'The Effects of Candidate Gender on Voting for Local Office in England'. *British Journal of Political Science* 18: 273–81.

Wessels, Bernhard. 1985. *Wählerschaft und Führungsschicht: Probleme politischer Repräsentation*. Berlin: Universitätsdruck der Freien Universität Berlin.

Wessels, Bernhard. 1987. 'Kommunikationspotentiale zwischen Bundestag und Gesellschaft:Öffentliche Anhörungen, informelle Kontakte und innere Lobby in wirtschafts-und sozialpolitischen Parlamentsausschüssen'. In *Zeitschrift für Parlamentsfragen* 18: 285–311.

Wessels, Bernhard. 1992. 'Zum Begriff der "Politischen Klasse"'. In *Gewerkschaftliche Monatshefte* 43: 541–9.

Whiteley, Paul. 1983. *The Labour Party in Crisis*. London: Methuen.

Whiteley, Paul F. and Patrick Seyd. 1994. 'Local Party Campaigning and Electoral Mobilisation in Britain'. *Journal of Politics* 56: 242–52.

Whiteley, Paul, Pat Seyd and Jeremy Richardson. 1994. *True Blues: The Politics of Conservative Party Members*. Oxford: Oxford University Press.

Widdicombe, D. 1986. *The Widdicombe Report: Conduct of Local Authority Business*. London: HMSO (Cmnd 9797).

Wilcox, Clyde. 1991. 'The Causes and Consequences of Feminist Consciousness among Western European Women'. *Comparative Political Studies*. 23(4): 519–45.

Willey, Fred. 1974. *The Honourable Member*. London: Sheldon Press.

Williams, Allan M. 1994. *The European Community* Oxford: Blackwell.

Williams, Philip. 1966. 'The MP's Personal Vote'. *Parliamentary Affairs* 20: 23–30.

Williams, Robert J. 1981. 'Candidate Selection'. In *Canada at the Polls, 1979, 1980*, ed. H.R. Penniman. Washington, DC: AEI.

Williams, Shirley and Edward L. Lascher. 1993. *Ambition and Beyond: Career Paths of American Politicians*. Berkeley, CA: University of California Press.

Woodhouse, A.S.P., ed. *Puritatism and Liberty: Being the Army Debates (1647–9)*. London: J.M. Dent and Sons.

Woolstencroft, Peter. 1994. '"Doing Politics Differently": The Conservative Party and the Campaign of 1993'. In *The Canadian General Election of 1993* ed. Alan Frizzell, Jon H. Pammett and Anthony Westell. London.

Wyatt, Woodrow. 1973. *Turn Again Westminster*. London: Andre Deutsch.

Yomiuri shinbun. 1992: July 27, evening edition.

Yomiuri shinbun. 1993a: July 5.

Yomiuri shinbun. 1993b: July 19.

Yomiuri shinbun. 1993c: July 20.

Young, Alison. 1983. *The Reselection of MPs*. London: Heinemann.

Young, Lisa. 1991. 'Legislative Turnover and the Election of Women to the Canadian House of Commons'. In *Women in Canadian Politics: Toward Equity in Representation*, ed. Kathy Megyery. Vol. 6 of the research studies of the

Royal Commission on Electoral Reform and Party Financing. Ottawa and Toronto: RCERPF/Dundern.

Zeuner, Bodo. 1971. 'Wahlen ohne Auswahl – Die Kandidatenaufstellung zum Bundestag'. In *Parlamentarismus ohne Transparenz*, ed. Willfried Steffani. Opladen: Westdeutscher Verlag.

Zuckerman, Alan S. 1979. *The Politics of Faction: Christian Democratic Rule in Italy.* New Haven and London: Yale University Press.

Zuckerman, Alan S. 1982. 'New Approaches to Political Cleavage: A Theoretical Introduction'. *Comparative Political Studies* 15(2): 131–44.

Index